LAMIA

LAMIA

LAMIA

by P. L. Thyraud de Vosjoli

LITTLE, BROWN AND COMPANY
BOSTON–TORONTO

LIBRARY OF CONGRESS CATALOG CARD NO. 70–121424

01363   W 0491   T 10/70

FIRST EDITION

PRINTED IN THE UNITED STATES OF AMERICA

1548053

*To my courageous and loyal
friend Frank M. Brandstetter*

Acknowledgment

I wish to thank Karen McLanahan for her patience in helping me through the difficulties of the English grammar; Dr. Henry King Stanford, president of the University of Miami, for allowing me to use the facilities of the Otto G. Richter Library; and all my former colleagues in French Intelligence for their support and precious information.

LAMIA

LAMIA

A man walked cautiously into my office. He wore a beige overcoat and clutched his hat nervously. He was of average height and appeared to be about forty.

"Excuse me for interrupting," he said, approaching me. "I am a friend of Mr. Bertrand. He gave me this letter." Putting down his hat, he fumbled as he extracted the paper from his wallet and handed it to me.

"My dear Philippe," wrote Bertrand, an old friend of my father, "I recommend to your special attention Mr. Meyer, manager of one of our factories. He is in trouble. I would appreciate whatever help you can give him."

I put the letter down, turned toward him, and motioned for him to be seated.

"What can I do for you?"

"I am a Jew, as you can see from my name," he said shyly, "I wanted to be able to cross the demarcation line before the Germans arrest me. Bertrand thought that since the line is so near, you might be able to help."

I was not surprised. I had known, deep within myself, that this would happen one day. I surely was going to help him.

Six months before, on June 14, 1940, German troops had entered Paris. I lived, at the time, with my parents in Romorantin, a small town south of the Loire. Geographically it was in the center of France. I was nineteen and awaiting my draft orders.

For days I had witnessed the sad spectacle of refugees fleeing before the invaders. I had seen French soldiers deserted by their chiefs, without arms or discipline, scattering in every direction in a shameful retreat. The defeat of the French Army and its sudden rout had come as a shock. I had always had an unshakable faith in the destiny of France and the gallantry of its soldiers. But . . . I had to face reality. In only a few days the Germans had overcome this French Army, which we boasted was the best in the world.

Orléans, the old city close to my hometown, had been bombed out by the Italians. Now everybody was running away from the Germans. The panic was contagious and my family succumbed to it. Taking all the cash and valuables we could pack with us in a car, we too had fled, going south, we did not know where.

In the town of Issyjeac, in the heart of the Périgord province, the radio brought us the news of the armistice. The French government, stunned and demoralized, had refused to regroup in North Africa in order to continue the fight.

The innkeeper where we were spending the night told us the London BBC had broadcast a speech by a French general, calling on the French people to continue the fight. I asked the general's name, but the man did not remember it. After a few days, discouraged, we decided to return home.

Marshal Pétain had stated on several occasions that an honorable armistice had been signed. Everybody knew it would be costly. The Prussians had defeated and occupied France before, and they had left after imposing financial and diplomatic penalties. But with the "Victor of Verdun" at the head of the government, it seemed certain that the armistice would be fair. Why else would the great military leader have gone to the pains of endorsing it?

Anyway, for the time being, the Germans were in conquered

4

territory and absolute masters of our destiny. When we arrived home, German officers had taken over our house. Others had ransacked it before them. The bedrooms were like a pigpen. Valuable antiques had been destroyed and used for firewood, the wine cellar had been looted, and an incredible array of wine and liquor bottles littered the floor. Such excesses are expected from troops in the midst of combat, but the Germans had entered our town after the armistice was signed. They certainly did not place much importance in it.

Curfew was in effect from 8 P.M. to 7 A.M. and travel was restricted. According to the armistice, signed by Pétain, France had been divided into two zones: one was to be occupied and administered by German troops; the other, a so-called Free Zone, was placed under the Vichy government.

A border had been established between the two zones and was called the Line of Demarcation. It was absolutely forbidden to cross the line without special authorization from the Germans, and communication was prohibited between the two zones. The Germans installed guardhouses all along the line, and their patrols arrested any person who could not explain his presence in the vicinity. Anyone trying to cross the line without authorization was fired on. It might be difficult for an American to imagine such a line dividing one's country. The only comparison would be a line drawn from San Francisco to Baltimore splitting the United States in two, with no travel or communication permitted between the two parts. Any violation could mean deportation to a concentration camp, or execution on the spot.

The line of demarcation ran a few miles south of my hometown and followed the Cher River. It could only be crossed by means of an ancient stone bridge and the Germans had set up a guardhouse in the middle of it.

I personally had no difficulty crossing the line. One of my former teachers was working as an interpreter in the Kommandantur and had obtained a pass for me. It was called an *Ausweis* and it permitted me to proceed back and forth across the new border. This whole area was very familiar to me since I had explored it often during my childhood and knew most of the people who lived along the river.

Helping someone "cross" the line under the noses of the Germans was not an easy operation, but it was nevertheless possible. The idea of defying the Germans was exciting, whatever the risks might be. More than a few had been killed by German patrols in their attempts to cross the river. We regularly heard of tragic accidents in which people had drowned trying to cross the treacherous waters.

The man named Meyer was looking at me with apprehension, awaiting my answer. The Germans already had started their persecutions of the Jews and I could sense his despair. He was feeling the trap close on him, and his only hope of escape depended on my decision.

Without knowing exactly how I could carry out the plan, I asked, "When can you go?"

"Anytime. Today, if possible," he answered, seeming to relax in that moment.

I was committed and had to devise a scheme.

I told Meyer to make himself comfortable while I tried to make some arrangements. First I visited my former teacher, the interpreter in the Kommandantur, and asked if he could get an ausweis. But when I gave him the name of Meyer he resolutely refused. "To facilitate the passage of a Jew is equivalent to a death sentence," he told me. He would not take the risk and looked at me oddly. I became concerned, immediately fearing that he would expose us. I decided to act quickly.

My best friend, Bernard Gaulier, had an uncle who lived near the demarcation line. Would he help? I didn't know, but I decided to try him. Bernard told me that his uncle could give me information on the frequency of the German patrols and offered to accompany me to see him. It only remained to find a means of transportation to cover the ten miles to the river. Because automobiles were prohibited due to the gas shortage, the only possibility was to use bicycles.

Meyer hadn't ridden a bicycle for years, and the one we found for him was old and in need of repair. We tied baskets to all the bicycles so that if stopped by the Germans we could say we were making the rounds of nearby farms for produce. In this period food was very scarce and it was common to see people going from farm to farm, buying or trading whatever they could at black market prices. We were lucky and reached the house of Chevet, my friend's uncle, without incident.

Chevet wasted no time. After hearing our story, he led us behind his house and pointed to the river. "The course of the river is erratic," he said. "The sands shift with the current. One day it can be forded here and the next there will be six feet of water. Deep sinkholes sometimes are filled with sand, but other times the sand washes out making crossing very dangerous. From my house you will be able to see the German patrol making rounds about every hour. There are also irregular bicycle patrols, but if you're careful they won't see you in the dark. Tonight there will be no moon." He pointed at the dark clouds obstructing the sky.

Meyer was looking back at the black unfriendly river with dismay he could scarcely conceal. He was probably wondering, like myself, about the temperature of the water on this cold November day. I looked at him and asked, "Well, shall we cross tonight?" He looked at me with the same expression that had touched me before when I had decided to help him. I could sense that he was now as frightened of crossing as of staying. With the kind of fatalism of one who has nothing to lose, he nodded affirmatively.

My friend Bernard offered to return the bicycle Meyer had used. This way I wouldn't have to run the risk of being spotted at night with two bicycles by the German gendarmes, who we used to call "prized cows" because of the chained breastplates they wore around their necks.

I left Meyer with Chevet and went out to explore the riverbank for a crossing place. The Cher was about 400 feet wide and its banks were covered with brush under which we could hide. A canal, no longer in use, ran along the river, and beside it the paths formerly used by the mules in pulling the barges were now used by German patrols. Our most dangerous moment in the night's undertaking would come in crossing the bridge over the canal and these patrol paths. After this, it would be easy to hide ourselves in the undergrowth. The hours passed slowly. We could see the German patrols at regular intervals, and I carefully timed their rounds.

Meyer was silent — slowly sipping a glass of wine Chevet had poured for him. Finally, around five o'clock, darkness came. No moon, no stars — heavy clouds hid them.

7

"It is time," said Chevet. "The patrol will pass in a few minutes." We turned out all the lights and went to the windows, where we soon could distinguish a dim light advancing slowly. The Germans carried a flashlight. We could hear the stomping of their boots coming near, then slowly receding.

As soon as all was quiet, and the rays of the flashlight disappeared completely, we said good-bye to Chevet. I silently led Meyer in the direction of the bushes I had spotted before. We crossed the mule paths and the wooden bridge without incident. When we were near the river, I undressed quickly and made a bundle of my clothing, motioning Meyer to do the same. His teeth chattering with cold and fear, he would only pull up his trousers and refused to undress further in spite of my insistence.

Grasping his hand, I pulled him into the water, which was ice cold and up to our knees. Meyer made every effort to remain silent despite the physical shock of the water. I could feel my limbs become numb. Moving slowly in order to make as little noise as possible, I cautiously explored the bottom with each step. Meyer forced himself to advance — I could feel his fear in the way he grasped my hand. When we reached the middle of the river, he suddenly cried out and disappeared beneath the water. He had stumbled into one of the sinkholes Chevet had warned us about. Resisting with all my strength in order not to be dragged down with him, I succeeded in pulling him back, shivering.

His screams had been heard by the Germans and their flashlight beams swept the river. Crouching, I dragged Meyer toward the opposite bank. Miraculously the Germans were too far upstream and didn't spot us. A few moments later we set foot in the Free Zone.

Meyer was staggering, all his clothes soaking wet. My own, which I had carried on my shoulders, were dry, so I gave him my jacket to wear and told him to exercise to warm up.

In Chabris, just across the border in the Free Zone, there was an inn where I stayed regularly when I crossed the line. The owner, Mariette, was a robust peasant woman, always in good spirits and ready to do a favor. I was sure she would give Meyer asylum and help him continue his journey. Indeed, as soon as we came through the back door, Mariette took him to a room, found him dry clothing, and gave him some hot soup. In a few minutes Meyer seemed revived and ready to put behind him those bad moments of our crossing. He talked animatedly, relieved to be in the Free Zone — and, he hoped, safe.

It was getting late, the clock showed 7 and time for me to go back. Leaving Meyer in Mariette's care, I headed for the river, which I crossed by the same route as before. Taking cover in the bushes, I waited for the patrols to make their rounds. Stopping at Chevet's to get my bicycle, I made it home before the curfew.

The next day a rumor was circulating in town that the Germans had seen two persons drowning while trying to cross the Cher. I relished the idea of having tricked the Germans; the thought of repeating the adventure enthralled me.

I didn't have long to wait. A few days later Meyer's wife and sister asked me to help them. Then one of my brother's friends, Chambon, then a friend of Chambon . . .

Several times a week my help was solicited by friends of those I had already taken to the Free Zone, or simply by acquaintances of my family who had somehow heard of other escapes.

I had discovered several other crossing points in the river and knew the exact hours of the German patrols. I was soon able to cross the river as easily at night as during the day. At the times when the water level was high, with youthful disregard of the danger, I would take refugees over an unused railroad trestle located about 100 yards from the German sentry post. It was built with steel beams which resounded with each step. When the night was very dark, I would wait until the German patrols were halfway across, then under cover of their loud marching we would follow. The disciplined Germans never looked back.

Mariette's place had become my headquarters. The refugees were welcomed there and helped to continue their journeys. For many months these crossings continued steadily.

The influence of the Germans over France was increasing, and so was the number of French people "collaborating" with the enemy. To see some of these Frenchmen fraternizing with the Germans for nothing more than material gain was for me a constant source of disgust. As a result of this, I felt an urge to make up for their actions and their cowardice.

Every evening my family, very careful not to attract the attention of the German officers quartered on the second floor of the house, gathered around the radio set to listen to the broadcasts from the BBC. De Gaulle, the once unknown general, had become the symbol of a France that would fight back. I drank in everything he and his lieutenants said — and with all the enthusiasm of youth. To me it was crystal clear. The Germans were occupying my country and a puppet government was giving them a helping hand in looting it. De Gaulle, a general and a former member of the cabinet, was in command of the French forces carrying on the fight from England. He was now the chief and I readily accepted his authority.

It puzzled me very much that de Gaulle always mentioned the "resistance," the underground movements. Every night I heard the BBC broadcast slogans and other mysterious messages. They seemed to be coded instructions or information for the benefit of these organizations. But in spite of my efforts, I was unable to locate or contact one of the underground groups. With my closest friends I often discussed many possible ways we could help the British and de Gaulle, but we had been unsuccessful in finding the right channel to offer our services.

By the beginning of 1941, it was clear to me that only a handful of agents from the intelligence services were working on French soil, and they were too well hidden for me to have any hope of meeting them. As for Frenchmen being members of the underground organization, I know now that there was very little organized resistance at this early stage. All anybody really did was to listen to the BBC.

In my district, in any case, I was the only one who had set up a regular system of crossing the demarcation line. I had not yet found an underground organization which could take advantage of my activities, and I was ready to consider the resistance as a myth. Then, at the end of August 1941, posters bordered in black and red appeared on walls of every village in the occupied zone. The Germans were announcing, as a warning, that Lieutenant Commander d'Estienne d'Orves and a man named Doornick had been executed for espionage against the Third Reich.

For the first time we had proof, tragic as it was, of clandestine action by Frenchmen against the Germans. Several days later I was to have more evidence of the existence of special operations.

10

I was in the common room of Mariette's inn with a group of refugees I had helped across when Mariette, peeking through the kitchen door, waved to me. I got up and walked to the kitchen. Bustling around the stove, she inquired, "Have you noticed the man sitting over there in the corner with the tan raincoat?"

In fact, I already had spotted this man, in his thirties, who had been staring at me ever since I came in.

"He checked in last night from Valençay or Châteauroux and asked me if I knew a way for him to get to the occupied zone," Mariette said. "His mother is dying in Paris. He looked to me like a nice man, so I told him perhaps you could help him."

It was an unusual request — the first time anyone had wanted my help in getting into the occupied zone. So far, they had all been concerned with escaping. Well, this was a case of filial love, and if this man wanted to see his mother for the last time, why not?

"If I can be of service, tell him to come and talk to me."

Mariette, wiping her hands on her apron, walked to him. She asked him to follow her into the kitchen.

The man's face was open and friendly, his voice pleasant, the type that inspires confidence. He explained what Mariette had just told me. I warned him that although the operation could go very smoothly, I could not guarantee a crossing without incident in spite of all precautions. The Germans might discover us at any time.

"If you'll take your chances, I'll take mine," was his answer.

He followed me out along the river. We went silently for about two miles. I showed him the spot where he would cross and explained to him: "You see that big oak tree on the other side? If I put my bicycle against it, that will mean it's clear for you to cross. But if, at any time, I walk away from the tree with my bicycle, it will mean danger. Then get back to the bank and hide. While crossing, be sure not to get your clothes wet, so that after we meet you can take my bicycle and go directly to Romorantin, and from there take the train to Paris."

I drew a rough map of the road to Romorantin on the wet ground, and gave him my parents' address so that he could leave the bicycle. I left the man, and using my ausweis, crossed into the occupied zone. An hour later he had joined me by the oak tree without any trouble. He thanked me warmly and went on his way. I never thought we

11

would meet again; however, two weeks later he came to see me. I inquired about his mother's health. She was doing better, he said, but it was urgent that he return to the Free Zone.

I already had guessed the purpose of his visit, and once again he crossed as before. I found him later at Mariette's sipping a hot beverage to warm him after his icy dip.

"You don't like the Germans do you?" he asked me abruptly.

"No, and what about you?"

"I came from London," he said lowering his voice.

I should have been surprised, but somehow I had been expecting this moment. The illusive resistance I had dreamed of since the signing of the dishonorable armistice had suddenly become a reality.

Without giving my interrogator a chance to continue, I heard myself say, "What can I do?"

It turned out that there was much I could do for him. First, of course, I could help him and his comrades in crossing the demarcation line. Then, I could act as a courier between him and his agents in the occupied zone. After a long talk, during which we tried to evaluate the advantages of one village over another, we decided that he would mail the letters to me in the occupied zone at General Delivery, Saint Christophe-en-Bazelle, a community of 400 located between Chabris and Valençay.

My new friend asked me to call him Marc, without mentioning his family name. He said he wanted information on the air base at Gièvres, and I was more than glad to promise him that I would get it.

The Gièvres air base had been set up during the First World War by the Americans. After the war, it was taken over by the French Army, which stored a great quantity of equipment there. It was one of the first French military air bases. At the beginning of the Second World War, the Germans cautiously bombed the base without doing much damage. They probably knew they would need it later on. After the armistice they moved right in with troops and a squadron of fighters.

I started my assignment the day after my meeting with Marc. Going back and forth in front of the air base, I tried to estimate its dimensions in order to make an accurate drawing. I appraised the approximate capacity of each warehouse, counted the number of fighters, and tried to remember exactly where they were parked. I watched takeoffs and landings of the planes to establish a flight schedule.

The Germans must have been overconfident not to suspect me. Otherwise my zeal as a neophyte secret agent, as well as my naïve and clumsy maneuvers, would have aroused their attention. After having spent some time drawing the sketches as accurately as I could, I mailed my first intelligence report to the address Marc had given me.

My work soon proved successful and, in fact, almost cost me my life. Sometime later, while I was riding my bicycle in front of the base, I suddenly heard a loud humming and the sky seemed to darken. I looked up; the sun disappeared behind a wave of English bombers. Like enormous bats they made a half turn above the base, the black bombs dropping in strings like slow motion from their fat bellies. Instinctively I threw myself into a ditch, and my speed saved me because a large-caliber bomb hit the ground not far from me. Fragments were falling all around. One hit my sleeve and burned a hole in my jacket. Fate had wanted me to be present at the bombing caused by my own information.

According to Marc's instructions, I instantly took note of the damage, noting which targets were hit and which buildings burned. The same evening I sent in my report.

Little by little, I was catching the intelligence fever, a virus I have never been able to shake. In spite of myself I developed this alertness which makes one "see" information in things which others regard as unimportant. The thrill of discovering what is hidden begins to haunt one. It is this permanent challenge which creates in certain individuals a passion for intelligence work. A mission is really interesting only when the goal seems impossible. Nothing is more exciting than to make the impossible recede by the use of wit and resourcefulness.

In those unhappy years, with England expecting the Germans to use France as a jumping-off place for invasion, every little detail was valuable as intelligence. But in our patriotic zeal and lack of professional know-how, I feel that we overdid it.

Mountains of miscellaneous information were sent out — the badges showing the unit and corps of German soldiers, how many bicycles they had, trivia about their daily activities. All this was mixed up with details about the construction of new shelters and locations of radio transmitters.

It was not very dangerous, or even very difficult, to gather intelligence. The risk started with the drafting of the report, and since special information was easy to collect, the tendency was to make voluminous reports which were difficult to conceal in case of search.

The danger was greatest when the information had to be carried from one zone to another by bulky envelope. To be caught carrying intelligence meant torture and execution by the Gestapo. It saddens me to think of how many useless chances were taken and how many brave people died for the sake of worthless information. Later, when I became more of a professional, I shuddered to think of the blunders caused by our amateurism.

Actually, our efforts were more a manifestation of resistance against the Germans than really effective action. We wanted to confuse the enemy and get a measure of revenge. The fear of arrest or torture added a certain spice to our lives which was necessary when all hope seemed lost. It also was a form of protest against the majority of the population, who followed Pétain's example and spent much of their time analyzing who was to blame for the French defeat.

Of course, they had the Jews at the top of the list. And the Vichy government, outbidding the Germans, promulgated laws forbidding them access to government offices and confiscating their belongings for the benefit of regime supporters. The position taken by the French government in the Free Zone eased the consciences of the French police in the occupied zone, who began to show a shameless zeal in helping the Germans in their dreadful persecutions.

I cannot think without anger about the horrible spectacle I witnessed one day in Paris as I was coming out of a friend's house on Rue Raynouard. A long line of buses was stopped in front of the deluxe apartment buildings overlooking the Quai de Passy. From each vehicle came groups of policemen — the same French policemen familiar to anyone who has visited Paris — with their capes, round caps, and white sticks. They entered the buildings, then a few minutes later reappeared amid screams and cries, pushing women, children, and elderly people. The women, some of them

14

wearing only a robe, were clutching children, many of whom could barely walk. Without pity, the French policemen were tearing the children from their mothers' arms and piling mothers and children in separate buses.

Swinging their sticks to keep the mothers back, they were throwing babies on the floors of the buses. Children of five or six were trying to help their younger brothers to their feet. All were screaming, crying, and calling for their mothers. Meanwhile, the poor women, with expressions of horror on their faces and crazed by fear, were pressed against the windows crying out the names of the children whom they would never see again. Paying no attention, the French policemen were pushing and piling and hurrying the innocents, sending them without remorse to certain death.

I could stand it no longer and came forward near one of the buses, only to be struck by a nightstick. In a daze, I could hear the words, "Get away and mind your own business." When I regained full consciousness, the caravan was gone and the street deserted. In a doorway two women were weeping. They told me they had heard one of the policemen mention the Palais des Sports. Wasting no time, I took the subway to the Passy Station, getting off at Lamotte-Picquet. The Sports Palace was close by. All around the outside wall policemen and gendarmes were patrolling. No one was allowed near the entrance, but the buses arrived continuously, letting out hundreds of children. No German was in sight. Only Frenchmen participated in this cruel and shameful persecution of innocent children.

Alone and powerless, I kept walking around the stadium looking for some possible way to enter, but the gates were few and every one well guarded. Since that day the vision of those little martyrs keeps haunting me. Twenty-five years later, the awful scene is still vivid in my memory.

I learned later that the prisoners were taken by the French gendarmes to a camp in Drancy, where many died from hunger and exposure. The survivors were handed to the Germans to be shipped to Germany and the gas chambers.

While the Jews represented the most persecuted faction, they were not alone in having been fingered by the Germans and the Vichy government as responsible for France's misfortunes.

15

The Freemasons traditionally occupied important positions in the French administration and in the Army. Because of mistakes made by some individual members, the whole organization was blamed. Fired from all official positions, their names posted as criminals, the 70,000 members of French Masonry had to seek safety in flight. I was frequently asked to help some of them escape to the relative safety of the Free Zone. Many joined the underground and performed courageously. Others, betraying their friends, played the sad game of informer.

The Germans, while triggering the persecution against the Jews and Freemasons, showed only moderate zeal during the first year of the occupation. Sure of their final victory, they were happy to leave the dirty work to the Vichy government.

Proud of their victory over all Europe, the Germans laughed at the idea that a French underground movement could present any danger for them, and at that time they were right. Neither the clandestine crossings of the demarcation line nor the handful of networks in the process of organizing were able to do them any harm. The majority of French people, disheartened by the defeat, were inclined to follow Pétain and collaborate with the Germans. They had many concrete facts on which to base their optimism.

The French workers were controlled by Communist-dominated unions, who applauded the pact signed by Stalin and Hitler and established contact with the Germans as soon as they entered Paris. They considered Germany and the occupation troops as their allies. Members of the Central Committee of the French Communist Party requested from the Paris Kommandantur the authorization to resume publication of their official newspaper, *L'Humanité*. Pending this authorization, *L'Humanité* came out in a semiclandestine form. Every issue exalted Franco-German fraternization.

Germans had no trouble, either, with the French bourgeois. Humiliated by the defeat, they placed all their hopes in Marshal Pétain, adopting the slogans in which he was so prolific. They believed that the Jews and Freemasons were responsible for the French disaster and that France's wounds would only be healed by returning to what they thought were the basic moral values. Work, family, and sacrifice were the only roads to national salvation. The bourgeois, blinded by their hidden guilt complex, had lost all critical

16

judgment and did not realize that the chief they were following was nothing more than a sly and proud old man handled by a team of cold and predetermined manipulators. Many of them belonged to the Synarchy and were experimenting with their theories under cover of the unsuspecting marshal.

Secret societies always proliferated in Europe in time of crisis. The Synarchy was one of them, created in the years following the First World War by Jean Coutrot. The complete name of the organization was "Mouvement Synarchique d'Empire." It was an offspring of the Martinism sect, a stem of early Freemasonry.

Synarchy literally means "the government of several leaders administering the various parts of a state"; thus, the Synarchic Movement was advocating the constitution of a government by several individuals. Coutrot, a graduate of l'École Polytechnique, the French M.I.T., believed that he and his schoolmates were the elite of the French people. Therefore, they thought the members of the government should be selected from among them. The organization took a highly esoteric shape. Each member knew only the one who had initiated him and the member he himself had instructed in the secrets of the organization. It took the form of a pyramid — ruled by those at the top. Any indiscretion on the part of one Synarch was punished by death. In a few years, because of the support the organization gave to its members, they succeeded in occupying key positions in the industrial and financial worlds.

One offspring of the Synarchy was the Secret Committee for Revolutionary Action (CSAR), generally known as the Cagoule, after the black hoods worn by its members during meetings. The Cagoule received a lot of publicity before the war, when as the organ of direct action of the Synarchy it perpetrated several political assassinations. After the French debacle, a great part of the Cagoule, following their chief, Eugène Deloncle, collaborated with Germany, while another faction rallied to General de Gaulle and were particularly noted for their activities in the secret services.

As for the Synarchy itself, the French defeat provided it with a long-desired opportunity to experiment with its theories.

Pétain had resolutely set aside all politicians from his government and surrounded himself with technocrats. Many of them were thought to be members of the Synarchy. I say "thought" because no list of members has ever been published, and the structure of the organization has never allowed its secrets to be penetrated. Nevertheless, I frequently had the opportunity to examine documents in the archives of the French Secret Services which did not leave any doubt as to the activities and membership in the Synarchy of many officials of the Pétain administration.

Sizing up the state of French affairs without emotion, these men decided that the defense of their own interests and the interests of the private firms to which they belonged should have priority. What was good for high finance should, in the end, be good for France. They conducted a series of surveys and concluded that France should collaborate economically with Germany if she was, in the future, to occupy a choice place in the European economic system. Pétain, lacking clairvoyance, met with Hitler in Montoire, and the official basis for the collaboration was set up. But the success of this policy depended on a determining factor — the victory of Germany. Without hesitation, the Synarchs — the technocrats — started to work toward this goal, while the mass of Frenchmen, not understanding what was happening, were putting their confidence in the "Victor of Verdun."

This does not mean that Pétain was surrounded only by traitors or collaborators. Far from it; the majority of the people in Vichy were decent men without malice. Accustomed to obedience, they were waiting for orders from the marshal without realizing that Pétain, prisoner of his age and of the team he had brought to power, was unable to change the course of events. Little by little, the faithful, acknowledging his silence, defected. Some joined the growing underground; others were eliminated or even arrested.

Certain chiefs of the Synarchy, panic-stricken by the direction taken by the organization, tried to warn Pétain. Jean Coutrot, the founder, made an attempt to furnish him with a list of membership. A few weeks later Coutrot died mysteriously; it has never been proved whether he was poisoned or pushed out of his apartment window. His secretary, Frank Théallet, had died a few months before, and the one who had replaced him, Yves Moreau, was to follow his chief to the grave six months later. Coutrot's brother-in-law, Alex Brulé, also died in suspicious circumstances. Then, within

18

a few weeks, Yves Paringaux, chief of cabinet for Secretary of the Interior Pucheu, and a friend of Coutrot, was found dead in a train.

The men at the top did not allow any indiscretions and did not tolerate any hindrance. The invasion of Russia by Germany was an excuse to increase their help to the Nazis under the pretext of fighting Bolshevism.

The French Communist Party, faithful to its allegiance to Moscow, had decided to reverse itself and oppose the Germans with whom it had fraternized for a year. It began to organize its own resistance. The Allies and the Free French had patiently begun implanting an intelligence network in order to help England to resist and bring about a German defeat. The Communists were setting up a very different type of network, and rather than confining themselves to the research of intelligence, they resorted to violence and terrorism.

By such methods the Communists suddenly created serious trouble for the Germans, but one cannot help wondering whether the results obtained were worth the price. For one unlucky German soldier murdered in a dark street, the Nazis executed at least fifty French hostages. To fight terrorism, the Germans set up a system of repression which enabled them at the same time to discover our intelligence networks and to arrest our comrades. The gathering and the transmission of intelligence became more and more dangerous. Besides this terrorism, the Communists made little contribution to the Allied cause in the form of intelligence.

In Vichy, the team which still gambled on a German victory decided to aid the Nazis in fighting the terrorists. Bousquet, former director of the Bank of Indochina and a Synarch, made an agreement with the Germans, allowing them to send Gestapo agents with French identification into the Free Zone to uncover and arrest the patriots of the resistance. The Free Zone became as unsafe as the occupied zone. The French honestly devoted to Pétain became potential informers. The resistance learned to be suspicious of everyone and everything. Germans were easy to detect, but the French . . .

As all this was happening, I continued to take to the so-called Free Zone both fugitives and increasingly voluminous bundles of intelligence. I had faked my bicycle in order to conceal letters and documents. Each tube that formed the frame of the bicycle was an ideal receptacle. For a measure of precaution, I had a friend make all sorts of metal caps to seal the tubes. This precaution saved my life when one day a suspicious German took apart the handlebars to examine them. It never occurred to him that behind the caps were numerous rolled-up reports.

The United States invaded North Africa, and the Germans occupied the Free Zone without, however, abolishing the demarcation line. So the obstacle remained and had to be crossed. But now the German patrols were on both sides of the river and the risk had become greater.

The posters announcing the executions of Doornick and d'Estienne d'Orves had long since been covered by others. The Vichy government team was constantly passing new laws against terrorists. Corrupted judges did not hesitate to enforce them, and death sentences pronounced by French courts were increasing. Naturally every member of the resistance was automatically labeled Communist. And the Germans had the satisfaction of seeing their adversaries killed by their own countrymen. Many times the Germans didn't even bother, in their haste, to wait for this pretense of French justice, and in the twenty-four hours following an act of terrorism, they proceeded with mass executions.

London had recommended that no sabotage of railroad or factory sites take place near a populated area, so that massive reprisals could be avoided. But the Communists ignored this — carrying out very often useless sabotage near important centers and provoking horrible massacres.

The Germans were forced continually to send fresh supplies of troops to the eastern front, and they had a pressing need for manpower in their factories. In agreement with the Vichy government, the Service of Compulsory Labor had been created. The mayors had to furnish lists of workers to be sent to Germany. Some refused and were severely punished. A member of my own family, a doctor and mayor of a small town, refused to comply with German requests. He was taken with his son, a medical student, to the town square, where his wife and the rest of his family were forced to watch their execution. First the son was shot and then the father.

Contrary to German expectations, these executions, instead of breaking the fighting spirit of the French, served only to intensify a desire for revenge. This feeling later stimulated the full development of the resistance. The more the Germans practiced deportation and execution, the more volunteers appeared to take up the fight.

The BBC was clever in exploiting each of the crimes committed by the Franco-German collaboration. Besides the organized networks, similar to the one I had joined, a great number of new groups spontaneously appeared and were striving for recognition by the Allies.

At the end of 1942, the arrests were multiplying, but none of us were really aware of the ordeal of those arrested. We knew only that the Gestapo was in charge and was merciless. They utilized a team of French policemen whose cruelty was equal to their own. It was much later that we learned the details of the tortures they inflicted on their prisoners. The torture of the bathtub was the most common. In this, the person being questioned was immersed in a tub full of water until he started suffocating, then his head was raised above the water and questioning was resumed. If he did not answer satisfactorily, the operation was repeated until the desired result was obtained or until he was dead. In other instances electrodes were attached to the genitals or the breasts and the electric charge was gradually increased. Or the victim's feet were burned with red-hot irons. New atrocities, impossible even to describe, were constantly invented by the sadistic criminals to get confessions out of their victims, who in the end were either shot or sent to concentration camps.

Everything has been done to hide the truth, but when the archives of the various local sections of the Gestapo were found after the war, we had to admit that for every German Gestapo member, there were some twenty French policemen to assist them in their sinister activities.

At the end of 1942, I received instructions to go to a certain location to pick up an envelope. The place was a bar located in Paris on Rue de Ponthieu called "The Parrot in the Nest." The meeting

21

was arranged for 11 P.M. The basement housed a nightclub where German soldiers and officers went to celebrate. One employee was a member of our network. The fact that the place was frequented by Germans and by black market traders made it relatively safe, for it was not, as a rule, under surveillance by the French police.

I took a seat at the bar and patiently waited for the contact who was to hand me the envelope. For some reason he was late. A few minutes after the hour I started getting nervous. The curfew was at midnight and it was dangerous to be caught without an authorization after curfew hours. But because I was leaving the next day for the Free Zone, I decided to wait a bit longer. Minutes were going by and still no one came. Finally, at a quarter to twelve my man appeared and slipped the heavy envelope into a pocket of the raincoat I had put next to me.

By the time I paid the bill, it was nearly midnight. I had two choices: either wait right there until six in the morning, or take a carriage home. Horse carriages were quite expensive; their customers were mostly black market traders who were known to pay off the police. For this reason, they were seldom bothered. Catering to wealthy clients, the coachmen were charging excessive prices, and a fifty-dollar fare for a twenty-minute ride was not uncommon. Although the expense was very high for my rather thin wallet, I decided to take a coach to the small hotel on the Left Bank where I planned to spend the night. Half asleep with the swaying of the carriage, I still noticed that we were taking the Rue de Berry, then the Champs Elysées. As we neared the Rond-Point, the carriage suddenly stopped and both doors were opened. I looked around surprised, expecting the Gestapo, but it was only two "Hirondelles," the bicycle-riding policemen.

"Do you have an ausweis?" they asked simultaneously.

"No, I'm from out of town and didn't know about the curfew," I answered trying to sound innocent.

They signaled the coachman to go ahead, riding one on each side to prevent my escape. I looked all around inside, trying to think of some way to get ride of the incriminating envelope. I couldn't throw it out the window. As a last resort, I hid it under the seat cushion. I didn't know its contents, but I was sure it concerned German installations and troop movements. It was certainly incriminating,

22

and no one would be fooled. The carriage slowed and then stopped. One of the doors opened and a policeman showed his head.

"Get down," he ordered.

I argued, "But officer, I've done nothing and I must get home."

He grabbed my arm roughly. "Hurry up, or I'll pull you out." He matched his actions to his words and I hit the ground. The coachman was standing there waiting.

"Pay him," I was instructed.

He asked 1,000 francs, or forty dollars, somewhat expensive for such a short ride. He no doubt had some arrangement with the policemen, and I had no choice but to pay.

"Can I go now?"

Instead of answering, they pushed me toward the door of the station.

"Another one without an ausweis," one of the policemen said, and then, paying no attention to me, began to divide some bills with his comrade. They were sharing their part of my coach fare.

"Your papers," demanded an officer behind the counter.

I got out my wallet in order to show my ID card, but he snatched it from my hand and spread the contents before him. Then slowly he started to fill out several forms. After a time he placed them in front of me.

"Sign here," he pointed out the line.

I was studying law and intended to use my knowledge by refusing to sign and by demanding to be set free immediately. I argued as a matter of form that I had not broken any French law, hoping by doing so to give some credibility to the out-of-town character, lost in the intricacy and injustice of the capital.

But I failed, and one of the officers grabbed me and pushed me into a large room where I found myself with some twenty people — the lockup. Besides a few drunks, the majority of my cellmates were, like myself, guilty of circulating after curfew hours.

"Don't worry," said one. "It's not my first time here. The coachmen and the drivers of velocycles (velocabs) have an agreement with the police. Instead of making long runs, they have their customers picked up by the police. Then they get the full amount of the fare and share it with the obliging cops. They're all bought off.

23

Look at them! All traitors!" He was pointing to a policeman selling cigarettes to the prisoners for outrageous prices.

"At 6 A.M. they will let us go. We only have to wait."

It seemed to me that the night would never end. I was furious with myself at having gotten rid of the envelope the way I did. I should have kept it; they had not searched me, only kept my wallet, which would be returned when I was released.

At six the door opened and we formed a line, waiting for our names to be called by the sergeant on duty. I was somewhere in the middle of the line when my name was called.

I rushed to the counter. Several policemen were talking together. The envelope I had hidden in the carriage was sitting there in the center of the desk, opened, with its contents spread out. From the distance I could make out lists and some drawings with figures. I felt myself grow weak, but tried to hide it and look indifferent.

"Is this envelope yours?" asked the officer who seemed to be in charge.

I looked at him questioningly, "What envelope?"

"This one," and he pointed out the opened envelope and papers.

"This? No. Why?"

"The coachman who drove you here found it under the seat and you were his last customer."

"Oh? Well, it's not mine." I made my face a blank, then asked, "May I have my wallet and ID now?"

Without looking up, he handed me my wallet, but kept the ID, which he carefully examined, inspecting all the stamps.

"You'll have to wait for the commissioner. The driver is sure this is yours because he checked the inside before he picked you up."

At this, I pretended to flare up in good Gallic tradition. "Listen, Sergeant, what is this all about? I said it's not mine — I've never seen it. For God's sake, what's the matter with this envelope anyway? If you don't want it, give it to me, but let me go. I just spent the night in a filthy cell and want to go home. You have no right to keep me here. My father's a lawyer and if I call him, you'll see some hell raised."

I emphasized all this by banging my fist on the counter. Raising my voice some more, I demanded, "When will your commissioner be here?"

Another officer, who seemed intrigued by the conversation, answered, "Not before 9:30 or 10."

I continued my pretense of anger, which was becoming more and more real: "Do you think I'm going to wait around here because of some envelope?"

The other policeman again intervened: "Sergeant, if this one says it's not his, after all, the driver could have made a mistake."

The sergeant was obviously embarrassed. He certainly realized that the papers before him were of importance and intended for the underground, but not being one hundred percent sure, he was worried about getting into trouble if he detained me.

"Look," he said after some thought, "the commissioner must see this," nodding to the papers, "and he will probably want to talk to you, but you can go now and come back at ten. I'm keeping your ID card here, so you'll have to come back. Where do you stay in Paris?"

I gave him the address of the small hotel where I had a room.

"All right, go on back, but I'll expect you here at ten. Otherwise we'll come and get you," he warned.

He didn't have to tell me twice, I rushed outside and got on the subway to the Left Bank and my hotel. I desperately tried to think of what I should do, knowing that the commissioner, upon seeing the papers, would immediately send for me. I had two hours to escape.

Going home to Romorantin was out of the question. The police had my ID card and knew my exact address. Orders would at once be forwarded to the local police to arrest me. The Germans would also start looking for me. I knew I could not contact the members of my network without giving them away.

Back at the hotel, I packed my suitcase and checked out. It was winter and still dark. I started in the direction of a hotel near the Invalides, where most of the clients were German. The police would not look for me there.

The Germans had forced the French to adopt Central Europe time, so it was dark until nine in the morning. I had complained like everyone else against this measure, but at this moment it seemed providential. The darkness was my only refuge.

For more than two years I had seen people in despair trying to escape from the Germans and their French collaborators. I had done what I could for them. Now I was the one being chased and badly in need of help.

Hidden in my small hotel bedroom, I could hear the German soldiers and their chippies coming and going continuously. There would not be any raids in this place; it was too popular as a recreation spot for the conquerors. For two days I stayed in my room. On the third, I decided to take a chance. I hadn't eaten for almost sixty hours and had to find food and help.

My brother was a college student in Paris. Watching my step carefully, I arranged a meeting and told him about the trouble I was in. Although he was five years my junior, he had always been my best friend and I could rely on him completely. He told me how the police had called on my father and had submitted him to a long questioning on my whereabouts. The officials had with them a sizable file on me — it seemed they had done a thorough job in only three days. My father had shrewdly answered that I was very independent and he did not know where I was or what my plans were. For the time being it seemed that he, being a lawyer with some prestige in our city, would not be harassed. But if I went back and was uncovered, they would accuse him of being my accomplice and send him to jail with me. I had to stay away from my hometown and not try to meet with any of my friends connected with the resistance. It would have been like pointing them out to the police. Since I couldn't spend the rest of my life in hiding, the only solution left to me was to leave France and join the Free French.

There were few ways of joining the Allied forces in England or in North Africa. Since the building of the Atlantic Wall, the crossing of the channel had become impossible. The Spanish border was the only practical route. Explaining my plans to my brother, I gave him a letter for Marc, my resistance chief, telling him what had happened and what I planned to do. I hoped he would be able to warn the British Embassy in Madrid of my eventual visit. Then I bade farewell to my brother, trying to look much more assured about my future than I really was.

Knowing no one along the Spanish border and being unfamiliar with the area, I had to find a guide to take me through the Pyrenees Mountains. Then I would try, one way or another, to get to Madrid and the British Embassy, where I felt I was certain to find help. The Germans had established a zone of surveillance along the border. Only the residents and persons carrying special permits were allowed in. The obstacles seemed almost insurmountable.

One evening I ventured out to visit a long-time friend and confided in her about my problem and my intentions. She told me about a former Air Force officer she knew who was also trying to join the Free French Forces. Why not get in touch with him and pool our efforts to find a way to leave the country? I hesitated about meeting the man. Who knows when one will meet a Gestapo agent or an informer? My friend eased my apprehension, insisting that she knew him well and was convinced that it was safe for me to talk to him.

Soon after, she introduced to me a tall, good-looking, likable fellow named Jacques Bagnère. He was from the southwestern part of France, a region called Landes near the Spanish border, and had been stationed for a time, as an Air Force officer, in Pau, a town near the Pyrenees. We talked all night. I explored with him the possibility of crossing the mountains and getting to Spain without being caught by the Nazis. He had a number of relatives in the region and through them there might be a chance of getting help from someone familiar with the area. Since I didn't want to waste a moment, we decided to catch a train to Bordeaux the next day. As agreed, I joined him at the Café de la Coupole in Montparnasse a few hours before our departure by train. We had picked this spot because it was near a station, and this would explain our suitcases.

Before leaving Paris, Jacques wanted to get some information from a friend, a beautiful girl named Geneviève who belonged to a network covering the southwest of France. She was already waiting for us. The conversation was tense. She had known Jacques a long time, but I was a stranger to her. As for me, I couldn't help feeling uneasy at hearing Jacques explain our project to a girl I didn't even know. In two years' time the only resistance people I had met were members of my own network. It seemed too much of a coincidence that Jacques should know someone from a network in the very place we were going. I have always been wary of coincidence. We talked rather guardedly for half an hour — she asked questions and I hesitated to reveal too many details about my intentions, which truthfully were still quite vague. She finally told us to see a friend of hers in Bordeaux by the name of Samazeuilh. This man was well-known in the region as editor of the local newspaper (*La Petite Gironde*) and a former tennis champion. I was to learn later that Samazeuilh was chief of her network, but at the time I had more than a few misgivings about contacting him. We said good-bye to Geneviève and took the subway to another station, transferring several times to be sure we weren't followed.

The Germans and French police made frequent inspections in the trains. Jacques was not wanted and had nothing to fear, but I was worried about being discovered in a train with no way to escape. Once more we resorted to the technique I had followed since becoming a fugitive — we sat in a compartment full of German soldiers. During the trip, which lasted the night, no one approached us, even to see our tickets. I considered this a good omen.

28

Bordeaux, one of the wine-producing capitals of the world, was filled with Germans. They had a submarine base there and the Gestapo was everywhere. The largest hotel, Le Splendide, which in 1940 had housed the members of the French government awaiting the armistice, was now completely occupied by Wehrmacht officers and members of the Kriegsmarine. The restaurant was open to the public, but at black market prices. All the decent hotels had been requisitioned and it was difficult to find a room anywhere. After several hours we ended up in a shabby rooming house with a rather questionable room, but at least a place to put our suitcases.

I was anxious to see Samazeuilh, for if he was unable to help us in crossing the Pyrenees, we would have to leave immediately in order to make our own arrangements. We avoided the telephone as a measure of precaution and right after lunch went directly to the newspaper office and asked to see him. He received us coolly, which, in a way, was understandable. I had many times myself had a stranger come to me giving only a friend's name, and it took some time to establish confidence. I explained our dilemma to him, but his response was discouraging.

"Look, even though I don't know you, I would be willing to help, but I really don't know anyone who could get you to Spain. The Germans patrol not only the border but the whole region, and you are running the risk of arrest even before contacting a guide. Besides this, many people have been arrested after being given away by so-called guides who had been paid their money in advance. Even if you succeed in getting to Spain, you have little chance of evading the police. They patrol the roads and all the public transportation. My advice to you would be to hide someplace in the country and to wait there for the end of the war."

We excused ourselves for taking his time and started to leave when Samazeuilh stopped us. "Wait a second."

From a drawer he pulled out a map and opened it on his desk. "This is winter and snow closes many of the mountain passes, so you must try to cross as near as possible to the coastal region where it is a little warmer. Also, you will need a valid excuse for going into one of the villages near the border. This is what I would suggest." He pointed to a dot on the map and continued, "This is Cambo, a station for TB patients. There are many sanitoriums and boardinghouses where people with lung diseases come to spend the winter. You can get there by train from Bayonne. If any questions are asked, one of you could pretend to be a patient and the other his attendant. Once in Cambo you shouldn't have too much trouble finding a guide willing to take you to Spain. That will be up to you. Once you have crossed the Pyrenees you will have to walk to Madrid. Neither trains nor buses are safe, but by the back roads you can get through. I am certain the peasants will help you along the way. They don't like the Franco regime and as a rule refuse to collaborate with the police. If you happen to be caught, destroy all your personal papers and claim you are British citizens. The Spaniards, being unable to prove that you are French, will not take you back to the border where you would be jailed by the Germans or Pétain's police. I'm sorry I cannot be of more help, but I have not visited this region for quite some time and I just don't know of any reliable person to whom I could recommend you."

His directions were nevertheless of great value to us, and we thanked him gratefully. Jacques Bagnère was already out of the office when Samazeuilh took me aside and said, "If you find yourself in trouble in Spain, write or phone Miss Campbell at the British Embassy using my name. But," and he held his finger to his lips, "not a word to anyone."

I was not to see Samazeuilh again; he died at the end of the war after having rendered very valuable services to the Allies as head of a most efficient intelligence network.

Time had passed rapidly. It was already January 5, 1943. The Americans had started the occupation of North Africa two months earlier, and Darlan had just been assassinated. Giraud was now in power in Algiers, and it was obvious that relations between him and de Gaulle were tense. Giraud represented the North African faction — people who had never seen combat and had rallied to Pétain. They had never resisted the enemy, only the American troops who had begun the liberation of Europe.

As for me, I had nothing but contempt for the Vichy military clique and couldn't wait to join de Gaulle and go into combat. I didn't want to waste a second and was rushing Jacques, who would have liked to spend more time in Bordeaux seeing friends. We decided to leave the next day.

We had changed trains in Bayonne. Comfortably seated in a compartment, I was reading about the difficulty of the Castilian dialect in a book I had bought the day before. Suddenly the door of the compartment opened and two *Feldgendarmes* wearing helmets and breastplates entered.

"Your papers," they demanded.

I tried to look natural while searching in my wallet for my driver's license. I had no ID card since the officer at the police station had confiscated it. I wondered if the license would satisfy the Germans or if they already had my description. Jacques, whose papers were in order, had given them his ID card, and one of them was examining it suspiciously. When I handed him my driver's license he barely glanced at it and returned it without comment. However, one of them then pointed to Jacques' suitcase on the rack above us and ordered him, "Open."

Jacques immediately obeyed and the Germans searched through it thoroughly. With my heart in my mouth I made a gesture as if to reach for my suitcase, when the other German nodded, "No, it's all right."

With unforgivable imprudence I had put in my suitcase a complete set of maps of the border region and several guidebooks on Spain. Even the dullest German would have guessed our destination. It was a close call and we both breathed our relief when they left.

Cambo is a delightful village, built on the side of a hill. The climbing streets are lined with pink laurel and small flower gardens. Even during this wartime winter Cambo looked cheerful. The first boardinghouse we came to looked remarkably clean and welcoming. There was only one vacant room, which we rented for a week and paid for in advance. I knew our presence would arouse the curiosity of the owners as well as the other boarders. But Jacques and I had agreed to say we were there to rest, and we tried to elude any personal questions.

The small village of Espelette was located halfway between Cambo and the border, a distance of about four miles. I decided to go there the same day and start looking for a guide. In the middle of the village was the gendarmerie and a little further, a café called Le Café Béraud. The streets were deserted and it seemed like walking in a ghost town. Stopping in front of the café, I entered and sat

31

down. A young girl took my order. I struck up a conversation with her and we chatted for a while. Deciding not to rush anything, I left shortly, leaving a large tip.

Back in our room, Jacques told me he had talked with most of the boarders but hadn't been able to get any information about crossing, which didn't surprise me at all.

For three days I went to Espelette and the Café Béraud. The waitress knew me by now and greeted me cordially. She went so far as to ask me what I was doing there. Feeling the time had come to take a chance, I invented a story of how I had been a prisoner in a German camp and had escaped with a friend. In order not to be caught, we had to cross over into Spain and I was looking for someone to lead us through the mountains. She didn't show too much surprise; my story seemed to correspond with her expectations. She told me she would speak to someone who might be interested in the job and for me to come at the same time the next day.

Jacques seemed happy to hear the news of my progress. He had become very popular in the hotel and everyone knew him.

The next day, when I got to the café, the girl took me to a table where a Basque was seated. He was about thirty, stocky and sulky-looking, wearing his beret pulled down over his brow. Without preamble, and looking not at me but at the table, he said, "You want to go to Spain?"

"Yes, and a friend of mine."

"It will cost fifteen thousand francs each."

The figure was very high. Today it would be about five hundred dollars each. It was no time to bargain, but just for the principle of the thing, I tried.

"It's awfully expensive."

But he was immovable: "That's my price."

I had no choice but to agree.

"O.K., be here tomorrow night at eight." And without any further exchange he got up, leaving by the back door.

This Basque didn't impress me too favorably. The man could be what he claimed or maybe an informer. In those days anything was possible, and many had paid with their lives for a mistake in judgment. I voiced some of my doubts to the waitress, but she told me not to worry, saying she knew him and he was honest.

Nevertheless, during the next twenty-four hours, I tried to form several plans of action to cover every eventuality I could imagine. I stayed in our room while Jacques socialized with his new acquaintances. Right before dinner he came in and approached me hesitantly.

"I've met someone — a former captain in the Foreign Legion. He wants to come with us."

I looked at him with alarm. "Come with us? You mean you told someone about us?"

"Don't worry! He's a former officer and can be trusted. He's outside in the hall. I want you to meet him."

I was furious, but what could I do? If Jacques had already talked to this man and he wanted to come, I couldn't refuse. It would be unwise to leave behind someone who could give us away in his discontent. Jacques returned with his new acquaintance. The man was emaciated — I guessed from tuberculosis. His eyes looked large and feverish.

"Captain Langlois," presented Jacques.

I was horrified. He didn't look as though he could last for more than a few days. I soon realized that Jacques had not only told him of our plans, but everything about me and my reasons for leaving France.

Langlois absolutely wanted to go. There was no way to avoid it. I told him the trip would involve a month of walking twenty miles every night and that we were leaving the same night. He knew this already from Jacques. I also mentioned that he would have to pay fifteen thousand francs to the guide, and he assured me this was no problem.

When Jacques and I were alone later, I spoke my mind. "Langlois is in no condition to make this trip. But now he knows too much to leave behind. Our chances of failure are increasing every minute." And my chances of execution, I added to myself.

I was beginning to realize that having a partner in this was a mistake — especially one who liked to talk as much as Jacques.

At seven we went down to the dining room for our last meal in France until the end of the war and our last civilized meal for a long time. Langlois came to sit with us. I kept my thoughts to myself, leaving Langlois and Jacques to carry on the conversation. At the

33

end of the meal, as our Cognac was served, all the other guests stood — about fifty in all — and proposed a toast, wishing us good luck on our trip! I was dumbfounded. It finally dawned on me that my partner had confided our plans to the entire boardinghouse. Even the waitresses and the chef took part in the toast!

For a while, too angry to speak, I debated whether or not to flee and hide somewhere while I revised my plans. With so many in on our "secret," it would be sheer luck if the local gendarmes didn't hear of it.

I left the dining room and went back to our room, leaving those two fools in the center of a group receiving congratulations and encouragement. I was packing my suitcase when someone knocked at the door. It was a doctor from Belgium who had come to Cambo for a month's rest. He had witnessed the collective farewell downstairs and told me of his concern over the indiscretion of such a widely known secret. I asked his opinion of Langlois' being able to stand the long hike. He was quite pessimistic.

"That's what I came to talk to you about." He showed me a box containing several vials of caffeine and a syringe. "In case one of you collapses, don't hesitate to give an injection. The stimulation will last an hour or two."

Many times I've thought with gratitude of this man, whose foresight contributed greatly to this already jeopardized expedition.

As he was leaving, Langlois and Jacques came in. They were beginning to worry over their imprudence. I told them to get their suitcases ready without wasting a moment and meet me outside. We had no time to lose after their carelessness.

I led the way and we walked rapidly to Espelette. The Basque was already waiting for us and motioned for us to follow him. He took us to a stable nearby, where he asked for the money. I paid my share and Jacques gave him his fifteen thousand, but Langlois had only ten thousand francs and started to dicker. The imperturbable guide refused to argue or accept less than the agreed price. Jacques Bagnère gave him the extra five thousand to avoid trouble, then bitterly reproached Langlois for saying he could pay his share.

The Basque left us for a few moments, probably to hide his money. He returned with a walking stick and set out at the measured pace of a mountaineer. Jacques was walking behind him, then came

Langlois. I was last. Avoiding the village, we took a path that one could hardly detect. An hour went by without incident. Then I noticed that Langlois was slackening his pace. An hour later, Jacques suggested that we stop, Langlois was exhausted. I gave him an injection of caffeine in the arm, and when we started walking again, my load was increased by the weight of Langlois' suitcase. The guide, showing no sign of stress, kept a steady pace without commiserating or offering his help. It was nearly three o'clock in the morning when the Basque pointed out a lighted house in the distance.

"The German guardhouse," he whispered. "Spain is over there," and he gestured in the night. "If you want to go further, it will be another twenty thousand francs each."

Never in my life have I felt such an inclination to strangle someone! This horrible creature, with no sense of shame, knowing that the least noise would bring out the Germans, was blackmailing us!

Langlois had no more money, Jacques had been left with two thousand francs. As for me, after taking care of all the expenses of our trip so far, I was determined not to waste away what I had left. Getting an extra five thousand francs out of my pocket, I told our guide this was all I had. Jacques offered the two thousand. The man hesitated awhile, but his greed for gain prevailed. Taking the money, he set out again briskly. Langlois was near fainting, so I gave him another shot of caffeine to keep him going. The Basque, indifferent to our tribulations, was walking on, indefatigable. The day was dawning. We were approaching the summit of a mountain where a sheepcote stood, built by shepherds out of rough materials. Our guide stopped and gestured in front of him at the hills and valley stretching to the line of the horizon.

"You are in Spain. The first Spanish town, Elizondo, is in the second valley, over to the right."

Jacques and Langlois had disappeared into the shack and fallen asleep on some loose straw. I told the guide that we could not possibly start walking again without a few hours' rest. He agreed, and I soon fell into a heavy sleep.

I awoke with a start. It was noon and the others were still sound asleep. As for the guide, there was no sign of him. I searched the vicinity but he was nowhere around and I finally had to admit he had disappeared, leaving us to our fate in the middle of the Pyrenees.

It took a while to rouse my two companions. Langlois was in poor shape. When told about the guide's disappearance, he sank into despair, and grabbing his suitcase, started to run down along the path toward Spain like a madman. Jacques and I followed him calmly. My friend, now realizing his mistake, was blaming himself for letting Langlois in on our plans, and was wondering what we should do now about this unfortunate fellow. We were walking at a short distance when, suddenly, Langlois lifted his suitcase and threw it into a ravine over a hundred feet deep. Then he took up his erratic running, like a wild puppet, until we lost sight of him. We discovered him almost an hour later on the side of the road, unconscious. I had no other choice but to give him another shot of caffeine to bring him around.

We could now command a good view of the valley, with another mountain chain rising behind. On the hillside was a dwelling. Although I could not accurately estimate the distance, the house seemed quite far away. My companions grew restless, anxious to get to the farmhouse, where they could rest and get food. They were convinced that one hour's walking would take us there. It was five hours later, after a strenuous walk, that we neared our goal. As we approached, dogs started to bark, and a frightened face peeked through the door. I can well imagine the surprise and fear of this girl, in her isolated retreat, when confronted with the spectacle of three bearded, dirty, exhausted creatures who were unable to speak her language. She spoke Basque and could say only a few words in Spanish. By way of gestures and the sight of money, we made ourselves understood and were able to get some corn biscuits and fried eggs. It was our first food of any kind in twenty-four hours.

She took us to a corn loft and we were soon overcome by a deep and consuming sleep. I awoke with a jolt when someone started shaking me vigorously. A man stood there, the eternal Basque beret worn low on his eyes, carrying a flashlight and staring at me sternly. He was the farmer and apparently he was indignant over the intrusion, during his absence, of three foreigners. Thank God, the man spoke French. I assumed him of our good intentions, explaining to him our need for a guide to take us to the vicinity of Elizondo without running into the local police. The offer of a certain sum of money was enough to convince him to help us.

The wife of a farmer in the area had just died, and the funeral was scheduled for the next morning. Our man thought that the three of us could easily pose as members of the family and follow the funeral procession to the cemetery in Elizondo. Once there, we could go on our way through the back roads and mountain tracks until we reached Madrid. The idea seemed a good one, and without bothering to wake the other two, I made the deal. The farmer left and I went back to sleep.

Around five the next morning, our host woke me again in his brusque manner. In turn, I woke Jacques and Langlois. They had not yet recovered from their extreme fatigue and it was not easy for me to convince them to follow the plan set up by the farmer. Brushing off the straw they had buried themselves in to get protection from the cold, they finally agreed and came into the kitchen with us, where the woman had prepared corn pancakes and hot milk.

Her husband was waiting to take us to his neighbor's farm. We walked for a good hour. The dead woman's body had not yet been laid in the casket and we helped the family with the task. Langlois sat in a corner, finding particularly to his taste the local custom of passing around a wineskin filled with a full-bodied Spanish red wine. Jacques and I declined politely. Such a beverage at this early hour would most likely have turned our stomachs.

When all was ready, two men stepped out and brought back two heavy branches they had cut from a tree and nailed one on each side of the coffin. Then, lifting this hastily improvised handbarrow, they carried it on their shoulders and the procession began. Jacques and I were walking immediately behind the body carrying our suitcases, posing as out-of-town members of the family. After half an hour, one of the bearers motioned us to come and take their place. We did our best, but were already so tired that we could not keep us with the pace and were advancing so slowly that two volunteers came up to relieve us after fifteen minutes.

I will never forget my state of mind while following this funeral procession. I was moved by the imposing beauty of the scenery and by the simplicity, the primitiveness, of this rustic burial. Then, as I would try to picture the grotesque spectacle presented by the three fugitives standing out against these peaceful people, the comedy of the situation would strike me. And I was hardly able to repress a laugh when, at a curve in the road, two uniformed men from the Guardia Civil, wearing their funny two-pointed hats made of pressed leather, stepped aside to let us pass and stood at attention while we proceeded. Jacques had a ghost of a smile on his face, and I dared not look in his direction for fear of bursting into laughter.

After three hours, we emerged on a paved road. The cemetery, surrounded by high walls, was on the right side. When the time came for us to cross the gate, the farmer nodded and I quite naturally stepped aside. Jacques and Langlois joined me. All was clear and we walked briskly around the cemetery.

My plan was very simple. Without losing sight of the road, we would walk through the fields to avoid the police until we reached Madrid. It was well known that the peasants had suffered a great deal from the civil war and from the restrictions of the Franco regime. I knew we could depend on them for food and shelter in exchange for money. The trip would no doubt be extremely tiring, but it was quite possible to cover the 200 miles to Madrid in about two weeks. Jacques and Langlois agreed to the plan.

We walked single file; Bagnère first, then Langlois, and then myself. We heard the sound of an automobile on the road not too far from us. Instead of hiding, Langlois unexpectedly announced he was too tired to walk. He ran down the embankment, stopped on the side of the road, and waved to the approaching car. Our instinctive move to stop him put us in the sight of the driver and after stopping to pick up Langlois, he motioned us to come along. Since we were already exposed, we went down in order not to abandon the incoherent Langlois.

In answer to my question, the driver said his destination was Pamplona. It was on our route, and if we could be driven that far, it would save us two days' walking. Another Spaniard was in the front seat next to the driver, and the three of us sat in the rear. The car started in the direction of Elizondo. Before entering the village, the driver made a left turn and stopped the car in front of a house. He blew the horn. Sticking his head out the window, he called, and three men ran out and surrounded the car. Our ride had lasted exactly five minutes and we were now in the hands of the Spanish police.

I was as furious over the stupidity of Langlois as over the betrayal of the driver. Langlois seemed not to mind the situation — he wouldn't have to walk anymore.

After crossing the mountains, I had taken care to destroy all my personal papers, and when the sergeant of the Guardia Civil questioned me, I declared my British citizenship and asked to see the consul. Bagnère and Langlois, who didn't speak a word of English, stated that they were Canadians. We were then taken to the local jail, which must have dated from the Middle Ages. The walls were five feet thick, the window nothing but a hole covered by an iron grille. Chances to escape were nil. All our hopes were now concentrated on the British consul, whose visit we awaited impatiently.

The next day the guards, armed with machine guns, took us by bus to Pamplona and the Carcel Modela or "model jail." Pamplona's jail represented one of the best urban realizations of Franco's regime. In a country devastated by civil war, Franco's concern was not rebuilding the shattered cities, but erecting jails to hold his political enemies. They were numerous, and the jails were overcrowded. This one was built in the shape of a Y. At the junction of the three wings was a hexagonal building of one floor housing the clerk's office. After our names were entered in the register, we were taken to the barber and our heads were shaved. Then we were assigned a cell.

Cell number 81 was located on the third floor of the main building. There were already four occupants in the 17 by 21-foot room. In the left-hand corner from the door was a toilet; on the right, dropped from the wall by chains, was a board. On the far side was a stack of straw pallets and an opening in the wall covered by thick iron bars. The four other inmates, Frenchmen and Belgians, were seated on the board. When the three of us came in we crouched on the mats, but after talking with the others, we soon set up an agreement whereby we took turns using the board.

The daily routine of the jail never varied: we woke up at six to a bugle call, then each of us washed hastily in a small basin with water from a pail. Then a guard came around carrying a long metal rod which he used to test the bars to make sure no one had tampered with them. Around eight we were brought a hunk of dry bread for breakfast. On Sundays an onion accompanied the bread! At ten we went out to a small yard, where we joined the other inmates. Every nationality was represented among them, but the majority were French, mostly of Jewish origin. No one knew how long our detention would last. We exchanged news about the war obtained from the guards and rejoiced over any Allied victories. At the same time we didn't want the war to end before we could participate in it again. After half an hour of fresh air we went back to the cell with nothing else to do but wait for lunch, which consisted of chick-pea soup. On the first day I cut one of the peas in two and found a worm inside. I then discovered that every pea had such an occupant. So, for a few days, we drank only the liquid, which was covered with a reddish-colored oil, but soon our hunger forced us to eat it all — devouring the peas without examining their contents. We spent the afternoon either sleeping or telling stories or trying to learn Spanish. At six o'clock we had another soup, thinner than at lunch. Then the guard returned and went through his routine with the iron bars. And we would try to sleep and forget our misery.

On Sunday mornings the cell doors were left slightly open so we could hear the mass being held on the roof of the registry building. A Spanish priest always delivered heated sermons praising the Nazis and Pétain and forecasting the fires of hell for us. This fanatic priest managed, I'm sure, to destroy the faith of many of the Catholic inmates. His grotesque attitude reflected the confused role Spain was then playing in the world.

During the first days of my imprisonment, following the advice of Samazeuilh, I had written from Elizondo to Miss Campbell at the British Embassy in Madrid, explaining my situation in veiled terms. I was also able to give another letter for her to a Spaniard who had promised to deliver it. Then, like the others, I had sent a letter to the English consul in Madrid. On February 19, 1943, I received a printed card from the military attaché of the British Embassy, acknowledging receipt of my letter to the English consul. I made every effort to keep my hopes up and to remain convinced that the British authorities, who then represented the Free French in Spain, would somehow intercede.

40

I had discovered by talking with the other French prisoners that with the exception of two of them, none had worked for a resistance network. They had escaped from France either to flee racial persecution or from a desire to fight for their country. One of the two resistants in Pamplona with me was a member of a Polish network working directly under the orders of the Intelligence Service, as we called the British service at the time. Another one was Henri Seignon, a hero of the resistance in Gabon, arrested after an aborted insurrection against Vichy. He had been sent to the prison of Riom, France, from where he made a successful escape. After crossing the Pyrenees, he was caught like the rest of us by the Guardia Civil.

The days and weeks went by and we refused to give up hope. Langlois, whose condition had worsened since his internment, was called one day and ordered to pack. His release had been decided. The Spaniards did not want to care for a sick man. I gave him another message for Miss Campbell, and he promised to do everything possible to help us regain our freedom. However, we were not to hear from him again. The irony of it all was that the one responsible for our capture should be the first to be liberated.

At last, toward the end of February, after two months of imprisonment, it was our turn to be called — Bagnère, Seignon, and me. We were to leave the next day with a hundred or so inmates for an unknown destination. For our last night we were transferred to underground cells, where our jailers gave us back our own clothes and suitcases and left us to sleep on the concrete floor. Disappointed, no doubt, at having us escape from their surveillance, they neglected to serve us dinner, but we were too excited to think of food or sleep.

Forgetting the anguish of our confinement and our own physical weakness, we could think of nothing but freedom. We talked and speculated through the night about England and the forces of the Free French, trying to brush aside our uncertainty about the Spaniards' plans for us. We didn't want to think that we might be handed over to the Vichy police in France or forced to join Giraud in North Africa, which to us was not much better. To our knowledge, the French in London were the only ones to have fought at the side of the Allies without interruption. Those in charge of my network were in London, and I was determined to get there at any price. The next few days would tell me if it would be necessary to escape again in order to do so.

At dawn the next day we assembled in the main building and were lined up in ranks and signaled to march through the gates. We thought we were free, but outside the gates more members of the Guardia Civil were standing in rows with machine guns at hand, as always, wearing their ridiculous little two-pointed hats. Surrounded by guards, we had to cross a section of the city of Pamplona. I looked all around for possibilities of escape, but the guards were too close together for me to see much. After a while we came to what looked like a depot. An ancient train was waiting and we were ordered to get on. What was our destination — north to the Vichy and the Nazis or south to freedom? Our guards refused to answer, and we looked at the sun with anxiety to determine the direction. The train pulled out of the station, and in spite of the meandering of the narrow tracks we soon realized that we were heading southwest.

"To Portugal!" someone shouted.

Puffing along with difficulty, the old engine was slowly pulling the cars. All along the tracks children and merchants were trying to attract the attention of the travelers to the food they were selling. One old man, displaying an unexpected agility, jumped onto the footboard of the car in which I was seated. He carried a gunnysack full of fresh loaves of bread — the large round ones weighing about six pounds we used to see in the country in France. I was starved and could not resist the appetizing sight. The old man, seeing our hunger, asked too much, but I paid his price. The man next to me did the same. With more pleasure than in the finest restaurant, I ate ravenously. Not seeming to be able to get full, I had eaten almost half the loaf, when my neighbor warned me, "You'd better stop before you get sick."

Curiously I looked at him. "I don't know you. What's your name?"

"Jean Rotter, and this is Guinsburger." He pointed to the man next to him. "Or if you prefer, Benoist, since everyone is changing names here."

42

My interlocutor was speaking in a quiet voice. He appeared tall and thin and was instantly likable.

"Look, I have given half of mine to Benoist. You have forgotten how it feels to be satisfied."

I looked at him with skepticism and continued to gorge myself.

"After all, it's up to you," he said disgustedly.

I nodded and kept eating.

Another Spaniard was selling cans of sardines. I bought one and ate the whole thing. Looking at me, Jean Rotter shrugged his shoulder but added nothing more, and leaning back, fell asleep.

All day we were jolted and tossed about by the train as our trip continued. It grew dark, and around eight in the evening the train stopped in the Logroño station, which seemed good-sized. In answer to my question, a Spaniard told me this was good wine country, and to demonstrate, he handed me his wineskin. Noting my clumsiness, he showed me how to use it. Holding the skin away and squeezing slightly on the sides produced a thin stream of red wine. My first try was rather sloppy, and the front of my shirt was stained with wine before I could imitate my instructor. The wine was dark and strong.

Buses were waiting for us. Exhausted and unable to distinguish anything in the dark, we rode along, no longer questioning, waiting for our journey to end. Occasionally someone would mention Portugal or a concentration camp in Miranda, but such utterances were received flatly and drew no response.

Shortly before midnight we came to a village. The first bus drew up in front of a hotel on the main street. The second, in which I was riding, drove through narrow cobblestone streets and stopped in front of an inn named La Fonda Marodan. We were in Arnedillo, a small spa famous for its mud baths, supposedly radioactive, for the treatment of rheumatism. How long were we to stay in Arnedillo? Our guards didn't know and answered with a meaningless "*Mañana*" our questions about when we were to leave for England.

This was not to concern me again for some time, since that night I came down with infectious hepatitis and lapsed into unconsciousness for forty-eight hours. When I came to my senses, Jean Rotter and Bagnère were at my bedside, worried over my condition. I was under the care of a local doctor, whose treatment included the use of leeches to bleed me. Only my strong constitution enabled me to survive both the illness and the treatment. Nevertheless, it took more than two months.

All this time we were the objects of special attentions on the part of the British. A delegation from the British consulate in Madrid had made the trip to visit us, and I had a long conversation with one of its members. Our liberation was being negotiated with the Spanish authorities. It seemed that the Spanish government, having previously shown a great partiality toward the Germans, had become more cooperative since the landing of the Allies in North Africa.

The sick ones were to be the first to be sent to North Africa, and others were to be released gradually in economic exchanges. The Spanish were short of wheat, and they agreed to free prisoners as deliveries of flour were made. The United States had promised to make the first delivery, and as a gesture of goodwill, the Spanish were going to release the first group of about fifty men. Due to the necessities of war, pilots were given an absolute priority. So, within our group, Bagnère and Jouare, the only two pilots, received orders to leave immediately for Madrid. The rest of us had to wait for the arrival of the first shipment of flour from the United States. Each bag represented freedom for one of us.

The British insisted that we should not try to escape, saying they would be unable to help us if we were caught again by the Spanish police. Besides, the tight security made chances of escaping very remote.

The British consul made an agreement with the hotel owners to provide us with food and lodging at their expense. We were also to get thirty-five pesetas a week as pocket money. In spite of the modesty of the sum, I thought it very generous of the British to keep us so comfortably.

In Madrid at the French Embassy was Pétain's representative, Pietri, who had been Secretary of the Navy before the war. Giraud also had a representative in Madrid — a Catholic bishop, Monsignor Boyer Masse, who was assisted by Colonel Malaise, a sort of military attaché. Some of the prisoners with families in North Africa, who didn't care whether they joined Giraud rather than de Gaulle, wrote to Bishop Masse asking him to help them. But neither the bishop nor Malaise answered or showed any interest in their condition.

One of the British representatives seemed particularly aware of my activities in the resistance and told me that a representative of General de Gaulle was in Madrid under cover of the British Embassy and was waiting for my visit as soon as I was able to get to the Spanish capital. His name was Morton and his office was located in the embassy building.

The events of the war were progressing so rapidly that I expected to learn any day that it was over without ever being a participant myself. Rommel's army had been crushed by Allied forces. Italy had requested an armistice, and de Gaulle had finally reached Algeria, and by doing so had given an impression of unity in the organization of the French fighting forces.

At the end of August the order came for us to be taken to Madrid. Our stay in the capital was very brief — only one day — but I had time to see Morton. He told me as soon as I arrived in Algiers to contact the BCRA, and in case of difficulty to get in touch, in Casablanca, with a certain Captain O'Byrne. I had no knowledge of the BCRA, and Morton was not too precise on the subject. He warned me, however, about the obstacles that the Giraud organization could create for me and advised me to be discreet with the members of military security who would interrogate me upon my arrival.

The evening of the day we arrived in Madrid we left for Málaga to wait for the French ship *Sidi Brahim*, which was to take us to Casablanca. At this time, German submarines were cruising the Mediterranean and Atlantic, so the arrivals and departures of Allied ships were kept secret. We waited for the *Sidi Brahim* for more than a week. The Spanish authorities, unconcerned about our comfort, had us sleep under the tiers of seats at the bullfight stadium, with no mats or even blankets. We were allowed, after many requests, to use some of the straw we found in the stalls to protect us from the cold. The sight of the *Sidi Brahim* flying the French colors made us forget all this, and it was with profound joy that we embarked on this old tub, which in other times would long since have been scrapped.

During the five days of the crossing, military security officers proceeded with a thorough interrogation as to our identities, our activities since the armistice, our families, etc. Following Morton's advice, I made sure not to reveal more than necessary. The interrogating officers belonged to the North African unit and had only vague ideas about the situation in France. They probably wouldn't have been able to recognize a German if they heard one speak. Sad, but at the same time it corresponded to the opinion we already had about these men of Giraud's who had never fought but were waiting for the end of hostilities in a colonial garrison.

Upon our arrival in Casablanca, the troops were deployed to receive us. There were detachments from all regiments stationed in the area. Soldiers of the Foreign Legion with their white caps, spahis in magnificent red and white uniforms, Zouaves wearing their wide red cummerbunds, fusiliers in white gaiters, and the infantrymen in khaki. They all stood at attention, the flag bearer dipped the flag as we passed, and the military band beat a lively march. We stood in file and General Giraud himself gave a welcoming speech, saying we would each receive a personal letter from him congratulating us on our escape and thanking us for joining the North African forces.

After these welcoming words, Red Cross ladies passed out mountains of indigestible sandwiches. We received all these attentions knowing that in a few minutes we would be free to walk, if not on the soil of France, at least on kindred soil. We were not prepared for what came next. When we left the harbor we were crowded into cattle trucks. The band and the general's speech suddenly seemed far away as we jostled and bumped down the road to a camp which was surrounded by barbed wire and heavily guarded.

So after all these months, thinking we had reached our goal, we found ourselves deprived again of the freedom we had come prepared to defend. From the trucks we had been able to catch a glimpse of the swarming crowds in the streets of Casablanca, but we could not mingle with them. Our disappointment and anger were acute, and we were completely bewildered. The official welcome and the Red Cross reception — why this comedy?

Leaning against the fence which separated us from freedom, I conversed with an officer wearing a British uniform but the red forage-cap of the spahis. He was on the other side of the fence.

"You just arrived here?" he asked.

"One hour ago — and I don't care to stay."

"Well, it will take a week or more."

"But for Christ's sake, why are they keeping us prisoners? We spent a year in Spanish jails in order to get here and fight. Now here we are; I don't understand."

"It's very simple. You are being detained here by Giraud's men to keep you from joining the Free French."

Jean Rotter, who was nearby and heard the lieutenant's statement, intervened, "But now de Gaulle and Giraud have reconciled. They're together in Algiers and there are no longer a dozen French armies. Right?"

"In principle you are right," said the lieutenant. "But you don't know the whole situation. Let me explain. General de Gaulle was the first and only one in 1940 to reject the armistice and to rally the few Frenchmen who had been able to escape from France before the total occupation of its territories. The Congo, the Cameroun, the Chad, and most of the African colonies decided to join him against the Germans. We were not many, but under the command of Leclerc and of Koenig we fought continuously along with the British, keeping France in the war, while here in North Africa the army, which numbered more than 120,000 men, was inactive. The career officers were leading the life of the garrison as usual — getting their promotions, living comfortable family lives, reporting to headquarters in the morning, going home for dinner with the wife and children. Most of them hadn't fought enough worth mentioning. Their consciences were at peace — they had sworn allegiance to Marshal Pétain. He had told them to collaborate with the Germans, so this is what they did. It was an ideal and safe situation. In their opinion de Gaulle and his followers were fools. Why choose to fight when one can live comfortably at home?

"Then last November came the catastrophe — the landing of

47

the American forces in North Africa and good-bye to the easy life. Those who were most pro-Nazi even fired on the Americans, who finally made an agreement with Darlan, Pétain's right arm. He was the one who had once had a meeting with Hitler and had prevented the French Navy from rallying to the Allies. After his assassination, the Americans brought Giraud to power. Actually, Giraud is not so bad, but he's a stubborn martinet of the old school, devoid of psychology, with an old-fashioned conception of war. All the Vichyite officers pledged their loyalty to him while continuing their daily military routine, waiting for the Americans to win the war. At this same time, we Free French were crossing the desert to attack the Italians from the rear in Cyrenaica; then, together with the British, we fought in Libya, at Bir Hacheim, and in Tunisia against the common enemy, German or Italian. Then, at the end of May, de Gaulle and Giraud came to an agreement. De Gaulle moved to Algiers and the Leclerc division has been quartered here near Casablanca so we can rest before going back to the front. This is the problem. The young men drafted by the Giraudists want to fight and not waste their time parading. They are reservists like ourselves, not career men, and want to get the war over with so they can go home. They rebel when Giraud's officers teach them horse riding and saber attacks. Rather than be a party to this idiotic play, they desert his ranks and enlist with the Gaullists. The Giraud camp is furious, and this explains your internment. They don't want any more such losses."

"I was in the underground with the Gaullists," I explained, "and am supposed to contact the BCRA as soon as possible. I hope to be able to do it without any trouble."

"Don't expect them to make it easy for you. But I'll give you a tip — before leaving this camp you will have to sign up for the duration of the war. As a volunteer you'll have your choice of units. Request to join a Gaullist regiment and you will have more freedom to make contacts."

"Which regiments are Gaullist?"

"I myself belong to the First Regiment of Moroccan Spahis [the first RMSM]. Why don't you enlist with us? You won't be sorry." He left after having convinced us to sign up with his unit.

The next day a security officer questioned me with precision on the resistance in France. I was asked to give the names of comrades as well as contacts where resistants would find refuge, also to point out on a map the spots suitable for parachute drops. Finally, the officer asked me if I would be willing to be sent back to France on a mission. The question surprised me — and I reminded myself that I was wanted by the Germans and Vichy police, but said yes nevertheless. Then I inquired about the possibility of contacting the BCRA, which according to Morton in Madrid was waiting for me. I was ignorant of what the initials stood for, but the reaction of the officer made me think I had pronounced a dirty word. He closed his notebook and said coldly that he would call me if there was anything further.

The days dragged by and we were still behind the barbed wire with no chance of communicating with the outside world. After going through a multitude of formalities and proceedings inside the camp, I finally succeeded in signing up for the First RMSM. I was anxious to join my unit in Rabat, hoping in the process to be able to steal a few minutes to make my contacts. After the customary physical, we were given khaki uniforms from the First World War. They were thick and uncomfortable, hardly suitable for the climate of Morocco. Puttees made out of the same material completed our uniform, adding to the discomfort by impeding circulation in our legs. The obvious disparity between our absurd uniforms and the good-looking and functional ones worn by the Germans and Americans showed more than anything else, and with striking evidence, the antiquated ideas of the French command.

Satisfied that our disguise would brand us as one of its members, the Army finally granted us what we had been yearning for — freedom; or rather, a glimpse of freedom, since ours lasted one day. But for that day we luxuriated in it, happy to roam freely in the streets without feeling uncomfortable at the sight of a policeman. I didn't forget, however, to placc a call to Captain O'Byrne to let him know of my presence in Morocco. He assured me he would immediately request my transfer to the BCRA. But considering the state of relations between Giraud and de Gaulle, this could take quite a while. He advised me to be patient and to let him know about any change of location, and invited me to come and see him if I got to Casablanca. Having done this, I decided philosophically

49

to content myself with being a soldier for the moment at least and to let others decide my fate.

Instead of having me rejoin my regiment, the Army decided to send me to officer's training in Camp Boulhau. After the war, Camp Boulhau was to become an important American air base, equipped with the most modern installations, but at this time it was nothing but an Arab village halfway between Casablanca and Rabat. The military camp consisted of wooden barracks with dirt floors.

The day after our arrival, a crusty sergeant set about teaching us the military profession — as it was then conceived, along the First World War lines.

With the escapees from France were the regular soldiers from the colonies; they were French, but their families lived in Morocco. They were well-fed and in normal physical condition, not having been exposed to the restrictions of the German occupation or imprisonment. They got through the military training with little effort, but the ex-prisoners, weakened by the hardships of prison life, lacked the physical strength to do what was required. I myself weighed only 110 pounds and was given no time to rest and regain some strength. The officers were unconcerned and didn't spare us. Some even took a certain pleasure in reducing us to a complete state of exhaustion.

One in particular would snarl, "So you wise guys didn't want to stay in France. You wanted to fight. Well, we'll let you fight, if you still can when we're through with you."

He was the son of the director of an important bank in Casablanca; he was the same age as we were and wore the bar of second lieutenant. Always dressed impeccably, he would crack his riding whip on his boots, and he especially relished, at the end of a tiring day when it was time to return to the barracks, to make us run for half an hour — or sometimes an hour, according to his whim. One day General Lattre de Tassigny, who later became famous in the French-Indochinese war, visited the camp unexpectedly. Having escaped himself from France and having spent time in jail, he asked that the escapees be brought to him. Our young lieutenant hurried us out. General de Lattre, seeing our enfeebled condition, became enraged, and in front of the assembled troops he put the lieutenant under close arrest and ordered that all maltreatment of us be stopped and that we be given time to rest before resuming our intensive training.

Unfortunately for me, the general had come too late. A few days later, succumbing to the fatigue and mistreatment, I was taken to the hospital in a complete state of exhaustion. What could have been a tragedy, however, turned out to be to my advantage. After several weeks of treatment, I was given leave to recuperate.

The beginning of December 1943, I left for Algiers carrying a letter from Captain O'Byrne. The captain had filled me in on the details of the situation. According to their agreement, General de Gaulle held the political power while General Giraud, in his capacity as commander in chief, held the military power. Relations between the two were far from cordial, and each incident which might infringe on the other's authority was magnified out of all proportion. In other times it would have been easy for the BCRA to request my transfer and send me to Algiers, but now it was necessary to ask for authorization for this transfer from Giraud headquarters, where it was naturally shelved. And if, without waiting for this formality, I had gone to Algiers on my own, this would have created an incident no one wanted. The sick leave I had just obtained, making it possible for me to go to Gaullist headquarters, was an unhoped-for solution to an embarrassing problem.

Captain O'Byrne had finally explained the meaning of BCRA to me — it was the Central Bureau of Intelligence and Action (*Bureau Central de Renseignement et d'Action*); in other words, de Gaulle's secret service in charge of the resistance in France.

The train was the only means of transportation between Casablanca and Algiers. The trip of 900 miles took three nights and two days — that is, if it was on schedule. There was, of course, no food served on board, and the passengers had to bring whatever they would need for the trip. The train stopped in every station, and the view of the Arab crowd was a colorful and picturesque sight.

The customs of the Arab world were impressed upon me when, as I was looking out, another train came to a stop beside us, blocking the view. Its windows were equipped with double screens which concealed the inside. It looked like a jail on wheels. Feminine voices could be heard — Arab, French, English, Italian and I don't know what else — calling the intrigued soldiers who crowded around trying to see in. The solicitations and derisive taunts didn't make soldiers blush, but the crude language would have been more appropriate coming from the mouth of some hardened Legionnaire. Someone said it was the private train of the sultan of Morocco and the cars were transporting some of the members of his harem — just enough to entertain him away from home, no doubt. The women must have been bored in the temporary absence of their master and were amusing themselves by jeering at the travelers.

The BCRA in Algiers was housed in an old administrative building known as the "Old Palace." The Minister of the Interior occupied the main part of the building, and scores of people hurried through the corridors trying to look important.

Major Bouheret, to whom I reported, greeted me warmly. He had expected me, and after questioning me about France and my activities in the resistance, he said he needed me on his staff. He asked one of his assistants to help me with the usual formalities. I first had to complete a form asking general personal information. Then I was given another, which I was told I was free to sign or not. If necessary, I would be given time to think it over before affixing my signature. It was a pledge to accept all missions entrusted to me, whatever the degree of danger involved. The text was impressive in its simplicity, as was the last routine question: "Person to advise in case of death." I filled it out and signed without hesitation. This seemed to be an unnecessary formality. We were at war and our lives were at stake, with or without our signatures on a printed form. I thought about all my comrades back in occupied France, each day taking considerable risks, the worst being the horrible torture sessions by the Gestapo. They had not signed any pledge. These formalities seemed somehow puerile, but were probably part of the inevitable red tape or maybe were meant to scare away the timid souls.

Then I was given notice to present myself the next day at the offices of counterintelligence, located in Rue de la Lyre. The remainder of my day was free, and I set out to find a hotel room. When I had gotten off the train that morning after three uncomfortable nights, I had been able to clean up a bit in the shop of an obliging barber. But now I could feel the accumulation of fatigue and was ready for a long, blissful sleep.

Algiers was crowded, and most of the hotels had been requisitioned for the officers. Having no luck, I decided to go for help to the welcome center of "Combat," located in an empty store. "Combat" was the name of the Gaullist resistance movement in Algeria. There I was told by a young girl that rooms were impossible to get in Algiers. She wrote a note recommending me to the superintendent of the Hospital for Deaf-Mutes, located on top of one of the hills overlooking the city. It was called Telemny, and it was the only place I could find a shelter. As a matter of fact, the superintendent showed me to a bed at the rate of five francs a night in the dormitory of the deaf-mutes. Although the place was peaceful and quiet, it was also depressing. However, it was to be home for me for many weeks, and it was there that I spent Christmas of 1943.

Rue de la Lyre, where the building of the counterintelligence services was located, was not far from the Casbah. With its arcades where Arab natives conducted their business of selling local goods, it was certainly one of the most picturesque places in the town. Its appearance of mystery and exoticism made it an ideal location for the headquarters I was looking for. It took me some time to discover the heavy wooden door that corresponded to the address I had written down. Squatting by one side of the door, a fortune-teller had in front of him a small amount of sand in which he was reading the future of an old man. On the other side stood an Arab at a wooden table on which he was cooking grasshoppers in a huge pan. His head was wrapped in a white turban. It occurred to me to wonder as I passed if they were really Arabs or French secret agents at the door of their sanctuary. I never found out, but the scene was certainly worthy of a respectable spy movie.

Once inside the door, I came upon a small patio where the ground and walls were covered with intricately designed ceramic tiles. In the center was a fountain spouting water and a profusion of plants and flowers. Wooden balconies with hand-carved rails surrounded the patio, and stairs to them provided access to the floor above. In this decor of the Thousand-and-One-Nights, servants descending the stairs in silky flowing trousers wouldn't have looked out of place. But the sight of a sergeant in khaki battle dress seated

53

behind a wooden table in a corner of the patio soon brought me back to reality.

He directed me to an office where Captain Lamartre was waiting for me. He was later to become a member of the cabinet of the first President of the Fourth Republic — Vincent Auriol. In a nice way, but with much more perspicacity, he questioned me along the same lines as the major had the day before. Then he gave me a kind of cabalistic formula — a code made up of letters and numbers — and asked me to give it to Major Bouheret. On my way out I stopped a few minutes to view the patio from the vantage point of the balcony, where a few weeks later a French Nazi agent would commit suicide by jumping when he realized he was uncovered.

Major Bouheret, after an approbating look at the counterintelligence visa, sent me to several other offices to complete more formalities. At last, after countless visits I was given my assignment to Company No. 1, which administered the soldiers assigned to the BCRA. I was now officially a member of the intelligence services of the Free French.

Reality seldom lives up to our expectations. I soon found this applied also to intelligence when, on that day in December 1943, I came to Major Bouheret to be given my first assignment.

For weeks I had been envisioning some kind of exciting mission in France or elsewhere. Intelligence work with its mystery brings to mind the image of extravagant adventures in exotic places, and I pictured myself in the center of a marvelously organized scheme conceived by a cold and brilliant chief with an encyclopedic knowledge of the world.

Bouheret greeted me with his usual courtesy and said, "Lieutenant Lucas is leaving for England in a few days. You will succeed him as the head of the section in charge of the Far East and the Western Hemisphere."

I looked at him blankly. "Sir, I was hoping to be sent on a mission to France or somewhere in Europe."

"The Germans and the French police want you. You would not last a week," he said with a smile, "and furthermore, we need you here."

"But," I insisted, "I know nothing about America or the Far East. And I really don't see how I could be useful."

"My dear friend," said Bouheret sharply, "this is war, and everyone of us must do as ordered and not what he chooses. No one here knows much. If we had intelligence experts on America and on the Far East, you would have been given another assignment. Each of us must do his best and learn fast. You will install yourself in the office assigned to you, and then see Sergeant David. He will give you all the files and archives. Study them and get to work. You will report to me every afternoon at five on the progress of your section."

Disappointed, I left Major Bouheret, reminding myself that I was only a private owing complete obedience to his superiors.

Sergeant David gave me the keys for the roll-shutter cabinet and the wood secretary in my office. The keys were really not necessary, since the shutter covering the cabinet would collapse at a touch, and a pin in the lock worked as well as a key for the secretary.

Inside, piled one on top of the other, were about ten cardboard files fastened with straps to hold the papers together.

Picking one at random, I opened it and skimmed over the pages. It contained a lot of reading material and many documents dealing with problems and situations unknown to me.

Step by step, by studying all the information I had and questioning those around me, I reconstructed the story of a group of men who, assembled in a foreign country, refused to accept defeat and decided to continue the fight against Germany. The picture of their activities, rivalries, and pettiness, as well as of their accomplishments, soon became clear to me and enabled me to grasp the real scope of my future work.

The first folder I opened contained copies of correspondence exchanged among de Gaulle, his staff, and the British authorities. After going through them carefully, I discovered how green I was.

For years I considered de Gaulle as a sort of idol but, along with all Frenchmen, I actually knew very little about him. His name appeared for the first time in the news a few days before the defeat, when from the rank of colonel he was commissioned a temporary general and was made a member of the cabinet as Under-Secretary for the Army.

After the German invasion and Marshal Pétain's decision to capitulate, de Gaulle became the symbol of the resistance, being the only member of the government to refuse to accept defeat. We listened religiously to him over the BBC and adopted him as our chief.

The documents I now had before me, and the explanations given by my new colleagues, showed him in a far different light from the man I had presumed him to be.

Back in France I had looked at de Gaulle as the natural leader of the handful of French soldiers and sailors who congregated in England to continue the war at the side of our British friends. He was a general, therefore a military chief fighting at the head of his men. I had never pictured him as a political leader, and my surprise was even greater when I realized that the British had never called upon his strategic knowledge or his military skills. He really never acted as a military chief, and had left to others the task of organizing and training the French troops which had gathered around him.

The French defeat had caused, understandably enough, a certain panic in England. Churchill, in an effort to salvage what was left of the French fighting potential, had suggested a union of France with England, and even a common citizenship. But the French politicians, blind with fear, had purely and simply refused. Only de Gaulle offered his support, and Churchill accepted it in the hope that this French officer would succeed in rallying part of the French Navy and encouraging other generals to come and join him with their forces. Churchill's idea was to set up not a French government-in-exile, but a kind of French organization which could act as a catalyst.

In order to be useful, de Gaulle had to be given a title, so the British recognized him as Chief of all Free French. This title allowed him to administer the French colonies which had refused to accept the defeat of France and decided to remain at war.

However, it did not take long for de Gaulle to realize that the small contingent of troops at his disposal in England plus the handful of territories recognizing his authority had only symbolic value. Not only was their tangible contribution to the Allied cause small, but they were, in a way, a liability.

De Gaulle had no intention of playing the part of an exiled general commanding an army of mercenary soldiers. He had higher ambitions. He wanted to represent France, and the only way to attain this end was to be recognized by the French people as their representative.

But France had a legal government, lawfully brought to power and recognized by many nations, one of which was the United States. France was also under enemy occupation, and communications were not normal. It was necessary for de Gaulle to take advantage of the general discontent caused by the defeat, and to bring the French to rebel against the Vichy government and the German occupying forces. Contacts with France were essential to the fulfillment of his plans, and two possibilities were open for him to establish such contacts. One was to address the French people over the radio, which he did very often. The other was by means of clandestine operations which required a special organization.

This is how the BCRA, which now counted me as one of its staff, was born. Its name clearly indicated what kind of activities would be expected from it. It was the agency entrusted with the collection of intelligence and the organization of "action" or subversive activities.

Agency headquarters were located at 10 Duke Street in London. Its founder and chief was Captain André Dewavrin, a graduate of l'École Polytechnique. Several of his classmates had joined him and helped set up the Free French secret organization.

In order to avoid reprisals from the Germans or the Pétainists against their families in France, they decided to take up aliases and made their choices from among the names given to the Paris subway stations. Dewavrin became Passy, Duclos chose Saint-Jacques, Lallier was Bienvenue, and so on.

This was an unfortunate choice, since the act of assuming the name of subway stations brought many people to believe that the members of the BCRA were connected with the Cagoule. Before the war, when the Cagoule had conspired to take over France, its members had planned to take as prisoners all the government leaders. To carry out their scheme, they intended to get access to the offices of the various government officials by means of the network of tunnels underlying Paris. The entrances to many of the tunnels were reached through subway stations, and some of the Cagoule members were known by the name of the particular subway station they were to use to execute their plans.

There is no doubt that several officers of the BCRA had been members of the extreme rightist organization, and some of them, for example, Duclos, alias Saint-Jacques, never attempted to deny it. But most of the BCRA personnel were devoted patriots eager to serve and, furthermore, attracted by the aura of romantic mystery which had, from the beginning of time, surrounded secret activities.

The BCRA, like all the Free French organizations, was completely dependent on the British for financial as well as other support. England, fighting for her survival, was in desperate need of intelligence on the German plans for an invasion of her territory, and the British intelligence service was only too happy to help a French organization setting up intelligence networks in France.

Colonel Claude Dansey, one of the assistants to the chief of MI6 (British Military Intelligence), gave the BCRA all the necessary assistance to carry out its intelligence task. But intelligence was only part of the mission assigned to the BCRA by de Gaulle. The agency, under the pretense of subversive activities, was establishing networks whose main purpose was actually political.

If the British were grateful for the intelligence work done by the BCRA, they also were reluctant to back de Gaulle in his ambition to overthrow the legal government of France. Being in a position of strength, they could easily find one excuse or another to slow down or even put a stop to certain activities on the part of the BCRA of which they did not approve. Such a situation created frequent clashes between the British secret services and their frustrated French partners.

The work of the BCRA was of such paramount importance to the fulfillment of his plans that de Gaulle often appealed to the leaders of the British government on its behalf. In a letter to Anthony Eden, then head of the Foreign Office, dated July 18, 1942, he stated:

The main goal of Fighting France is to encourage, in France and in the French Empire, people to resist the enemy and to oppose

59

Vichy; to organize on the national soil forces capable of participating actively in an eventual effort of the Allies on their territory, and, finally, to prepare the mobilization of the country as fast as it will be liberated.

I believe that greater support to Fighting France on the part of His Majesty's Government, as far as the Secret Services are concerned, would facilitate, in the present situation, France's participation material as well as moral, to the joint effort of the Allies. I dare hope that Your Excellency will be in agreement with this point of view.

But the British turned a deaf ear to de Gaulle's conception of the task of the secret services, and were suspicious of what was not strictly intelligence. One of de Gaulle's close aides, André Philippe paid a visit to Anthony Eden and handed him a memorandum summarizing the Free French position:

The main mission of the secret agents had gone through a change in two years. In the fall of 1940, the task was above all to obtain military intelligence on the German potential for invading England. There was not much mention of an organized resistance in France. To-day the main target is the Allied landing in France and, without neglecting the gathering of military intelligence, the involvement of French patriots in the action.

It is worth noting that, at the time, de Gaulle's concept of what was to be known later as the resistance was not shared by the Allies. Realizing that the BCRA's main concern was political, the British organized their own intelligence networks in France and supported only the Free French endeavors thought to be useful to their military operations. This would bring de Gaulle, with more and more irritation, to reproach Anthony Eden:

During the month of July [1942] about fifty missions were arranged on France, out of which only ten were on behalf of Fighting France. And still, the British services are reserving for themselves the right to decide the relative importance of the missions and of their order of priority.

60

Anthony Eden, although always very favorably inclined toward the Free French, decided to clarify, once and for all, the British position and to answer at one time all the grievances of de Gaulle and André Philippe. He wrote, on October 26, 1942:

In your letter of the 18th of July you suggest that, in order to organize forces in France to assist any eventual operations on the continent, the Fighting French Secret Services should have complete freedom of action and should dispose of their own means of communication. Mr. Philippe in his memorandum suggested that in addition, the whole work of preparing the French cooperation should be placed under your exclusive control. I think I must make clear that we should find it impossible to agree to these proposals. In the first place, His Majesty's Government would not feel able in any circumstances to abandon their own means of communication with France or to take these communications out of the channels which have been carefully prepared and which correspond with those in use for communicating with other countries. This applies both to our Intelligence Service and to the organization of the special operations which supplement in various ways our military operations against the enemy.

. . . it is necessary that the means of communications and transportation, which must be organized in this country and for which the materiel must be supplied largely by us, should remain under British control. . . .

In spite of all the stumbling blocks, the BCRA was very successful in obtaining political support for de Gaulle in France. Through its agents, contacts had been made with all the outlawed political parties, and the fact that they were rallying around him gave him the appearance of legality of which he was very proud.

In April 1942, Colonel Billotte, de Gaulle's Chief of Staff, was delighted to write to Major Morton, Churchill's personal liaison officer with de Gaulle, trying to interest him in meeting several Frenchmen recently arrived in England. First on the list, he named:

"Mr. Pacot, who had come from France to inform General de Gaulle that the Communist party, in its entirety, was ready to enlist under his command to fight the invader."

Major Morton's answer to Colonel Billotte was not without a touch of humor:

I was particularly interested in your description of the first name on your list, but having made most discreet inquiries, I find that he is already in close touch with one of our Secret Departments to which he gives all information. . . .

Many Frenchmen living in London were concerned over de Gaulle's drive for power. One of the most outspoken was Admiral Muselier, the first Navy officer to have joined de Gaulle. It was Muselier who had chosen the Cross of Lorraine as the emblem of the Free French. He had shown great efficiency in the reorganization of the Free French Navy. A convinced democrat, Muselier was appalled by de Gaulle's political ambitions, and very critical of the BCRA's drive to build him up.

His remarks naturally created friction within the group of the London exiles. Many plots to get rid of him were concocted, and he was even arrested by the British Security Services and accused of passing intelligence to Vichy. This charge turned out to be a fabrication, and the admiral was freed with apologies. His accuser was, in turn, jailed.

Muselier accused the BCRA of contriving this whole affair to discredit him. This was the last straw. De Gaulle decided to relieve him of his high command of the Free French Navy and appointed him to the meaningless position of Inspector General. Muselier refused to accept and was forced to retire. But de Gaulle's resentment was to follow him for a long time. While he carefully abstained from mentioning it in his war memoirs, his letter to Anthony Eden, in June 1942, illustrated the tenacious hatred de Gaulle is capable of nourishing against those who oppose him. In fact, after informing the British Secretary for Foreign Affairs of his intention to have Muselier court-martialed after the liberation of France, he requested him to keep the admiral away from London and to assign him a residence.

Eden's reply, advocating moderation on de Gaulle's part, is an example of the usual British concern for fair play and an illustration of the constant annoyance caused them by their ally, the chief of the Free French.

In going over the next file, I was confronted with another angle on our war leader and his inflated pride.

Lieutenant Commander Jubelin, hero of an extraordinary escape from Indochina, had proposed to General de Gaulle that he fly to Paris in a Spitfire and drop the tricolor on the Arc de Triomphe. De Gaulle had submitted the idea to the British Air Minister, Sir Archibald Sinclair, who, when the opportunity presented itself, gave orders to a British pilot not only to drop the French flag on the Champs Elysées but to machine-gun the German military parade which, ironically enough, presented arms daily to the French unknown soldier.

Sir Archibald Sinclair immediately informed de Gaulle of the success of the operation:

Flight Lieutenant Gatward took his Beaufighter across France to Paris and back at a height of about twenty feet, without getting so much as a bullet hole through it. He passed down the Champs Elysées, below the level of the tops of the houses, but he saw German troops. He then peppered the Ministère de la Marine with cannon shells, circled around the Arc de Triomphe again in order to make certain that the German troops were not hiding in any corner, flew again down the Champs Elysées, gave the Ministère de la Marine another peppering, and came home. He dropped two tricolors — one at each end of the Champs Elysées.

It occurs to me that you might like to see this young officer and some photographs which he brought back with him. I am therefore asking my private secretary to enquire about this from your aide-de-camp and, if so, to make the necessary arrangements.

De Gaulle immediately answered the British Air Minister:

The flight over the Arc de Triomphe at a specific time by a French pilot had been, as you know, requested several months ago by our groups of action in France for moral and psychological reasons which cannot be overlooked. This is why I had the honor

63

to write you about this matter on November 5, 1941 and June 5, 1942.

A different operation having been nevertheless executed, I can only express regret that the British Royal Air Force did not see fit that a French officer could drop a French flag over the capital of France.

I was in Paris when Flight Lieutenant Gatward accomplished his mission, and I remember the jubilation among those who witnessed it. Of course, no one had been able to identify the pilot and, really, no one cared whether he was French or English. The psychological effect had been fully realized, and the ability of England to machine-gun the Germans at will had been demonstrated. De Gaulle's making an issue over the fact that the plane was piloted by a British rather than a French pilot was another exercise in futility by a man who, great at times, could not stand any obstacle to his will.

One could easily understand the irritation of Sir Archibald Sinclair when he politely wrote: "I interpreted your letters to mean that your chief concern was to get the tricolor dropped in Paris . . ."

With all his arrogance, de Gaulle received the worst affront of his career when, on November 8, 1942, the Allies landed in North Africa. De Gaulle had been given no advance notice, and the BCRA was taken aback.

Operation Torch — the name given to the American landing in North Africa — presented, from a diplomatic point of view, an unprecedented problem. The United States, after having declared war on Germany, was starting its military operations by forcefully invading a French territory ruled by a government with which it had normal diplomatic relations. This territory had to be administered, and the United States had a choice between establishing an American military government or entrusting the French with its administration. In any case, the French population did not have any say and were not consulted. Decisions were made on their behalf by the representative of the President of the United States, Robert Murphy.

From the beginning, Murphy had designated General Giraud to

take over the Army and the administration. Admiral Darlan's accidental presence in Algiers at the time of the invasion forced a change in American plans, and the admiral, who a few months before was discussing with Hitler an eventual alliance between France and Germany against the Allies, was given the title of High Commissioner and placed at the head of the administration. Giraud was entrusted with the position of Commander in Chief of the French Forces engaged in the battle of Tunisia.

Six weeks after assuming his new post, Admiral Darlan was assassinated by a young fanatic, Bonnier de la Chapelle. The assassination took place on December 24, 1942. On December 25, a Court Martial issued a death sentence against the murderer, and at daybreak on December 26 he was executed.

On the evening of December 25, a group of people tried to meet with Robert Murphy to request that he intercede on behalf of the accused, at least until all the facts were known, but he remained inaccessible. General Eisenhower, Commander in Chief of the Allied Forces, held the power of pardon since the sentence had been pronounced by a military court whose jurisdiction extended into his theater of operations; Robert Murphy was the link to him.

The day after the execution, news got around of the presence in Algiers of the Comte de Paris, pretender to the throne of France. He had come from Morocco under the name of Monsieur Robin. A group of conspirators among the party who helped Murphy in setting up Operation Torch had suggested replacing Darlan with the Comte de Paris, the only person, according to them, able to unite the French.

Many reports mentioned later that "Robert Murphy had submitted this project to his Government with favorable recommendations," but President Roosevelt and General Eisenhower refused even to consider it. Giraud was also firmly opposed to it.

The speedy execution of Bonnier de la Chapelle before he was able to explain his motives, and Murphy's refusal to intercede for a postponement of the execution, gave substance to the now widespread belief that Murphy's intentions at the time were to reestablish the monarchy in France.

True or false, this belief, based on unexplained facts, immediately alienated the democratic-minded leaders in North Africa against the United States.

De Gaulle enjoyed the uproar. The United States had not even contacted him and pretended to ignore him even though French troops were fighting next to the British in North Africa, and most of the French colonies had recognized his authority.

The situation could not go on like this. There were now three Frances, Pétain's France occupied by the Germans, de Gaulle's France supported by the British, and Giraud's France politically organized by the United States.

The need for unity among the French in fighting the Germans was felt by the entire world. The two resistance leaders could have made an effort to work out an understanding, but pride kept each from making an overture. De Gaulle was completely wrapped up in his mission, which he believed was divinely inspired, and Giraud, a good man and a brave soldier, listened too readily to the advice of men around him whose only purpose was to justify their previous lack of involvement.

It took the decision made by Churchill and Roosevelt to meet in Casablanca for the two French leaders to agree to come together and exchange views. The handshake reluctantly exchanged under the amused gaze of Churchill and Roosevelt on January 24, 1943, for the benefit of photographers, was interpreted throughout the world as a symbol of unity. In reality, no accord had been reached between the two generals except for the setting up, in Algiers, of a Gaullist mission which was headed by General Catroux. He was charged with finding common ground for an agreement between the two.

Roosevelt believed that the problem had been solved. He was unaware of the fact that the BCRA, with agents in the right places, had obtained detailed reports on his conversations with assistants. De Gaulle in this way had confirmation of Roosevelt's interference in French internal affairs which should have been of no concern to him. Roosevelt was taking it upon himself to decide on appointments and promotions within the French administration, as if he were handing out patronage jobs in the United States after an election. He would seize every opportunity to declare his intention of stripping France of her colonial possessions. All his statements, faithfully reported to de Gaulle, served to widen the breach between America and the Free French.

De Gaulle was then in an inferior position compared to Giraud. He had no control over rich or well-organized territories such as North Africa, and his army was considerably smaller than his rival's. Also, he was not in the favor of the President of the United States, who used Giraud against him, helping Giraud with money and political advice.

The British, in order not to antagonize the Americans, grew cool toward de Gaulle, who had become the underdog.

His partisans, however, stood faithfully behind him, and others, uncommitted before but angered at having a foreign power decide the fate of a divided France, came over to him. De Gaulle's material inferiority was largely compensated for by his BCRA, which was his major instrument in reestablishing his prestige and defeating his adversaries.

When the Gaullist mission headed by General Catroux arrived in Algiers, one of its members was Commander Pelabon, a graduate of l'Ecole Polytechnique and a friend of Passy. Pelabon was the BCRA's representative. He carefully studied the situation and reported:

The public opinion here seems, as a whole, similar to what I indicated to you before my departure, with the following distinctions. Much more Gaullists than I thought among the civilian population, but the kind of Gaullists susceptible to be scared by the least threat and whose demonstrations are usually stopped by small numbers of opponents. No Giraudists (Giraud is a nonentity). The Pétainists are few among the civilians but they are resolute. There are more of them than I thought in the Army and they seem to include the totality of the Navy officers. The Pétainists seem to be ready to do anything to prevent Fighting France from taking over Algerian affairs. The promise to shoot de Gaulle, if the occasion presents itself, is heard often among the pro-Pétain officers in the various units. They have even drawn lots to decide who should have the honor of the first try.

Pelabon, an indefatigable worker of high intelligence and wit, set to work in spite of all the difficulties he encountered. He had a network of informers located in strategic places, previously recruited by Bienvenue. They kept him up to date on the contacts between Murphy and Giraud. By advising Combat, the only Gaullist organization in Algeria, he skillfully brought its leader, Capitan, to a more practical view of the problems. Then he kept a close watch on how Catroux was carrying on the negotiations. He supervised everything, and without deviating from his good common sense, he knew how to use both prudence and audacity simultaneously.

Drafts for an agreement were constantly being exchanged between London and Algiers, the main idea being the establishment of a committee presided over by de Gaulle and Giraud at the same time. However, Giraud, under the advice of the Allies, wished to play a preponderant role in this double-headed organization. But the word "preponderant" was not clearly defined and could mean everything or nothing. Naturally, de Gaulle would not hear of this clause. In a conciliatory spirit, Catroux was critical of the rigidity of de Gaulle's position, and de Gaulle, furious at this, wanted to recall him. Pelabon wrote to the BCRA:

Marchal [one of the members of Catroux's mission] *believes that a break between General de Gaulle and Catroux would be disastrous in all respects. He suggests that de Gaulle recall Catroux immediately to London, by a friendly cable, and that they come back together in order to bring the negotiations to a successful and rapid conclusion. According to Marchal, these negotiations can, as of now, lead to an agreement granting to Giraud the prestige of Chief of State and delegating to de Gaulle the authority as Chief of the French Government, as well as all powers, civilian and military. Such an agreement would be, in Marchal's point of view, the most Fighting France could hope to obtain for the time being. Marchal has faith in Catroux' loyalty toward de Gaulle while not always approving of his methods. I am inclined to think on the same lines as Marchal but will add that, obviously enough, Catroux does not like de Gaulle.*

In case de Gaulle decides to come right away he should, in order to get the maximum support in the way of public manifestation, plan to arrive on Saturday, and the day after to lay a wreath on the

War Memorial in front of the Central Post Office. The demonstration could take place at the site of the ceremony. I am still unable to evaluate the impact of such manifestation. In my opinion, providing I receive word forty-eight hours in advance, this could be quite a turnout. Be on the lookout for sabotage or assassination attempt.

This note was sent on April 7, 1943. On May 30, de Gaulle finally entered Algiers. It was a Sunday morning, and Giraud had kept the news of his arrival secret. Over luncheon the two generals exchanged sour remarks. Then de Gaulle left for the Villa des Glycines, the residence which had been requisitioned for him. But instead of going directly to the villa, as planned, he asked to be taken to the War Memorial, where an impressive crowd had gathered and waited for his appearance. Relating this event in his memoirs, de Gaulle commented: ". . . although this ceremony was quite extemporaneous, unmentioned by any newspaper, unattended by any troops, thousands of patriots alerted by the Combat movement had gathered swiftly and welcomed me with great acclamation."

This "spontaneous" manifestation took place, as suggested by Pelabon, on a Sunday, and de Gaulle knew that, although "there were no troops in this country [Algeria], no police, no officials, no funds, no fitting means of making [his] voice heard," he could rely on the BCRA, which was there to ensure the success of his ventures better than any army.

Giraud, in his capacity as Commander in Chief, had under his command the traditional military intelligence organizations whose networks in France were made up of former French Army officers. Therefore, it was possible for the Commander in Chief to direct subversive activities in France independently of de Gaulle.

De Gaulle had already opposed the absolute control of the British over the activities of the underground. Giraud, by interfering, was paving the way for his downfall. In fact, six months after de Gaulle's arrival in Algiers, Giraud was obliged to resign as co-President of the French Committee of National Liberation. De Gaulle became the only President, with Giraud assuming only the functions of Commander in Chief. The bicephalous leadership of the Committee was replaced by a homogeneous organization, at least in theory.

To understand what was involved, a better knowledge of the history of the French secret services is essential.

Until 1940 the French services were exclusively a military operation. Located at 2 bis Avenue de Tourville in Paris, they were divided into two branches: the intelligence division and the counterintelligence division, both directly under the control of the Army Chief of Staff.

The intelligence division's main concern was the gathering of information on the composition and movements of foreign troops. As a military intelligence service working for the 2e Bureau (French G2) it had never been able to reach beyond the routine required by the General Staff, and paid but little attention to the political or economic aspects of countries whose military secrets were being sought. The intelligence division claimed to have provided the French Chief of Staff, at the beginning of World War II, with detailed intelligence concerning German designs. This assertion has never really been proved, but even if true, it remained that its chiefs failed to convince the High Command of the enormous German power which, in only a few days, was able to destroy all French defense.

Following the armistice, the Army was held in great contempt by the French population, whose fresh memories of officers abandoning their men to flee among women and children were not easily forgotten.

The Germans had authorized the Vichy government to keep an army of one hundred thousand men, commonly called the Armistice Army. In the framework of this army, the secret services tried to survive, but the officers making up these services were all ardent partisans of Pétain and never opposed his policies.

Some among them, in order not to lose contact with foreign countries, were willing to pass some intelligence to Colonel Schow, the United States military attaché. At the time the United States was a nonbelligerent country. Others prudently kept just enough contacts with British intelligence networks. But no liaison had been established with de Gaulle and the Free French, who were considered rebels. The French intelligence services lived sparingly, with very few resources and a blurred objective.

By contrast, the counterintelligence services, under the leadership of Captain Paillole, undertook the remarkable task of identifying German agents and destroying their networks. Captain Paillole, under the assumed name of Monsieur Perrier, had set up, as a cover, a company called Entreprise des Travaux Ruraux (TR), whose headquarters were located in Marseille. The company's main objective was supposed to be the development of rural districts, and its "executives" set up branches all over the country; and so counterintelligence stations sprang up in various places. The Paillole team turned out to be very efficient in the hunting of German agents, but it was working for the Pétain government, nursing the hope that, at long lost, Marshal Pétain would resort to the decision to resist.

In the wake of the American landing the Germans invaded the remaining part of France — the so-called Free Zone — encountering very little opposition on the part of the Armistice Army. With the collapse of the Armistice Army, the intelligence officers went back to civilian life, only to realize, after a while, that they had to get together and join the underground. Their chief, Colonel Rivet, went to Algiers and took charge of Giraud's intelligence, made up of the networks set up in France by former members of his service.

The officers of the counterintelligence division were already underground. Living under civilian covers, they were prepared for any eventuality, but following the disintegration of the Armistice Army, their funds had been cut off. To alleviate this, Paillole gave the direction of his service to his assistant Laffont, alias Verneuil, and succeeded in getting to London by way of Spain. He immediately met with General Menzies, chief of MI6, through Commander Dunderdale, the former British Intelligence Station Chief in Paris. General Menzies readily offered to Paillole all the financial and material help he needed. Paillole met also with Colonel Passy and discussed with him the merging of his organization with the BCRA's counterintelligence division. Then he got back to Algiers, where, as a career officer, he found himself under General Giraud. Entrusted with the direction of the Military Security Service, however, Paillole continued to control his organization in occupied France.

On the arrival of de Gaulle in Algiers in March 1943, Giraud was in contact with the French underground through his intelligence service headed by Colonel Rivet and through his counterintelligence under Captain Paillole. On the other hand, the BCRA had been de Gaulle's only instrument in organizing the underground since 1940. Obviously, the resistance movement in France suffered from being led by three different organizations, and unity was essential.

De Gaulle entrusted Jacques Soustelle with the task of merging all services into a single agency called Direction Générale des Services Spéciaux (DGSS), or the Special Services Agency. But this task proved to be almost impossible. The traditional military services wanted to be left alone and remain under the Commander in Chief, General Giraud, while the BCRA refused to have anything to do with those it considered Pétain's followers.

Jacques Soustelle showed an incredible amount of patience and used the utmost diplomacy in trying to convince everyone of the absolute necessity for coordination and unity. When all his attempts had failed, Soustelle took the only course of action left to him next to persuasion. He cut off appropriations.

The Soustelle plan was very reasonable. Merging the Giraud intelligence, directed by Colonel Rivet, with the BCRA, he was stripping the BCRA of its counterintelligence division and placing it under Paillole's command.

General Giraud, following the advice of his entourage, decided to intervene personally in the quarrel and insisted on maintaining the absurd existing situation. On February 5, 1944, he sent a letter to de Gaulle:

My idea is to maintain the intelligence service and military security in a strictly military position, proven by experience and tradition, for my only desire is that they continue the combat with me at the side of the Army, as much against the enemy as against anyone, French or foreign, whose activity would be an obstacle to the liberation and interest of France.

In other words, Giraud, together with the Army and Special Services, intended to liberate France, and it would just be too bad for anyone to interfere.

This declaration came as a slap in the face to de Gaulle, and from that day Giraud lost all chance of returning to France as Commander in Chief at the liberation.

De Gaulle's answer came the next day. He wrote bluntly:

I have the honor to confirm to you that the government has made the decision to achieve the effective merger of all special services into a higher level board under the direct authority of the President of the French Committee for the National Liberation, and the President of the Action Committee in France.

De Gaulle's position was clear and left no doubt — Giraud was out. To prevent any rebellion among members of military intelligence, de Gaulle, in another letter the same day, dealt with a matter which was embarrassing to the Commander in Chief.

The military attaché to the Vichy Embassy in Madrid, Colonel Malaise, had joined Giraud after the American landing in North Africa. He had been detailed immediately to military intelligence and, in this capacity, had returned to Madrid to set up an office in the U.S. Embassy. There, under the cover of technical counselor to the U.S. military attaché, he unofficially represented Giraud and his intelligence services. He also controlled, on their behalf, several underground networks. The BCRA somehow got word of instructions given by Malaise to his agents in France, reflecting his hostility and distrust toward de Gaulle.

De Gaulle demanded Malaise's recall to Algiers and forbade his return to Spain, but Malaise, feeling protected by Giraud, ignored the order.

The occasion was ripe for de Gaulle to show his authority and discourage any defiance among the officers standing behind Giraud. He gave them the simple choice either to obey or to face prosecution by a military court, without even trying to soften the blow. He wrote:

As I had the opportunity to mention to you during our meeting this morning, I had been informed that Colonel Malaise had returned to Spain in spite of the interdiction of the government that I brought to your attention on January 17.

I am also advised that Mr. Dungler (alias Schneider), whose return to France had been equally forbidden, had nevertheless been taken there through the good offices of an American service called the

OSS, following repeated intervention coming from either yourself or one of your staff officers (General Ronin, General Chambre).

I add that the government has decided to put a stop to such acts opposing its authority. I asked this day the Commissioner for the Army and Air Force, to immediately summon Colonel Malaise, Mr. Dungler and their accomplices before a court martial.

The following day, Colonel Rivet was notified that his service was now part of BCRA, under the name Technical Division of Special Services, and Paillole received the order to take over all counter-intelligence organizations.

At this point, Giraud should have sensed that further interference would be deadly, but listening once more to ill-advised counselors, he decided to go on fighting de Gaulle.

A Consultative Assembly, a sort of advisory chamber of representatives, had been set up in Algiers to advise the provisional government. Giraud approached its Defense Committee and asked for its arbitration in his conflict with de Gaulle. Within the Defense Committee, the Communist votes were decisive. In order to win those to his side and permanently disgrace his rival, de Gaulle decided to accede to a Communist request: the trial of Pierre Pucheu, former Secretary for the Interior in the Vichy government.

Pierre Pucheu had served Pétain faithfully up to the time of the American landing in North Africa, when he became convinced that Germany would be defeated. Fleeing from France, he went to Spain and wrote to Giraud, asking to be allowed to serve in the North African Army. Giraud answered his request affirmatively and authorized him to come to North Africa. But the presence of Pucheu in Morocco created quite a commotion, and Giraud had to restrict him to his quarters.

Pucheu had previously been sentenced to death by an underground Communist court, under the accusation that he provided the Germans with a list of fifty Communist hostages to be executed in reprisal for the assassination of two Kommandantur chiefs in Nantes and in Bordeaux. He was also held responsible for the reorganization of the French police, which resulted in their increased efficiency in hunting underground fighters, and in giving more help to the Germans. Those accusations were later to appear well-founded, but at the time, no proof was on hand.

De Gaulle set up a military tribunal to hear the case. This court was not in accordance with French law or the French constitution but only with de Gaulle's concept, "Justice is a state matter and it should be dedicated exclusively to the service of France."

The tribunal was composed of one civilian judge and three generals, one of whom had previously been entrusted with the coordination of the special services but had failed in his endeavor. The prosecutor, a former Air Force general and ex-Vichy follower, wore heavy makeup. He brought the charges in a voice that was shrill and biting. Giraud appeared before the bar as a defense witness, but his testimony, vague and embarrassed, was not convincing and caused many of his supporters to lose confidence in him. In spite of the vehemence of the Communist accusation, the judges hesitated in pronouncing the death sentence against Pucheu.

In line with his very special concept of justice, de Gaulle was using Paul Coste-Floret, the eminent jurist, as unofficial liaison between himself and this unusual tribunal. Following the proceedings closely, Coste-Floret informed de Gaulle of the judges' reluctance to pronounce the capital punishment. De Gaulle told him to persuade the judges — because of *raison d'Etat* — that Pucheu had to be sentenced to death, but that he would use his power of pardon to commute the sentence.

Impressed by Coste-Floret's assurance, given in de Gaulle's name, the judges complied and Pucheu was sentenced to be executed by a firing squad. Still, to emphasize the guarantee given by de Gaulle's representative, the tribunal carefully recommended clemency.

Disregarding Coste-Floret's promises made in his name, and ignoring the court's recommendation, de Gaulle refused at the last minute to grant the pardon and had the former Vichy Secretary of the Interior executed. The Communists were delighted and showed their gratitude by giving de Gaulle their full support.

A few days later, he resorted once more to the method he used so successfully in getting rid of Admiral Muselier and took away from Giraud the title of Commander in Chief. He appointed him to the honorary position of Inspector General of the Army. His partisans, disappointed by his poor performance during the Pucheu trial, deserted him, and Giraud resigned and left for Morocco, in exile.

De Gaulle was now alone in a position of power, and with the support of the BCRA he would be free to realize his ambitions.

My discoveries about de Gaulle's true personality, his ambition, his art in creating dissension among the Allies, his deceit, and his tenacious hatred came as a great disappointment. But we were at war, and the first and most important concern was the liberation of the motherland. With all his faults, de Gaulle was nevertheless a great leader and there was no other. He was undependable and at times even dangerous, but the last word would rest with the French people.

To be a member of de Gaulle's own secret service was very exciting, and I fully enjoyed the close comradeship of the BCRA team. Seldom has there been assembled a group of men of higher caliber, working so fervently toward the goal set for them.

Our boss was Jacques Soustelle, and even his worst enemies couldn't deny his extraordinary intellectual capacities. His orders were always calmly voiced and well defined. He was a quick thinker and would grasp a problem even before we finished explaining it. In his dealings with the members of Giraud's services, he had shown a great deal of understanding and patience in trying to conciliate the differing points of view.

The London branch of the BCRA was headed by its founder, Colonel Dewavrin, alias Passy. Passy was a skillful organizer, showing no hesitation himself in undertaking dangerous missions in occupied France. His intelligence networks spread all over France. At the time, he was also successfully coordinating all the French underground organizations which had spontaneously sprung up in the country. In spite of frequent clashes with British intelligence — clashes inherent in the nature of the problems being negotiated — Passy had developed with the British a good relationship based on mutual esteem.

The head of the BCRA in Algiers was Commander Pelabon, whom we mentioned earlier. Gifted with an incredible capacity for work, he was most adroit and showed kindness to those around him. His wife had organized a welfare program which proved to be of great support to the escapees setting foot in unhospitable Algeria. Pelabon's right arm was Reserve Captain Guillaumat, who was to become the most influential man in the French oil industry. Guillaumat was very sharp and was feared by the military personnel, whom he showered with sarcasms, but he was more tolerant toward the reservists and volunteers. The head of the intelligence division was Major Bouheret, who had been flown recently from France. He had been an aide to General Beynet, chief of the Vichy delegation in Wiesbaden, and had been for a long time a priceless source of intelligence for the Allies.

The Committee for Action in France determined the directives and support to be given to the underground movements. It was presided over by de Gaulle and included a limited number of his most trusted aides, as well as representatives of some of the movements involved. The committee's decisions were handed to the Director of the Special Services to be carried out by the London branch of the BCRA for all actions concerning Paris and the North of France, and by the Algiers branch for everything concerning the South.

The political importance of the Special Services increased with the prospects of the liberation of France. A new administration was to take over, and the Special Services recommended to the committee candidates to fill all the important positions. The candidates were mostly selected from among members of the underground organizations working under the control of the committee, and the recommendations were always approved. The Special Services were selecting an administration devoted to de Gaulle, whose members would have good reasons for being grateful to their sponsors.

Intelligence networks working in foreign countries were directed from Algiers. Since de Gaulle's Special Services originally had been set up to work exclusively on French territory, the work accomplished in foreign countries was of little importance. Except for several networks in the Balkans and the Middle East, the only sources of intelligence were benevolent informers.

America was under the authority of my division. We had, as correspondent in the United States, Bienvenue, one of the founders of the BCRA. He regularly sent us press clippings and reports on the activities of French refugees in the United States. Two of them were very active against de Gaulle and were supposed to have the ear of President Roosevelt.

One was Camille Chautemps who, before the war, had several times been Prime Minister of France. A member of the Reynaud government in 1940, he had supported Pétain's request for an armistice and later had come to Washington as his unofficial representative. After his final break with Vichy, he remained in the U.S. capital, bitterly campaigning against the Free French government. The Gaullist organizations laid on him the responsibility for Roosevelt's attitude toward France.

The other one was Geneviève Tabouis, a very well-known journalist with access to the White House. She was said to be a friend of Mrs. Roosevelt and to have used her influence to oppose de Gaulle's politics. Her links with Soviet intelligence were revealed after the war and made some people wonder if she was a Soviet agent at the same time she was a frequent guest at the executive mansion. She published a weekly paper, *For Victory*, and had been able to obtain the help of the very famous French journalist Henry de Kerillis, himself in exile in New York.

Kerillis was of a completely different caliber. A member of the French House of Representatives, he had always opposed any agreement with the Germans and had been in touch with de Gaulle since 1940. When he recognized de Gaulle's dictatorial propensity, he refused to go along with him and, from New York, tried to awaken the nation's conscience. His influence was widespread, and the president of the French Committee of National Liberation was trying, without success, to get his support.

The Gaullists were led by Henry Torres, one of France's great lawyers, and to counterbalance *For Victory*, he published another weekly, *France Forever*.

Conflicts between the two groups were typical of the hatred and jealousy always present among immigrant groups. This was unfortunate and not worth the time or money spent to keep an eye on their activities. But de Gaulle wanted to know, and we kept him informed.

There was also another category of Frenchmen we had to watch in the United States. They were the former members of the French

Embassy representing the Vichy government up to the time it broke diplomatic relations with the United States. Some of these diplomats had gone back to France, but others asked the American government to stay and were interned in Hershey, Pennsylvania, as enemy aliens. The actual French Ambassador to the United States was one of them until he repented and later joined Giraud's representation in Washington. Since this small group had advocated Pétain's policy of collaboration with Germany, it was necessary to check if they had any direct link with the enemy. They presented an obvious counterintelligence problem. I left to an aide the task of filing all the reports we kept receiving on these various matters and of passing them to the interested parties.

Another problem was de Gaulle's chief worry at the moment. Several unconfirmed pieces of intelligence had reached him, mentioning the creation by the United States of a military organization giving special training to officers in anticipation of the administration of European territories after their liberation. This organization, which was called American Military Government for Occupied Territories (AMGOT), was supposed to house a special section in charge of the control and the organization of France once it was rid of the German occupants.

My orders were to ascertain the reliability of this information. I immediately contacted all my correspondents and the French Military Mission in the United States. Information started to arrive which confirmed the training, at a fort near Washington, of officers for the future administration of Germany, Italy and . . . France.

These various intelligence reports lacked details, and I tried to get an accurate account of the situation. An officer on the General Staff of General Eisenhower, after a few drinks in an Algiers bar, became talkative and explained the role he would play after the liberation of France, as head of a section of AMGOT. The officer spoke good French, and his remarks immediately found their way to my office.

Some time later, a reserve officer and member of the French Military Mission in Washington, upon receipt of my questionnaires, asked to be allowed to report to me in Algiers. The request was granted and I conducted a complete debriefing. This officer, whose name I choose to withhold, since it is not my intention to create any difficulties for him, had lived in the United States a number of years before the war. His wife was American and belonged to a prominent family in the United States. Her brother had, through the best of coincidences, been recruited for service in AMGOT and had disclosed to our French officer what his duties would be, come the liberation of France.

I now have no doubt that President Roosevelt and his collaborators had the best of intentions when making their plans. After some twenty years in the United States, I can now understand the American President's wish to give the French people the chance to choose freely their system of government and the men to govern them. But . . . as well intentioned as the President and his advisers were, they simply overlooked the fact that France's firm desire was to take care of her own affairs *"en famille."* It was a time in France when no one was eager to see the German Kommandanturs replaced by officers of the AMGOT. The French wanted no more foreign interference in their affairs of state. They would rather be governed by Frenchmen they did not particularly like than by friendly and well-intentioned outsiders.

With his talent for creating dissension, de Gaulle had clearly sized up the problem and used it much later to justify his actions.

I received de Gaulle's congratulations for the results I had obtained. Looking back, I often wondered what would have happened if I had not produced this hard intelligence. Would de Gaulle have made the same arrangements when the liberation came? And if not, France, under America's influence, might have become a true democracy.

I was confronted, in the same period, with another interesting experience dealing with American problems. One day the guard on duty at the reception desk called to say that a gentleman was asking to be received by the officer in charge of intelligence on the Western Hemisphere. My secretary went down to see what it was all about. The name she repeated to me was unknown, but the visitor had told her he wanted to show me certain important documents in his possession. I wondered for a while if it might not be an agent of some foreign country trying to penetrate our organization, but I was curious.

When the man entered my office, his appearance and accent made me guess he was Lebanese. Self-assured, he calmly handed me a large brown envelope.

"You will find several documents inside," he said. "I will leave them with you so you can study them and convince yourself of their authenticity. I will come back tomorrow to tell you why I brought them to you."

I asked where he could be contacted and he gave me the address of a small hotel, then left; I was puzzled and intrigued.

The envelope contained several letters on White House letterhead and bearing the signature of Franklin Roosevelt. They were addressed to Perón, who, it appeared, although he did not hold an official position at the time, was nevertheless the real power in Argentina. Also enclosed was a draft for an agreement between the United States and Argentina, sent by Roosevelt, as well as several letters to Perón from Nazi officials. I was greatly surprised by this correspondence which, while not of direct interest for France, was certainly very informative. I forwarded all the documents to the proper department, asking for a report on the authenticity of the signatures and on the official stationery used. The answer came back: affirmative.

I waited for my visitor the next day. He showed up as promised.

"Were you interested?" he asked.

I told him I was, without commenting on the matter.

"I wanted to prove to you that I have the full confidence of Peron. I can be of great help to France in Argentina and see that she enjoys a privileged position. In exchange, I would like to be guaranteed that after the liberation, with the population undernourished and the food demand enormous, I would be granted a monopoly on the frozen meat market. I can provide, ship, and arrange for the necessary credit for considerable quantities of meat."

I passed along the terms of this unusual offer made by the Lebanese. I never received any answer nor did I hear from the man again.

My first experiences in foreign intelligence taught me how the clever maneuvers of politicians can result in failure when the secret of their intrigues is not tightly kept. I learned at the same time one of the basic rules of the trade. Many people are willing to give away secrets they have been entrusted with for ideological purposes or simply to derive a profit. But seldom do they know to whom to go. Intelligence officers, in their desire to be cautious, disguise the nature of their activities more than necessary and miss tremendous chances to come upon valuable information. If our Lebanese had not known at what door to knock, or if I had refused to see him for fear of compromising myself, I would never have obtained copies of this rather interesting correspondence.

The Western Hemisphere, as far as intelligence work was concerned, did not offer to me the challenge presented by the Far East, which was also under my responsibility. I had arranged to have with me as deputy my good friend Jean Rotter, who had shared the long months of captivity in Spain. He took care of all problems dealing with America and I devoted almost my entire time to the problems of French Indochina.

"This is the dog skin report," said the noncommissioned officer, putting a thick file on my desk.

Surprised, I looked at him, wondering if this was some code word or if the man, who had seemed rational until now, had suddenly lost possession of his faculties.

In answer to my look, he pointed out the file. "I mean the report," he said as if it would explain everything.

I nodded noncommittally, going along with him. "Yes, I see the report, but why 'dog skin'?"

Looking at me condescendingly, he explained: "That's right, you're not familiar with the story. This is the last report we received on Indochina, and believe me, it's not recent. It was written by a public works engineer, Bourgoin, who escaped from Indochina some time ago. In order to conceal from the Japanese the information he had for us, he shaved his dog and, using indelible ink, wrote down the most important facts on his skin. Then he waited for the dog's coat to grow out before fleeing the country. When he reached India, he shaved the dog again and was able to write his report."

The officer couldn't help laughing at my surprise. "It's no joke. I remember everyone's amusement when it happened. The thing is, we haven't had a report since. Maybe dogs are in short supply — they say the Chinese eat them."

As soon as he left my office, I opened the file and quickly ran through the famous report. The information contained in it might have been of value at the time, but it was now over a year old and obsolete. So it seemed that the Far Eastern Intelligence Section of the Free French Special Services consisted only of one old report, originally written on a dog skin, and a 23-year-old youth whose knowledge of the region was quite superficial. There was something wrong. Why didn't we have more information on the area where France had one of her most flourishing colonies? I had been too busy with the Germans to pay a lot of attention to what was happening at almost the antipodes.

Taking advantage of the defeat of France, the Japanese in July 1940 had obtained from General Catroux, Governor of Indochina, authorization to set up a border inspection on the frontier between Indochina and China in order to prevent the passage of strategic materials to Chiang Kai-shek's army. After trying, without success, to bring Indochina to the Allied cause, Catroux, finding himself alone, went to London to join de Gaulle. Vichy appointed another governor, Admiral Decoux. The French forces in Indochina were so absurdly small that the new governor was unable to oppose Japanese demands. The Nipponese troops occupied, little by little, all airfields and ports, leaving the administration of the country to the French and tolerating an army composed of 12,000 Europeans and 35,000 natives. The French Air Force consisted of about fifteen planes. Ammunition stocks were very low, with fewer than 300 cartridges per rifle.

Without being directly engaged in the war that was raging in the Far East, Indochina was used as a base of operations by the Japanese in their attacks against British possessions and against China. For the French, life in Indochina was relatively normal. The administration, following Vichy rules, showed hostility toward England and the Allies in general.

In China, the Pétain government was represented by an ambassador, but General de Gaulle's appeal had been heard by the handful of Frenchmen living there. One of them, Jean Escarra, professor of law, was an adviser to Chiang Kai-shek in charge of preparing a code of Chinese laws. He had joined de Gaulle's cause immediately after the armistice of June 1940, and had created a Free French committee to represent de Gaulle unofficially with the Chinese government. Escarra was assisted by a French explorer, Guibaut, who, after an unsuccessful expedition to the source of the Salween River, had barely escaped a group of Tibetan bandits and returned to Chungking. A few officers of the French Army in Indochina had fled in order to rally to Free France and joined the small team organized by Escarra, thus constituting the core of what would later become the French Military Mission in China.

During the same period in Malaysia, the director of a rubber plantation, François de Langlade, had also rallied to de Gaulle, along with several of his planters, and had been instructed to help the British resist the Japanese. In collaboration with British intelligence, he undertook several missions in Indochina, where he began to form a network with some of his friends. The potential for obtaining intelligence on Indochina from Malaysia soon was recognized, and de Gaulle sent Lieutenant Colonel Tutenges to Singapore as chief of the Free French Intelligence Service in the Far East. In January 1942, a few weeks after Tutenges' arrival, the Japanese occupied Malaysia, and Tutenges, de Langlade, and the members of their group were forced to flee the country by the famous Burma Road.

De Langlade's assistant, the well-known author Pierre Boule, has related this epic incident in his book *My Own River Kwai*.

When Tutenges arrived in China, he reported to the French Military Mission in Chungking and began to set up an intelligence organization on Indochina. He soon met rigid opposition on the part of the Chinese. Since de Gaulle was not recognized as head of a government, his representatives could not claim diplomatic immunity. They were only tolerated and were under the constant surveillance of the police.

Thanks to his friendly relationship with the Generalissimo, Escarra was able to obtain for the military mission a more or less official recognition, but on one condition — instead of dealing with the military commission in charge of the relations with the other Allied military missions, the Free French were to communicate only with the Bureau of Investigation and Statistics (BIS). This was nothing less than the Chinese secret police, headed by the powerful Tai Li.

Tai Li's name is now almost forgotten. With the exception of those living in China at the time or of intelligence experts, very few have heard of this extraordinary man. A student at the Whampoa Military Academy in Canton, he caught the attention and interest of Chiang Kai-shek, then head of the academy. When Chiang decided in 1926 to lead the National Army from Canton toward the North, he entrusted Tai Li with the organization of his intelligence. Tai Li obtained remarkable results, and Chiang later acknowledged him as one of the major elements in the success of his campaign.

Tai Li then devoted himself to the creation, for Chiang, of a secret service with such divisions as intelligence, action, politics, and counterintelligence. His agents were spread all over China, in the smallest villages as well as the cities. He also had agents in foreign countries. In Washington, D.C., his representative within the Chinese Embassy, Colonel Hsiao, contributed to the creation of what has since been called "the China lobby."

This powerful apparatus was operating under the innocent name of Bureau of Investigation and Statistics. An enormous amount of money was needed to keep such an army of agents. To finance it, Tai Li engaged in a large-scale traffic in opium. When Japan invaded China, he took control of the black market, and did not hesitate to deal with the enemy whenever important business could be negotiated.

Tai Li granted the monopoly for smuggling along a certain part of the coast to two leaders, Chang Kuei Fang and Chang Yi Chiu, who ruled over more than 25,000 pirates. In exchange, they kept him informed on everything that went on in their area and occasionally agreed to carry out jobs for him.

Leading a rather simple life personally, Tai Li was renowned for his lavish receptions, where he provided his guests not only with the rarest of delicacies and best wines but with the most beautiful

Chinese girls. In 1942, Tai Li had already become a legend, but his power was to increase still more in the following year.

In the meantime, members of the French Military Mission were placed under Tai Li's complete control. Colonel Tutenges and de Langlade were free to go where they pleased, but only in the company of an interpreter-guide provided by Tai Li. They were also given transmitter equipment and operators, so that the Chinese were able to have absolute control over all communications. The situation was more than uncomfortable, but the French had no choice. It was either give in or renounce the mission they had committed themselves to.

In the spring of 1942, de Langlade, accompanied by Pierre Boule, decided to go near the Indochinese border in the hope of making contact with some French officers in border outposts. After numerous adventures, the two Frenchmen settled temporarily in Muong-La, hoping to meet a certain Major Fourmachat, in command of the Laichau district, who they thought was favorable to the Allied cause. After a long waiting period and no results, Boule made up his mind to enter Indochina clandestinely, but he was arrested on orders from Major Fourmachat, who turned out to be a devoted supporter of Vichy. Boule was terribly maltreated and sentenced to twenty years' imprisonment.

Following this failure, the morale of the French Military Mission sank very low, but their troubles were far from over.

After the Japanese attack on Pearl Harbor, the United States had recognized the necessity of being kept regularly informed on the movements of the Japanese Navy and weather conditions along the Chinese coast occupied by the enemy.

Rear Admiral Miles, then Commander, had been sent to Chungking to set up an intelligence ring to gather this information. He spoke Chinese fluently and was well acquainted with China, having spent many years there. This clever and courageous American made friends with Tai Li and was able to gain his confidence. Together they toured the territories occupied by the Japanese, setting up networks of informers and installing radio transmitters. The results were remarkable and drew the attention of General Donovan, director of the recently created Office of Strategic Service (OSS).

OSS's intentions were also to organize intelligence rings in China, but Tai Li, upon Miles' advice, would not agree.

After arduous negotiations, an agreement was reached and signed in Washington on April 11, 1943, between the OSS, the Navy, and Tai Li, resulting in the creation of the Sino-American Cooperation Organization (SACO). Tai Li was appointed head of the organization, with Miles as assistant. Considerable means, both financial and material, were now put at the disposal of the chief of the Chinese secret police.

In the wake of the creation of this new organization, the French mission's difficulties with the Chinese increased. This was attributed to the friction between de Gaulle and the Americans. But the French representation was not aware that two major decisions had been made — the importance of which was unsuspected even by their authors.

President Roosevelt, without seeking advice, made a personal decision that Indochina was to be withdrawn from France's sphere of influence. As a result, all cooperation with the French in the Far East was to be terminated. But as Indochina represented one of Japan's most importance bases, it was of primary concern to the United States to receive information on what was going on in Indochina. Therefore, Tai Li and Miles agreed on the creation of networks composed of Indochinese.

Tai Li was on the lookout for someone, preferably an Annamite, able to take charge of those networks. He decided to ask a certain Nguyen Ai Quok, who was serving a prison term in Lieu Tcheou for Communist activities. Nguyen Ai Quok already had run into serious trouble in Indochina and was well known by the French. So it was decided that he should change his name. He chose for himself the name Ho Chi Minh.

In the meantime, Free French officers finally had been able to make contact on the Indochina border and establish a system of radio communications with certain of their friends. Naturally this communication was handled by Tai Li's operators, and the French Military Mission immediately conveyed the intelligence received to the Allies.

Colonel Tutenges had been replaced as the head of the Intelligence Division by Colonel Emblanc, and General Petchkoff had been appointed by de Gaulle as chief of the French mission in China. Upon his arrival in Chungking, Marshal Chiang Kai-shek received General Petchkoff with all honors normally bestowed on an ambassador and thereafter called him by this title. This brought Petchkoff's enemies to say ironically, "General Petchkoff, French Ambassador in China, who is neither General, nor Petchkoff, nor Ambassador, nor French."

It is a fact that he was only a colonel and the title of general had been given him by de Gaulle for the duration of his mission. He was the adopted son of Gorki, the famous Russian author, and had taken the real family name, which was Petchkoff. He was not ambassador since this title had been given him by Chiang Kai-shek, not by the French government. And lastly, he was technically not French, since he had never been naturalized, but was considered as such, having served as an officer in the Foreign Legion.

His adoptive father, Alexis Petchkoff (and some claim he was his real father), had chosen the pseudonym of Gorki, which in Russian means "bitter." Difficult and unpredictable as his life had been, Petchkoff was never bitter. After a very poor youth spent in Nijni Novgorod, his birthplace, he followed Gorki to Italy. The easy life of Capri and Sorrento did not suit him, and when World War I broke out he enlisted in the Foreign Legion. A year later, gravely wounded in combat, he lost his right arm. This did not prevent him from continuing his military career, and twice more he was wounded in Morocco, during the War of the Riff.

Extremely clever, the proverbial soul of discretion, Petchkoff seemed born with a flair for intrigue common to many Slavs. He was entrusted by the French government with many confidential missions during the years preceding World War II.

Following the defeat of France, he joined General de Gaulle and spent some time in America, where he had many friends. He was on particularly good terms with General Donovan, and more than once stayed in the general's home on his frequent trips to the United States. General Petchkoff once told me he had met General Donovan, then a lawyer, in Russia before the war.

Immediately before coming to Chungking, Petchkoff acted as de Gaulle's representative to Marshal Smuts in South Africa. In China, his personal charm and wit won him Chiang Kai-shek's recognition with a title he did not really hold. This indirectly increased de Gaulle's prestige; and de Gaulle, grateful in his own way, placed in Petchkoff a confidence he usually sparingly bestowed.

Thanks to the restraining influence of Petchkoff and to his relationship with Chiang Kai-shek, a modus vivendi would certainly have been worked out if an unsuspected event had not aggravated an already deteriorating situation.

One day in August 1943, a group of French officers and non-commissioned officers headed by Commander Meynier came to Chungking without being announced. Mrs. Meynier accompanied her husband. The group came directly from Washington, together with officers of the U.S. Navy. They were instructed to create, in the framework of SACO, an intelligence ring on Indochina — another one.

Commander Meynier was quite remarkable in more than one respect. He had made an extraordinary escape from France with his ship, and had landed in Casablanca. Through his contacts with the U.S. Navy he was able to convince the experts of the Office of Naval Intelligence (ONI) of his wide knowledge of Indochina. The ONI asked General Giraud to detail him to work with them. Later, it appeared that Meynier was far less knowledgeable on the Indochinese problem than his wife. Mrs. Meynier was an Annamite related to the reigning family of Annam, but she had not been able to escape with him and was still in France.

After several requests from American sources, as well as French politicians, a special operation was planned to pick her up and bring her to North Africa. One dark night a Lysander landed in a field in France, and Mrs. Meynier, escorted to the plane by members of the resistance, was taken to London and then to Algeria to her loving husband.

BCRA officers did not hide their annoyance over a dangerous operation being undertaken only to reunite a husband and wife. Mrs. Meynier, irritated by the cold reception she received, showed toward the French the same ill feelings as did many Eurasians at the time, holding the French responsible for all her troubles. She had also witnessed the defeat and humiliation of France, which, as far as she was concerned, had lost face completely.

On the other hand, she developed an immediate attraction for the

United States, whose immense power could be seen and felt throughout North Africa. When her husband told her of his contemplated assignment with ONI, she was greatly enthused and, using her influence over him, gradually took over the direction of the operation.

The whys and wherefores of Meynier's mission have never been clearly understood, but it is a fact that before leaving for the United States with his wife and a group of his officers, he had been entrusted with codes by Giraud's intelligence and by the BCRA. What Meynier accomplished in the States is not known, since he failed to report on his activities.

One day he showed up in Chungking and paid a visit to General Petchkoff, who demanded that Meynier hand over his codes and that all his communications be made through the embassy. Continuing his round of visits, Meynier went to see Colonel Emblanc and informed him that he intended to set up a separate intelligence ring in liaison with the U.S. Navy. Exactly what took place during this meeting remains a mystery. One thing is certain — from that day Meynier ignored completely the existence of the French mission and its intelligence division and started making contacts of his own in various circles. Assured of the backing of Tai Li and of the U.S. Navy, he worked hard to establish contacts with the French element in Indochina and to implant, through these Frenchmen, intelligence networks.

When Emblanc was informed about Meynier's efforts to recruit agents in the French colony, he declared that Meynier was not working for his country, France, but for the United States, and that everything should be done to prevent the success of his enterprise.

This got back to Meynier, of course, and soon a split developed among the French in Chungking. Pro-Emblanc and pro-Meynier partisans wasted their time in futile and stubborn quarreling.

Because of his close connections with the U.S. Navy, Meynier's views and decisions carried more weight with Tai Li, and he was free to do what he wanted. Furthermore, Meynier gradually succeeded in convincing Chiang Kai-shek's secret police chief of the French Military Mission's ill will toward him. As a result, at the beginning of 1944 Tai Li ruled that the French mission would be forbidden to use any transmitters for its communications with Indochina and with its stations in China. Because of a rivalry among the French, all the good work accomplished in the past four years had come to a halt.

Mrs. Meynier, too, was very active along the Indochinese border, using her personal charm and relationship with the imperial family of Annam in trying to win over the Annamites she met. She was escorted by several U.S. Navy officers whom she won to her cause. Rumors then began to spread that SACO and the U.S. Navy were planning to place Mrs. Meynier on the throne of Annam after Indochina was rid of the Japanese.

In Algiers, reports kept pouring in on the possibility of an American scheme to put Mrs. Meynier in a royal position. This did not seem far-fetched to people who had already heard rumors about American support in putting the Comte de Paris at the head of the French government.

Such was the situation when I was placed at the head of the BCRA Far East section.

In Algiers many different people were dealing with the Indochina problem, but because they had no information on the situation there, no policy had really been established.

In theory, the Commissioner for Colonies, Mr. Pleven, was in charge of Indochina, but he had no communication with Hanoi or Saigon. The Commissioner for Foreign Affairs, Mr. Massigli, and the Chief of the Asian Desk, Gilbert, who a few years hence was to distinguish himself as French Ambassador to Israel during the Suez crisis, deplored the situation existing in China, but they could do nothing about it.

Within the National Defense Staff, Colonel Escarra was in charge of all military missions in foreign countries. The French mission in China, with its intelligence division, gave him greater headaches than all the others put together; but although he knew something had to be done, he was unable to figure out how to go about it.

In anticipation of an eventual participation of French troops in the Asiatic theater of operations, de Gaulle had gratified General Blaizot with the sonorous title of Commander of the French Expeditionary Forces in the Far East. In his headquarters located in the Pins Maritimes, a few miles from Algiers, General Blaizot had gathered a staff to work on the organization of two divisions to liberate Indochina. This staff based its plans on two assumptions: first, that after the liberation of France there would be enough troops available to make up the two divisions; second, that the Allies would provide all the equipment for these divisions.

The first assumption had a good chance of proving true, but there was no indication that the Allies would supply the equipment needed. Still hopeful of American assistance, General Blaizot planned one of the divisions on the U.S. Marine pattern, and splitting his bet in case of American refusal, he planned the other one on the British model.

In case of a victory over Japan before the liberation of France, he was organizing, also, a First Intervention Force made up of a handful of officers and men, confident that he would get reinforcements if the need for action arose.

In my eagerness to seize hold of the Indochina situation, I showered with questions every person whose competency and knowledge got me a step further in my work. I was soon known by all the specialists. One day Colonel Tutenges (who had set up the intelligence division in Chungking) called me. In his new position as head of General Blaizot's Second Bureau, he asked me to lunch with the general, who wanted to meet me. I was interested but not at all impressed. General Blaizot belonged to that military clique, none of whose members had fought during the war. Instead, he had been in Dakar with Governor Boisson, refusing to join the Allies up to the day Darlan persuaded him to rally to his command.

In the officer's mess of the Expeditionary Force in the Far East, the ritual and inevitable jokes were exchanged. The food was good, and General Blaizot very courteous. He talked about his projects and his current task of setting up a political section able to take over the Indochinese administration after the liberation of the country.

General Blaizot displayed four stars on his sleeve. I was only a private (not in uniform, thank God), and this was enough to arouse my audacity. I systematically refuted all the general's points, knowing fully that I was forfeiting all chances for future invitations. I needed to prove to myself that all his theories were antiquated as far as this war was concerned, and I was sick and tired of these career officers letting civilians do the job for them. Furthermore, their idea of combat based only on their pre–World War I military academy schooling was alarming. They had not yet conceived what members of the underground knew by instinct — in today's war all means were good if results were obtained. The ultimate goal was to win the war and not to parade troops according to the drill instructor's manual.

One of the guests at this luncheon understood my point of view and supported it. He was Commander Jacquelin de la Porte des Vaux. A legend was already attached to him. He liked to call himself a warrior "because of his taste for battle and blood," but his eccentricities were many and tended to overshadow his military exploits. Seldom would anyone mention his heroism during the defense of Dunkirk, but everyone knew about his behavior when, as a guest of Admiral Dowdin in Plymouth, he plunged his hand into the fish tank and ate a live goldfish under the horrified eyes of his hostess.

Jacquelin de la Porte des Vaux was in training to lead a group of Navy commandos in a landing on the Indochinese coast. With no one under him, he was going through the training all by himself. More than one civilian had been baffled at the sight of this Navy officer, in peculiar uniform and armed to the teeth with pistol, knife, and grenades, climbing telephone poles and cutting wires in order to improve his sabotage technique. A staff officer told me that once, upon hearing strange noises coming from a steel cabinet in his office, he opened it and found Jacquelin de la Porte des Vaux inside, unconscious. He had locked himself in for several days to see how long he could stay without moving or eating.

All this was very funny, but at the same time it was frightening. If Indochina was to count for its liberation on officers trained to fight an antiquated war or on a warrior who seemed to lack the sense of balance necessary to a leader, others besides the French would have to be responsible for it.

I was powerless, of course, and chances for a solution were very slim. Then new developments gave me reason to hope.

I would meet once a week with Professor — or rather, Colonel — Escarra and go over this dead-end issue with him. Because of his personal experience, I suppose, he was still more suspicious than I of the plans prepared by the military, and he was appalled by the existing confusion. The establishment of a special division coordinating actions of all departments dealing with Indochina was badly needed. We had to find the right man to help us set up the organization we were trying to outline.

One day Escarra told me, "I have heard that Lieutenant de Langlade is arriving here. He is coming to report on his liaison with Mountbatten's staff in Kandy. I would suggest that you have a long conversation with him about our problems and I will do the same. If anyone can help us find a solution, he is the one."

I had some plans ready, based on the merging of Giraud's intelligence with the BCRA. The decision to merge the two services inside the Direction Générale des Services Spéciaux (DGSS) provided that the new organization would assume control of all intelligence and counterintelligence and other similar activities wherever they were carried out. All Free French actions in the Far East were in these categories. Therefore, the intelligence division, working now in China, as well as the special operation force set up by General Blaizot, had to be under the DGSS authority.

In war and in peace the French military have a propensity for wanting to increase the scope of their authority. Plans to reduce it were unthinkable and would give way to endless debates. When my proposals were presented, the official response was always the same — the official would look at me with a long face and patronizingly say, "All this is very fine, young man, but we know from experience that it cannot be done. The research of intelligence in the Far East is a military operation and the military alone can do it."

Still, the intelligence coming from Chungking was so poor it was worthless. Intelligence is organization, and until a real organization could be set up, the Free French government would not know the facts necessary for the making of a policy.

I needed an ally to achieve what I had in mind, and when de Langlade arrived, I was at the Maison Blanche airport in Algiers to welcome him.

When he had first started as an intelligence agent in China, he had assumed the name of Long. Seeing him in his fitted British uniform, with the stripes of a lieutenant, I could not help thinking how appropriate the name was. He appeared to be taller than he really was. His looks, so typically British, took one by surprise, but his warm voice, along with his extreme kindness, made contacts pleasant and easy.

He had come straight from the Far East and ignored all the political schemes flourishing in Algiers. The DGSS, which I represented, was new to him. I set out to bring him up to date and he, in turn, taught me a great deal. He knew better than anyone the need for a coordinated policy, and he endorsed my plans with enthusiasm. At the particular time the Special Services seemed the only one able to bring unity in the existing confusion.

De Langlade's personality won over Captain Guillaumat, Commander Pelabon, and finally, Jacques Soustelle. The three men agreed that if all the sections dealing with Indochina could be united, de Langlade would head the new organization in the Far East.

But the merging remained to be done, and the military was unyielding. After working with me for days, de Langlade went on leave, and I kept on knocking at the doors of the officials responsible for this poor state of affairs.

One morning I got a call from Colonel Escarra asking me to come to see him right away. His office was located in the Summer Palace (Palais d'Été) and it took me a good fifteen minutes to get there. The spahi on duty showed me in immediately. Colonel Escarra was seated at his desk, his face red with anger. In front of him, an American general, appearing to be in the same disposition, was punctuating his words by banging his fist on the desk.

Without bothering to introduce me, Escarra nodded to a chair. Another French officer was also present and trying to remain unnoticed. I do not know how long this dialogue had been going on, nor how it all started. I turned my complete attention to the words being exchanged.

"The United States is at war with Japan. You, the French, are not engaged in any of the Far East theaters of operation. We are fighting with our Chinese ally, and whether you want it or not, we will conduct our intelligence operations as we please," said the American.

"Indochina is French territory, and we cannot tolerate both the Chinese and yourselves raising all kinds of obstructions to prevent our officers from establishing contacts with Indochina. We are willing to work with you, but as an ally and not as a subordinate," answered the colonel.

"The Chinese are free to act as they please in their country and we have nothing to do with their decisions."

"This is a joke. The Chinese are completely dependent on the United States for all their needs, and you can make them do whatever you want. It is you, the Americans, and not the Chinese who wanted Mrs. Meynier to be Empress of Annam," said Colonel Escarra accusingly.

"Mrs. Meynier, Empress of Annam? What does this mean? Are you crazy?"

"Don't pretend to be surprised," continued Colonel Escarra, who was becoming more and more excited. "Your maneuvers are no secret. We also have secret services," he was pointing in my direction, "and they can be as efficient as yours. And it would not take long for them to get rid of your organizations over there, if I instructed them to."

The American general was as aggravated as the colonel. The discussion went on in the same key for a few more minutes. Then the general got up and took his leave.

"Who is he?" I inquired after his departure.

"General Donovan, Chief of OSS. I have known him for a long time. He is a very good lawyer in New York, but since he has been in charge of the American secret services, he has constantly tried to create trouble for us everywhere. In Spain, he took Malaise under his protection, and after the French government's order for him to get back to North Africa. It looks like Donovan induced him to rebel. With Meynier we have the same story. I order him to come to Algiers immediately, and he argues that this is impossible because the Americans need him. Who gives orders now, the OSS or the French government? I will call your boss, Commander Pelabon, to inform him of my decision to put the intelligence section on the Far East under his authority. This will show the Americans. . . ."

So General Donovan was indirectly responsible for the decision to place the Far East Intelligence Service under the control of DGSS. My plans were becoming a reality.

I hurried back to my office and immediately prepared the draft of a letter to General Bethouart, Defense Chief of Staff, Colonel

Escarra's senior officer. The letter was signed by Commander Pelabon, and a few days later an affirmative answer reached us. This decision took effect on July 1, 1944.

De Langlade was back, quite pleased with the new developments. He agreed to head our organization in the Far East. However, in order to work with the most efficiency and to run a smoother operation, he requested that every organization working on Indochina be subordinated to him. He had explained his views to General de Gaulle and to the Commissioner for the Colonies, René Pleven. His request was granted. In a letter, Mr. Pleven informed General Blaizot that his Special Forces were now placed under the authority of the secret services: "As far as the political action in Indochina is concerned, I leave it to the Special Services, and will issue a memorandum with my precise and imperative instructions . . ."

Never before had secret services officially been given as much authority on French territory, and if concrete results were not obtained, the blame could not be attached to lack of full government backing.

Before de Langlade was to assume his new post, de Gaulle entrusted him with a delicate and dangerous mission.

At the end of 1943, the representative of the BNCI (Banque Nationale pour le Commerce et Industrie) in Saigon, Mr. François, had been allowed to leave Indochina. He came to Algiers and passed to General Giraud a message from General Mordant, Chief of the Armed Forces in Indochina. Later, the military mission in Chungking, through radio contacts with French military elements in Indochina, got confirmation of General Mordant's desire to collaborate with the Algiers government.

At the beginning of February 1944, de Gaulle wrote a letter to Mordant, assuring him of his confidence and trying to secure his complete support for Free France. The letter was to be entrusted to Mr. François, who was supposed to go back to Indochina. But some complications arose and François did not return. De Gaulle's letter had remained in Algiers, undelivered, and now de Langlade had been chosen to accomplish this mission. De Langlade was to see General Mordant and give him de Gaulle's instructions to assume the leadership of the resistance in Indochina.

The best way to enter Indochina clandestinely was to be parachuted in. De Langlade had no previous training, but he was game, and the element of danger in the mission, far from daunting him, presented an attraction. Chances of being captured by the Japanese or the Vichyites were great, and in either case he could be made, under torture, to reveal secret information. Also, the security in Algiers was poor, and the Japanese could easily be tipped about his trip. To cut down on the risks, two decisions were made. First, de Langlade would stop working on the planning of the new Special Services setup until he returned from Indochina. In the meantime this task would be carried on by a reliable person of his choice. Second, he would be offered the post of French Minister to the legation in Australia. This piece of news would receive a wide coverage, so this trip to India could be interpreted as a stopover on his way to assuming his diplomatic functions in Australia.

In fact, General de Gaulle had made it clear that upon his return from Indochina, de Langlade was free to accept the Australian post if he desired. De Langlade designated one of his former assistants in Malaysia, Leonard, to continue working with me on the organization of the services in the Far East. Then he left for India.

The difficulties created by the Chinese and Americans made it impossible for the French to operate from Chinese territory on a large scale. India was the only other country offering facilities to set up a base for our secret services. The British seemed to understand our problems and were willing to help. On the other hand, de Langlade and his team had done many favors for the British services during the battle of Malaysia and had gained their confidence. They could certainly count on their support, at least inasmuch as England's policy would coincide with Free France's.

We decided to set our base in Calcutta because of its proximity to Indochina. It was also an important aviation center, where Dakotas flying over the "hump" were taking supplies to China twenty-four hours a day. This heavy air traffic would be favorable for our communications. Activity by radio was also great, increasing the chances for our clandestine transmissions to go unnoticed. One last advantage was that it would be possible to house a certain number of people in the city who would blend in with the cosmopolitan population during this time of war. The French colony was small, and everyone had joined the Free French at the beginning of the hostilities, thus reducing the risk of surveillance by Vichy agents.

Leonard, like de Langlade, was a man of great resources. Because of his courage and energy, we gave him the nickname "Lion"; de Langlade was "Lutece" and General Mordant "Narcisse." All these pseudonyms were used in the correspondence in order to confuse unauthorized readers.

Leonard was gifted with a talent for organization and an iron will, which he disguised with mildness and patience. He set out to recruit personnel, but found it impossible, in most cases, to convince people of the usefulness of fighting in the Far East. Nearly everyone wanted to remain in Algeria to take part in the campaign to liberate France.

At times, personal problems made it difficult to assign people where they would be the most useful. For example, there was the case of the officer who spoke Chinese fluently and had a perfect knowledge of the Far East. Leonard wanted him to head our station in China, but his wife and children were in Indochina, and the poor man was ignorant of the fact that his wife had taken up with a well-known Vichyite. Sooner or later, he would have stumbled over the truth and his good judgment could have been impaired. This officer had been designated to participate in the landing in France, and after much thought, we decided not to ask for a change in his assignment.

With great pains we finally assembled a small group to start what we had officially called Section de Liaison Française en Extrême Orient (SLFEO). This name didn't mean much but was as good a cover as any.

Every day brought new questions to be resolved. Some, which appeared simple, were the source of many headaches.

Leonard, as well as de Langlade, held the rank of lieutenant in the reserve. In their new positions, they would have to deal daily with Allied officers of a much higher rank. The only solution was to give them the temporary rank of major. This would permit them to wear the insignia of that rank on their uniforms, but they would continue to receive their lieutenant's pay. Furthermore, at the end of their mission, they would go back to their original rank.

The authorization was granted, but raised quite a storm when the two officers showed up in the Far East with the insignia of their temporary rank. Most career officers took it as a personal blow to their dignity and campaigned violently against the secret services, "which was handing around bars and stripes." I was held personally responsible for those temporary promotions, and this created many difficulties for me in dealing with career officers. As for de Langlade and Leonard, they had to endure shuns and bitter remarks from high-ranking officers who thought that the insignia of a rank showed a man's real ability.

The Allied landing in Normandy had started, and the liberation of France was only a matter of weeks away. In our theater of operations in Asia, victory seemed more distant. The underground in France received its directives from the Committee for Action in France. Following this example, we laid down the outlines of a similar project for the Far East involving the creation of a Committee of Action for Indochina, with de Langlade as Secretary General in charge of carrying out the committee decisions. This would take care of the political directives to be given to the Indochinese underground.

But what exactly was the underground in Indochina? What networks had been set up? Who were the personnel working for us under cover of the military mission in China? We did not know and we could not get any answers to our numerous inquiries. True, we had a decree giving us authority over that mission, and we were to set up a new organization, but we could not go on with our work until we knew what we already had. This is why it was decided that I would leave as soon as possible for China to make a careful survey of the situation and to propose to the director of the Special Services a course of action to improve the intelligence organization there and to reorganize it if necessary.

I welcomed this opportunity for a close look at what was going on. Regardless of my negligible knowledge of the Far East, for months I had worked hard to collect every available piece of documentation and intelligence, and I was sure I had gathered everything to be found in Algiers on the subject. Still, it was very little.

I had gone so far as to obtain information from the OSS. Through our liaison with David Rockefeller, who represented the American intelligence in Algiers, I collected several reports of a very general nature but reflecting, nevertheless, the enormous research job conducted by the Americans. I was convinced that by setting up an intelligence division able to give the Allies substantial help in their fight against Japan, they, in turn, would share with us their own intelligence.

I was also concerned about our complete ignorance of the feelings and reactions of local populations. In May I had studied a report coming from Royère, unofficial representative in Kunming of the Governor-General of Indochina. The report referred to the activities of a group of Annamite refugees in Kunming. They were former members of the old revolutionary movement, Vietnam Quoc Dan Dang. Royère explained in detail the group's intentions and named its more important members. This document was the only one of its kind received in Algiers, and I thought it was of such interest that I forwarded it to General de Gaulle. The report was received by Mr. Palewski, de Gaulle's director of cabinet, who returned it to me a few days later with the comment, "There have always been revolutionaries in our colonies, and your service had better work on the Japanese rather than waste time on such nonsense."

The remarks of de Gaulle's close collaborator failed to convince me, and I resolved to go on finding out everything I could on the attitude of the native population toward the Japanese, the French, and the Chinese.

The feeling prevailing among members of the government in Algiers — unaware of the decisions made at the Conference of Quebec — was that the Chinese intended to get hold of Indochina and that American policy was to leave them a free hand in their endeavor to replace the French. All the so-called experts I consulted predicted a violent reaction from the people of Indochina against the Chinese, who through the years had made a practice of looting neighboring territories.

I left for India at the beginning of July 1944 as inspector of the French Military Mission, very much aware of the difficulties I would encounter. Upon my arrival in Calcutta, the French consul, Raux, whom I already knew, told me about de Langlade's being parachuted over Indochina. The operation had been successful, but there had been no news since. A symptomatic incident had taken place before his departure: de Langlade had radioed General Mordant telling him that he was to be parachuted with a letter from General de Gaulle. General Mordant had shown a certain reluctance at first, but after an exchange of messages gave his O.K. He insisted, however, that de Langlade come without de Gaulle's letter, stating that it would place him in a dangerous position in case of capture by the Japanese. Acceding to his request, de Langlade had radioed the letter in a coded message before his departure. We knew he had landed safely, but General Mordant's attitude seemed far too cautious, and I feared for de Langlade's safety.

The British outfit charged with carrying out the operation was the SOE (Special Operation Executive), which, oddly enough, was under the authority of the Minister for Economic Warfare (MEW). When Colonel Brandt, the MEW representative in Kunming, cabled that de Langlade was en route to Calcutta, without stopping in Kunming, we all felt relieved. He had accomplished a tremendous job in a very short time and was bringing with him a detailed report from Mordant on the situation and the needs of the underground.

Before heading for Algiers and London to report to de Gaulle on his mission, de Langlade held several meetings with the British. While recognizing the need for establishing our base in Calcutta for operations in Indochina, the British were imposing two conditions. The first, that the operating team would be small and inconspicuous, was reasonable. The second, however, was that all communications would be sent and received through their services. This would make us completely dependent on British intelligence, which could stop or delay our communications at will. Every effort to get them to change their position was in vain. The British put forward as the reason behind their decision orders from New Delhi and London, where America — they said — was against the French conducting any kind of operation dealing with Indochina.

Were we to abandon our project of a base in India and to continue our action from China despite the increasing difficulties created by the Chinese? After giving the problem some thought, we came up with a solution. Since the seventeenth century, France had several protectorates in India. One of them, Chandernagor, was located about thirty miles from the center of Calcutta. Chandernagor was French territory, administered by a gendarme who was the only representative of the Governor of French India. We would be at home there and could set up all our radio communications without any interference or special conditions on the part of the British. Delighted by the idea, Leonard lost no time in organizing the base, while I left for China.

The staff of the French Military Mission in the Far East, after learning of their new status under the Special Services, were curious about the arrival in Chungking of the service's first representative. My curiosity was still greater, since my findings would show if our plans were workable or if they had to be revised.

Did a resistance movement really exist? De Gaulle had named General Mordant as its head, but this did not mean too much.

It took me a few days to break the ice, but finally Colonel Emblanc showed me on an old map of Indochina the locations of the trans-mitters with which he was in contact. One was in Saigon, another in Tourane (now Da Nang), two more in Hanoi, and one in Langson. He told me something of the group connected with each one and gave me a list of the members, totaling fifty-three persons.

Fifty-three resistants in Indochina in August 1944, after three and a half years of Japanese occupation? I paralleled this with the resistance in France. It was small, but next to it the proportion for Indochina was meager. Even to call it a resistance was a joke. There were some agents, but not really an underground movement. Still, most of the members were officers and could, in case of an uprising, carry their troops with them. Their goodwill and desire to help were real, but they did not know exactly what was expected of them.

Communication with Chungking was impossible following Tai Li's interdiction. Although French Intelligence had a transmitter hidden in the Odent barracks, no one dared to use it for fear of detection by Tai Li. Based on what I had seen in Chungking, I had my doubts about the effectiveness of Tai Li's goniometry. Even if we used the transmitter and were discovered, we were not running any great risk. The worst that could occur was the expulsion of several officers who were idle anyway until communications were restored.

It was therefore decided to reestablish radio communications with our groups in Indochina. This increased appreciably the flow of intelligence on Japanese military movements, which was immediately given to the U.S. naval attaché, Commander Jarrel. In several instances Japanese warships were met upon their departure from Saigon or Haiphong by American submarines alerted through our intelligence.

A liaison was also operating with Colonel Dickey, General Still-well's G2 chief, but contacts were rather cool, since Colonel Dickey's orders were not to cooperate with the French. He was above all anxious to be informed about France's designs toward Indochina. The tension in Franco-American relations was uncomfortable and could not be blamed on French officers, who were always seeking contacts with American representatives and supplying them with the intelligence they received. We were to learn later that Washington orders were imperatives.

In Kunming, the representative of French intelligence, Major Bonnet, had excellent connections with the 14th Air Force, under General Chennault's command. Staying out of politics, General Chennault's only goal was to fight the Japanese. His pilots needed to know weather conditions over Indochina as accurately as possible. Having no intelligence setup of his own in Indochina, General Chennault had to rely on the information provided by SACO and Tai Li, but they were usually late. Therefore, he authorized the French to operate a transmitter within his headquarters in exchange for regular weather bulletins. In addition, the French reported to the general on the results and accuracy of his bombings. Several times the French network helped American pilots shot down over Indochina to escape the Japanese and get to Kunming safely. Agreements such as this one should have been in effect with all other American groups, but General Chennault was probably the only one to refuse to get involved in politics.

General Petchkoff's friendship with General Donovan brought a happy ending to the problem presented by Commander Meynier's undisciplined actions. Meynier and his wife finally departed from the Chinese theater of operations. I met them in Calcutta and, during a dinner I had with them, learned much about the activities of the Indochinese revolutionaries. Commander Meynier was the first one to recognize the importance of the movement led by Ho Chi Minh.

If passions had not been so exacerbated and rivalry between the different French coteries so fierce, his contribution to the defense of French interests in the Far East would have been priceless.

I was in Chungking the day Paris was liberated, and a few weeks later I flew back to Algiers and then to France to turn in my report.

In Paris, thousands of former resistants, experiencing difficulties in adapting to normal life, volunteered to go to Indochina to pursue the fight. Whereas several months before I was alone in the Special Services and it was almost impossible to assemble a handful of officers, there were now almost too many. People everywhere were hunting for jobs and positions. I had just reached my twenty-fourth birthday, and was not too surprised to learn that Major Bouheret, having been replaced as head of the intelligence division of Special Services, was now in charge only of the Far Eastern Section. Wishing to devote all his time to the Indochinese situation, he assigned me to be in charge of intelligence on all Asiatic countries outside Indochina.

De Langlade and Leonard were working miracles in overcoming the thousands of daily obstacles, and the underground in Indochina was growing steadily. The original fifty-three members of August 1944 had multiplied into several thousand. No Japanese ship could leave or enter an Indochinese port without being reported immediately. Often French agents in the various harbors even were able to communicate the exact course of the ship. Airports were under constant watch and plane movements reported. Japanese communications were under close surveillance, the telephones tapped, their cables intercepted. All this intelligence was immediately given to the proper American authorities.

Still, relations between the French and Americans were more and more strained. The French were still unaware that at the Quebec Conference, President Roosevelt had voiced his decision to eliminate the French from Indochina and to entrust Chiang Kai-shek with the administration of the country. On several occasions Chiang Kai-shek, overcome with problems, had expressed his doubts about the wisdom of this, but President Roosevelt was unshakable. This was his way of punishing France for having lost the war.

I received several reports stating that many responsible Americans in China, realizing the good work being accomplished by the French, had intervened with representatives of the State Department, but the diplomatic adviser to the chief of the theater of operations stressed repeatedly the orders not to collaborate with the French. Many cables were exchanged between Chungking and Washington over this matter — and these cables were to start an awful storm in a very strange way. Who would have thought the Japanese were reading Washington's cables?

Japanese intelligence maintained good relations with Finnish intelligence, based on their common hatred of the Soviets. The Finnish had long ago begun specializing in the deciphering of foreign codes, particularly Soviet codes. During the winter of 1939–1940, the Finnish code-breaking services were able to interpret successfully the coded instructions of the Soviets, even before they reached their recipients. The victories of Finland over the Soviet Union were all based on the good work of their decoding services. Greatly impressed, the Japanese had arranged, in an agreement with the Finns, for one of their officers to work with the Finnish operators. In return, the Japanese offered financial help as well as information on the Soviet codes in the Far East. So Colonel Hirose of the Japanese deciphering service went to work in the Finnish General Staff section busy with uncovering Soviet codes.

However, the Finns were not working exclusively on Soviet codes. They succeeded also in deciphering a code used by the U.S. State Department, following a mistake made by the coding room of the American Embassy in Vichy. After refusing several requests from Hirose, the Finns agreed in 1943 to give him the code. This same code happened to be used by the American Embassy in Chungking, allowing the Japanese to read all cables exchanged between the State Department and the U.S. Embassy in the Chinese capital.

Informed of American policy, knowing that no support would be given to the French, and aware of the harm caused them by the efficiency of the French organizations, the Japanese, on March 9, 1945, arrested and jailed all the French in Indochina. French troops took to the jungle and tried to resist. They radioed Calcutta and Kunming asking for support from the U.S. Air Force. Nothing happened. The French ran out of ammunition while desperately

107

waiting for promised arms to be dropped. American forces were located only a hundred miles from the battleground. The 14th Air Force headquarters was no more than one hour by air, but the planes did not show up. Why? General Chennault, in his memoirs, explained:

Soon after the Japanese struck, I sent 14th Air Force Intelligence officers to make contact with the French troops. Flying in tiny grasshopper planes, they landed in cleared jungle strips and had made arrangements for air drops of ammunitions, medical supplies and food to the retreating French, when orders arrived from theater headquarters stating that no arms and ammunitions would be provided to French troops under any circumstances. . . .

I carried out my orders to the letter but I did not relish the idea of leaving Frenchmen to be slaughtered in the jungle while I was forced officially to ignore their plight.

From Calcutta, de Langlade and Leonard did their best, and the British, lacking planes and equipment, still gave all the help they could. But Calcutta was much farther away than Kunming, and it was not enough. Several thousand French soldiers were slaughtered within a few days, while American planes altered their courses in order not to impede the Japanese in their bloody massacre.

No one in France was ready to believe that the American action was the result of a predetermined decision. America was our ally, and we had once more fought the Germans together. Her present behavior was attributed to lack of organization or shortage of equipment. Yet intelligence received from our agents in Southern China revealed that SACO was using groups of Indochinese Communists to carry out missions in Indochina. Such actions were not surprising on the part of the Chinese, but we could hardly figure out how America could be directly involved in such undertakings. Could they be explained as isolated acts concocted in the shadow of Happy Valley, Tai Li's nest, by officers in quest of personal gain or privilege? Or was Washington behind the action?

With the end of French activities, a vacuum had been created in American intelligence. To fill the gap and keep intelligence from Indochina coming in, Indochinese Communists were sought to take over the task of the French services. But we had learned that in several instances, the Communists had been in contact with the Japanese secret services (Kempeitai), and we had little doubt that the help given to the American General Staff was illusory. The leaders of those revolutionary groups had also made contact with representatives of our services in Chungking, and although they requested independence, they showed their readiness to discuss terms with France.

At the end of July 1945, the U. S. Ambassador in Paris informed the French government of the decisions reached at the Potsdam meeting. It had been agreed in substance that after Japan's surrender, the Indochinese territory would be occupied by China in the northern part, and by the British in the south. De Gaulle, infuriated by the fact that he was kept away from the Potsdam conference table, did not realize fully the broad implications of this agreement at the time.

France, who had not yet been able to raise the required military contingent of two divisions, agreed that her Allies would act as substitutes but greatly resented the occupation of Tonkin by Chinese troops. France would not have raised any objection to the occupation of this part of Indochina by British or American troops.

On August 16, immediately following the capitulation of Japan, Ho Chi Minh declared the independence of Indochina. The Vietminh was taking over. The French imprisoned in Hanoi remained under Japanese custody. French government envoys were either assassinated or arrested and guarded by Japanese, with American representatives refusing to intervene on their behalf. The question of whether these Americans were acting as their country's true representatives and were following orders has never been cleared up. The head of the group of American officers was a member of the OSS, Major Patti, who had provided arms to Ho Chi Minh and later organized the training of his guerrillas. When Ho Chi Minh tried to negotiate an agreement with the French government, Major Patti came in and promised him the support of the United States

109

if he would stop negotiations with the French and demand complete independence for Indochina.

At the same time, several American officers with the Patti mission came to the Vietminh with offers to substitute for the French. One had already drafted contracts granting himself exclusive rights in dealing with all public works in Vietnam. Another had planned to direct the education system and bring American teachers to this country where English was not spoken.

When the French showed some progress in turning the tide, the Vietminh initiated a fund-raising campaign among the patriots, urging them to give generously so that arms could be bought from the United States. The money collected at the end of the "Gold Week" was handed to Major Patti prior to his departure from Hanoi. The Vietminh received none of the arms Patti had promised, and a rumor soon circulated that he had been arrested upon his arrival in the United States.

From Paris I was kept informed of all activities of the American advisers to Ho Chi Minh. One by one, they were returned to the United States and fell into oblivion. But the harm caused by their maneuvers and mistakes continued to spread long after they were gone, obviously playing a part in the evolution of the situation leading to the present state of affairs in Vietnam. Still, it would not be fair to place the entire responsibility for the unfortunate events in Vietnam on American actions.

In conformity with the Potsdam agreement, the Chinese troops, under command of General Lu Han, cousin of the Governor of Yunnan, had entered Indochina for the so-called purpose of disarming the Japanese troops. Their first action was to loot and ransack whatever the Japanese had not already taken, reducing the country to a state of famine and making it easier for the Vietminh to recruit followers among the population. The territory occupied by the Chinese extended to Tourane, today known as Da Nang. This zone was to become North Vietnam. The Chinese General, Lu Han, who with his American deputy General Gallagher had organized the Chinese occupation, soon after joined Mao Tse-tung.

Tai Li is said to have died in 1946 in a mysterious plane accident. All Western intelligence services knew at the time of his dealings with the Communists, and in many counterintelligence services the

Tai Li file is still open. The possibility of his still being alive and helping Communist China in her worldwide subversive activities is believed in many quarters.

As for the French government, the lack of vision and the absence of political wisdom greatly contributed to worsen a situation which in the years following would needlessly cost the lives of hundreds of thousands of people.

The day was cold and gray and the city of Orléans seemed gloomy and desolate. The beautiful streets once lined with arcades were hardly recognizable now. A succession of bombings had demolished most of the buildings, and even the magnificent Gothic cathedral had not been spared.

Carrying my suitcase, I followed the stream of travelers through the station, which also lay in ruin. The train could take us no farther, since the bridge over the Loire had been destroyed. We had to walk through the city, then take a ferry across the river, where we could get another train south of the Loire.

I had returned to France two days earlier, coming from China via Algiers. In North Africa complete confusion reigned. Paris had been liberated three months before, and still no fast means of transportation existed between what had been the temporary capital and the real capital of France. Traveling by plane was restricted to a few privileged officials, and I was not one of them.

An endless waiting period had followed my return from Chungking. Finally, I embarked on the *Batory*, a Polish ship converted for the transport of troops. To void encounters with German submarines, the *Batory* had joined a convoy under the protection of several destroyers. Instead of heading directly for Marseille, the nearest harbor, our convoy, for security reasons, zigzagged toward the coast of Normandy.

All the members of the Free French Special Services were on board, and I couldn't help being amused at the sight of them lounging on the deck of a foreign ship around a sign labeled "Secret Services." Also on board were a large number of the foreign diplomats accredited to the Algiers government and their families. Among them was Bogomolov, the Soviet Ambassador.

Eleven days after our departure, we sighted Honfleur. We transferred to barges for crossing the channel to the old fishing port. The peasants of Normandy welcomed us, showing their enthusiasm by throwing us apples. After all, Normandy is the apple orchard of France. The Bogomolovs had taken the first barge and a peasant, in his excitement, threw one directly at Mrs. Bogomolov's face. So it was with a black eye that the wife of the Russian Ambassador set foot on the soil of France.

As soon as I reached Paris, I tried to call my family, but the old telephone system wasn't functioning and most lines had not been repaired. I requested a leave and boarded the train to make the trip home to see my parents. It had been two years since I last heard from them.

This was the reason for my presence now in Orléans. As I stood near the embankment waiting for the train to Romorantin, I became aware of someone staring at me. Looking around, I recognized the owner of the local jewelry store in Romorantin who had been for many years president of the Commerce Court in our district. He looked so puzzled that I went to him.

"Are you really Mr. Thyraud?" he said in disbelief.

"Of course," I answered, wondering at his expression and fearing that something had happened to one of my relatives. "But why are so surprised to see me, Mr. Tondu?"

"Well . . . that is, we . . ." he stuttered, "everyone thought you were dead."

It was my turn to be shocked.

The explanation turned out to be very simple. None of my letters from China had reached my family, and since France had

113

been liberated for more than three months, they had been forced to assume that I would have returned by now unless I had been killed.

So that my parents, who were getting old, would not have the shock of seeing me with no forewarning, Mr. Tondu offered to have me wait in his store while he prepared them for my return. Thus, even after my prolonged absence, I once more had to make a secret entry into my hometown so as not to risk an accidental meeting with my father.

The elation of my family was no less than the surprise of all our friends over the news that I was alive. I really felt like a ghost. Messages and expressions of sympathy over my death had reached my family in great number, and to tell the truth, I almost felt out of place among the living.

It took me some time and made me a little sad to realize that my disappearance, although mourned, failed to change the course of family events and daily routines. This realization about the relative importance of individuals greatly influenced the decisions I was to make later on in my life.

In our small town almost every man wore a uniform, few ranking below second lieutenant. Captains were even more numerous. This rank seemed to have a particular attraction for combatants of the last hour. In the few weeks preceding the liberation of France, men who previously had not dared to commit themselves sensed the necessity of demonstrating their desire for an Allied victory. In great numbers they joined the underground, where they were hastily organized into incongruous units. Those units were to become the French Forces of the Interior, commonly known as the FFI. The organization had many more officers than soldiers, and after the liberation the display of such a multitude of stripes was reminiscent of a comic opera.

These brave soldiers, who for the main part had never seen battle, suddenly discovered a new vocation as dispensers of justice. They hunted collaborators, making arrests indiscriminately with no regard for the legal process. They started immediately after the Germans departed with the arrests of women suspected, rightly or wrongly, of having consorted with them. As a rule, the poor girls were carried up to the city hall, where, from the balcony, they were stripped and their heads shaved. Then, under the insults of a hysterical crowd, they were paraded naked through the streets before being thrown in jail. One of those women, supposed to be the illegitimate daughter of a prominent businessman of the town, was for that reason the particular victim of the sadism of the FFI patriots.

Many of the FFI belonged to the Communist organization Francs-Tireur et Partisans. Under the pretense of punishing the collaborators and those who had fraternized with the Germans, the Communists were able to get rid of many of their adversaries. A friend of mine, who on several occasions had helped me get hunted men to freedom, was shot, along with several members of his family, in a nearby town by a band of wrathful Communists.

The jails were filled with people arrested under the most fallacious pretexts. The legal authorities could only look the other way and let it all go on. Gendarmes and policemen, who a few weeks before were arresting real patriots to hand over to the Gestapo, were now zealously arresting their former associates.

One day some members of the Francs-Tireur et Partisans arrested a family under the feeble excuse that their manor had been requisitioned by the Germans. They took the father, mother, and eighteen-year-old daughter into the Troncay Forest where a dozen men raped the mother and then the girl after first torturing them by burning their breasts with cigarettes. They then beat to death the father, who had been a powerless witness to the scene. Among the hoodlums guilty of these atrocious crimes, besides Frenchmen, were many Communist Spaniards, and Slavs of undetermined origin.

The Communist underground organizations, besides receiving orders from de Gaulle, had also been getting instructions from Moscow, often brought in by messengers. These messengers were sometimes Soviet citizens infiltrated through German lines, or often Polish or Czech members of the Communist underground in their own countries. Many of them were instructors and remained with the French organizations to train their members and take care of communications. Speaking good French and familiar with all methods of deception, the Slavs eventually were completely assimi-

115

lated into the networks, and the other members soon forgot that they were not French.

This infiltration of the resistance networks by the Communists was later to be of paramount importance, since many of them assumed the identity of missing persons and were recognized as French citizens. For the time being, their main concern was to create a climate of terror in the villages as well as in the cities by getting rid of any who opposed them. By infiltrating the government and administration on behalf of the KGB, they were paving the way for a Communist takeover.

Certain regions were completely under the control of these groups who owed their allegiance to Moscow. Towns such as Toulouse, Lyons, and Limoges were a problem for de Gaulle, whose power was at times only nominal. If the Allied troops had not been in France, and if Moscow had been ready, a Communist regime could very well have been set up in Paris.

Besides the official jails, each town had numerous secret jails where the Communist groups were holding those they arrested. Revolutionary courts pronounced death sentences after obtaining confessions from their victims by means of torture as horrible as any devised by the Gestapo. The decisions of these improvised tribunals were followed summarily by executions. No exact census has ever been made of the number of French executed by their compatriots, but the figure listed in a Department of Interior report which I read later was 500,000 deaths during the six months immediately following the liberation. This was without customary legal procedure — 500,000 people killed out of personal revenge or assassinated by the Communists. The figure is equal to half the total number of Frenchmen killed in five years of war. Of course, the executions which took place by court orders are not included in this figure.

My exaltation in returning to France was dimmed by the disgust I felt over events in my home district, which was only a small-scale example of a national situation. After a week of trying to familiarize myself with the changes that had taken place, I left my family for Paris to resume my duties with the Special Services.

The BCRA had changed names and was now called Direction Générale des Études et Recherches (DGER), meaning Central

Agency for Studies and Research. The offices of the DGER had been set up in a group of buildings at the beginning of Boulevard Suchet, recently vacated by the Kreigsmarine and once the most luxurious apartments in Paris. The Far East Division, which six months earlier had one office occupied by one staff member (me), was now an extremely busy place with a staff of about fifty spread through an immense suite of fifteen rooms.

The basement of our headquarters had been converted into a restaurant, where utter confusion and disorder prevailed. Lavish meals were served at all hours, with wine and liquor flowing abundantly. Everything was free and there was no identification check at the door. This meant that in this period of extreme rationing, anyone could get a remarkably good meal in the basement of the DGER. Needless to say, the place was crowded, and several thousand meals were served daily at the expense of a government which was itself in need of everything.

The DGER, successor of the BCRA, inherited the networks it had run in occupied France. Now the network members wanted some kind of recognition for the services they had performed. Those with a desire for a military career wanted to be integrated into the military complete with their self-conferred ranks. Others wanted to be given positions in the secret services. All expected decorations and a regular salary as their due, since they had "liberated" France. With the battle over, they expected a share of the loot but were unwilling to bend to any authority or follow any orders.

I recall one day being with the officer in charge of issuing permits for transportation and providing cars and gas coupons to authorized personnel. A young man in his late twenties or early thirties came into the office and requested a permit to take a car to Limoges with five of his friends. The officer refused his request, since he needed written permission. The man left abruptly, slamming the door behind him. He returned a few minutes later with his five friends, all carrying machine guns. Pointing one at the officer, he said, "Now do you have the authorization?"

The officer naturally complied. He knew that he was in no position to call for help, since some of the menacing men were his own guards.

117

With such a large staff to accommodate, there was not enough room for my section at headquarters and I was assigned the entire floor of a superb building located on Avenue Foch. The former tenants had been none other than the Gestapo. The sumptuous apartment in which I set up the intelligence section of the Far East division was furnished with priceless antiques. As we were moving in, I noticed about ten cars in the courtyard of the building. "What are all those cars for?" I asked one of my assistants.

"They're yours," he said. "They were left by the Gestapo."

"But we don't have registration papers," I protested.

Pointing to a gun lying on the front seat, my assistant declared, "This new Luger is better than a registration certificate."

This mixed atmosphere of county fair and revolution was not conducive to serious work. However, I tried to carry out the organization of a research service covering all the Far East, with the exception of Indochina, over which Major Bouheret had chosen to retain authority. After classifying all the intelligence and counter-intelligence data we had on hand, we were able to pinpoint our weak spots and organize specific missions to fill the gap.

Daily I was contacted by volunteers eager to be sent to China or neighboring countries. All these young men had acquired a taste for clandestine work in the underground and were now ready to carry on the fight against the Japanese in the same manner as they had against the Germans. Their desire to serve was genuine, but unfortunately most of them just didn't qualify, and we were not equipped to train them adequately for missions in Allied, or supposedly Allied, territories. Still, we did single out several suitable men to supplement our sources of information in foreign countries.

In France, we had come across the archives of the Vichy Ministry for Foreign Affairs and the Ministry of Colonies, which gave us a fairly accurate account of the situation in Indochina. The archives of the Japanese Embassy in Paris had been destroyed by the representatives of Japan before their flight to Germany. But the Sûreté had searched the homes of the Japanese diplomats and discovered valuable documents that put the police on the track of some of their agents.

One Japanese military attaché who was married to a French

118

girl had left behind a suitcase full of papers. The documents were written in Japanese, and we were in the process of translating them into French. They had already revealed his connections with Japanese intelligence and also several addresses he had used to conduct secret meetings with his agents.

Two addresses had been checked when our translator came in with a list of about thirty other Paris locations. Were we about to uncover a network of Japanese agents? The prospect was exciting to all of us. I immediately contacted the Sûreté. Soon a police official armed with search warrants set out to investigate the given addresses. One of my deputies accompanied him. To their amazement, the first address on the list proved to be a brothel. The second was the same. So were all the others. It seemed that since the brothel's clientele was mostly German officers during the occupation, the Japanese military attaché would meet his agents there. He also, we discovered, used certain prostitutes to supply him with information they were able to obtain because of their intimacy with the German officials. This method, used by the Japanese to keep a close watch on their Nazi ally, was certainly not original, but to my knowledge it had never before been used on such a large scale.

The investigation by the Sûreté of the Japanese movements in France uncovered other activities which greatly annoyed the French government. The police found out that OSS officers, ignoring the French authorities and regulations, had proceeded with searches in the homes of French citizens who were suspected of having contact with representatives of the Japanese Embassy. The United States government had officially recognized the French government in October 1944, and the action of the OSS, acting in France as if in conquered territory, brought a strong reaction against the American services. They were warned that if such acts were repeated, they would be prosecuted for violation of the domiciles of French citizens. The Sûreté offered to collaborate with the Americans on all investigations they required.

The OSS office was located on the Champs Elysées above the famous Mimi Pinson dance hall. Its activities were at least as confused as the French service's. Many members of the underground who thought they were working for Free French networks had learned since the liberation that their activities had not been recognized by the Gaullists and that, in fact, they had been working on behalf of foreign governments. Many of them came to see the OSS representatives, hoping to obtain the same advantages given to their comrades who had worked under the authority of the Algiers government.

Long negotiations began between the American and British services on one side and the DGER on the other regarding the termination of these networks. An agreement was reached so that this would be done on an equal basis. The members of the American network, however, did not share all the advantages granted to the members of the Free French network and were bitter that they had been shortchanged. For years they were unable to get security clearances because of being labeled "foreign agents" and were unjustly kept from occupying sensitive positions.

The difficulties that arose between DGER and OSS did not keep the French from collaborating with the Allies on military matters. A few days before Christmas 1944, several farm families living in the eastern region of France reported to their gendarmerie that low-flying planes had been circling their fields and parachutists had been dropped. Some of the farmers had cooperated in the underground by hiding and aiding Allied parachutists. They knew what they were talking about, and their testimony was taken seriously. Gendarmes were sent to patrol the fields where the drops had been observed, and one patrol arrested two suspects wearing French uniforms.

French and American counterintelligence officers, working together, interrogated the men, who after questioning admitted being Germans. They disclosed that their chief was the famous Colonel Otto Skorzeny, who had planned the kidnapping of Mussolini. Their orders were to penetrate, under cover of their disguises, the various Allied headquarters and to assassinate the main military chiefs — American, British and French. The alert was immediately given, and the security of General Eisenhower, the commander in chief, and his assistants was reinforced. Military patrols aided by former underground members scoured the same area and turned up more Germans.

A court martial was immediately called, and several of the prisoners were sentenced to death and executed soon after. Impersonating foreign soldiers was contrary to war codes and put them in the position of foreign spies.

At exactly the same period — that is, before Field Marshal Von Rundstedt launched his counteroffensive in the Ardennes — an extraordinary affair was uncovered in England thanks to the vigilance of an American officer.

Captain Frank Brandstetter was intelligence officer for General Matthew B. Ridgway, commander of the 18th Airborne Corps. He and another officer, Captain Hoelzl, were training a group of American intelligence officers in England. They were perfecting their professional skills by interrogating German prisoners interned in several important camps in the London area.

Captain Brandstetter's team was operating mainly in the Devizes prison camp located some hundred miles west of London. The camp held about 7500 prisoners captured during the first days of the Normandy landing.

On November 9, 1944, the escape of ten Germans was reported. This was not unusual, since others had broken away before, but escapees were likely to be spotted on the island sooner or later. The camp authorities alerted the local police and waited confidently for the return of the fugitives. A few days later, during roll call on November 13, guards discovered the ten men back in their respective barracks among their comrades.

The incident would have had no further consequences if Captain Brandstetter, sensing something significant, had not decided to proceed personally with the interrogation of the prisoners. Speaking fluent German as well as six other languages, he questioned the men in their native tongue for several days, but without much consequence. They claimed that their attempt to escape was motivated simply by the strong desire to be reunited with their families. After realizing their escape would not be successful, they had decided to give up and get back to the camp, hoping they would receive no punishment. The explanation was quite plausible, but it did not fully satisfy Brandstetter. One prisoner named Baier seemed to be particularly tense during the interrogation and quick to lose his temper. Captain Brandstetter decided to center his attention on this

121

man and to break down his resistance by bringing about one of his tantrums.

One day, when he had been asked the same question for the hundredth time about the reasons behind his escape, Baier, unable to control himself, barked at him, "*Aufklarung!*"

Scouting! But scouting what? Baier had told too much and not enough.

Bombarded with questions from Brandstetter, who was assisted by Captain Hoelzl, several of the Germans finally admitted that the reason for their false escape was to explore the area in view of a general uprising by all prisoners.

Captain Brandstetter, still skeptical, alerted MI5 (British counter-intelligence). British and American security officers, in close collaboration, succeeded in introducing into the camp a handful of under-cover agents posing as recently captured German soldiers. This maneuver immediately paid off. The bits of information obtained seemed to complement one another.

Feeling some urgency, Captain Brandstetter worked tirelessly analyzing the information and interrogating the prisoners. On December 7, 1944, he had reconstructed the plot and was faced with the astonishing truth. The prisoners in Camp Le Merchant in Devizes (Wilts) had planned a general uprising on Christmas Eve 1944. A few of them were supposed to use the rifles and light arms they had succeeded in hiding to subdue the guards at the time they would be relieved. Then, locking up those guards and taking their uniforms, they planned to free all the other inmates.

The prisoners who were previously members of armored units would immediately take over the hospital vehicles, while the former paratroopers would form two groups. One group was to storm the Wilshire Barracks, which housed the regiment guarding the camp, in order to seize the arsenal. The other group, which was to include many pilots, would attack the neighboring Air Force base, where they would take possession of the planes.

The group which had occupied the barracks, after dressing in British uniforms, would then meet the other prisoners, and they would all go by hospital vehicles to the 17th British Armored Camp, where a large quantity of equipment was stored under a minimum guard. Since they were to be dressed in British uniforms, the Germans had decided on a password to identify their fellow conspirators. One would say *"Hans drei,"* and the response would be *"Gustave vier."*

With tanks and planes, the next step would be a surprise attack on London, which was unprotected against this kind of invasion. The prisoners of two other camps located in Bourtom and Spring Hill were to revolt at the same time and join forces with their Devizes comrades for the attack. The number of POW's implicated in this scheme was more than 75,000.

The British government, alerted immediately, decided to wait a few days before taking any action.

Other intelligence collected by Allied services reported that on the island of Helgoland near Hamburg, specially trained German troops were ready to be transported by air. Several paratroop units in Holland were also preparing for some operation. Brandstetter, pursuing his investigation, discovered that the prisoners were in contact with Germany, and that those troops were waiting to reinforce the POW units as soon as the attack on London started.

Prime Minister Winston Churchill was briefed on the conspiracy and kept advised on all developments. He postponed making any decision in order to give the secret services time to uncover all loose ends. However, on December 14, one of the undercover agents told Captain Brandstetter that the prisoners had moved the date of their revolt up from Christmas Eve to December 16. The Prime Minister then ordered the arrest of the ringleaders. British commandos and paratroopers were dispatched into the camps with fixed bayonets and seized them — Fritz Frischimger, Hans Hacker, Westerman, and about thirty others.

Two days later Von Rundstedt launched the famous Battle of the Bulge. If Captain Brandstetter had not uncovered this revolt scheme, Hitler, it was learned later, was counting on the actions of the POW's in England to open the third front (*die dritte Front*), gaining the advantage over the demoralized Allies by striking London.

For their action, Captain Brandstetter and Captain Hoelzl received the Bronze Star from General Ridgway.

While Allied intelligence concentrated its activities on the Germans and endeavored to help win the war in Europe, French intelligence (DGER) was trying to put its affairs in order. The situation had gone from bad to worse — more than 110 buildings had been requisitioned in Paris to house its various branches. All the former members of underground networks who had been idled had succeeded in securing jobs in one division or another of the DGER. Using their DGER identification cards as if they were police badges, they went on with arbitrary arrests and did not hesitate to use coercion and torture to get funds.

Whatever their rank, the former resistants encountered difficulties in adapting to normal life. Accustomed to shady deals involving false identification and ration tickets, many continued to live in illegality as they had in the past. Some blackmailed former collaborators of the Germans or accepted bribes from them to fix their trials and assure innocent verdicts. Others, taking advantage of their connection with DGER and of the transportation facilities at their disposal, violated all exchange regulations and trafficked in foreign currency. Diplomatic pouches meant to carry confidential documents were in fact filled with gold, dollars, and other scarce currencies.

One day early in 1945, we were informed that a former network chief known as Franklin had been nominated to head the intelligence section of DGER. He was a pleasant man, known to be familiar with all the tricks of the trade. This news gave us a sense of relief. At least order would prevail and we would be able to get on with some serious work. Three weeks later we received a cable from our representative in London:

Financial Attaché informs me that Franklin during his last visit to London requested from Bank of England the exchange in small denominations of two 500-pound notes which he believes were illegally brought into England. The British Treasury, in agreement with Financial Attaché, intends to bring the matter to court. Have succeeded in stopping the action provided we furnish full explanation about the origin of the notes and Franklin's reputation.

There is no need to comment on the lamentable impression this embarrassing affair produced not only with the various French missions in London but with the British services as well. Try to imagine for one second Dansey (Deputy Director for MI6) being prosecuted by the French Treasury Department for traffic in foreign currency! Soon the members of DGER in London were labeled "traffickers."

A few days later Franklin had vacated his office and a new candidate was sought to fill the post of Chief of French Intelligence.

I was told one day that it seemed unusual for a young man of only twenty-four to have full responsibility for a section as important as Far East intelligence, which, due to the situation in Indochina, was continuously expanding. A new man with contacts in government circles was put in charge. I became his deputy. A week or so later, I ran into my new boss in the hall of the building, being escorted out by two security men. Charges of traffic in licenses were brought against him. It happened that, taking advantage of his new position, he had befriended an official in the Paris police headquarters. Since licenses were required to set up any business, our man was able, for a certain price, to obtain licenses for members of the underground eager to go into business.

Someone else was then appointed head of Far East intelligence. His first day on duty he became very impatient because the diplomatic pouch had not arrived on time. The next day, when the bag containing the mail from our stations in Asia was brought in, he insisted on opening it himself and went hastily through the stack of envelopes. He found the one bearing his name and address. It contained a small metal box no larger than a pill box. He opened it and his face reflected a keen excitement at the sight of an extraordinary collection of diamonds resting on a bed of white cotton.

"Two years of work," said the officer, who had recently returned from a tour of duty in Indochina.

I mentioned this incident to one of my superiors, who raised his arm in a helpless gesture. "What can I do?" he said. "Most of the men in this section ought to be locked up."

There were honest men in the group — a minority with good fighting records during the war, who refused to become involved in illegal operations. They deserved credit for resisting the temptation which was everywhere. Each day lists were passed around, and one simply had to enter one's name to be a candidate for one

125

decoration or another. We could feel nothing but contempt for the pseudo-soldiers around us yearning for the coveted medals.

In this peculiar war, those of us first denounced as rebels and then praised by our country as her defenders had responsibilities far more important than our real military rank, justifying the award of temporary ranks. Twenty-four-year-old colonels were not an unusual sight, and generals no older than twenty-eight were not uncommon. Naturally none of the so-called brass had any idea of the military profession as taught in the academies, but all knew it through experience. Committees had been created to convert into permanent status the temporary ranks held by the former members of the underground. A mere signature on a form was all it took to effect the promotion. Some among the BCRA members simply could not let pass such an opportunity to satisfy their vanity.

In our small group we took pride in purposely ignoring opportunities for what we considered puerile compensations. I was very proud of having a military record showing that I held the temporary rank of captain, but was discharged a private second class. The fact that we were after no personal favors gave us the independence to fight openly for the realization of our common dream — the organization of a French intelligence capable of effectively aiding the government in restoring France's international position and protecting her interests.

With an army she could not equip, with many scientists and engineers dead in battle or concentration camps, and with her stock of resources and heavy materials stolen by Nazis, France could only count on the astuteness and devotion of her citizens. We had astuteness and devotion to spare in the secret services ready to be used for the good of the country, if only we were given the chance. Alas, in the government, too many were only trying to promote their ambition.

De Gaulle had long wanted power and now was ready to take it. Upon his arrival in France when the Allied troops had barely landed, only one thought occupied his mind — to be recognized as the chief of France. To accomplish this he used a method which he would later repeat many times. He pushed aside his supporters — the members of the National Council of the Resistance — and initiated closer relations with the Communists, who at the time were in a position to block his ascent to power.

As soon as he arrived in Paris in August 1944, de Gaulle named two Communists to his government. One, François Billoux, member of the governing board of the Communist Party, became Secretary for Public Health and took control over the tentacular Social Security organization. This government agency refunds all medical expenses and employs tens of thousands of civil servants in offices all over France. Billoux immediately placed party members in key positions, thus making Social Security one of the strongholds of French Communism.

Another Communist, Charles Tillon, became Secretary of Aviation. France had almost no aviation, and the new Secretary set to work creating state-financed corporations to rebuild the French aeronautical industry. Of course, the boards of directors as well as the engineers and executives of the new corporations were mostly Communists, and the French aviation industry was to be forever Communist-controlled. The Soviets' unveiling of a supersonic jet strangely similar to the *Concorde* several months before France should come to no one's surprise. It was child's play for the Soviets to procure the plans and formulas developed by the French technicians working in the nationalized French factories.

The presence of several Communists in his government failed to ease de Gaulle's apprehension and fear of being deprived of the power he prized so highly. Of course, the United States had at last recognized him, although half-heartedly, as President of the French government. But he knew he could not count on Washington to help him establish his strong rule over France. His fears were intensified by the Communists' latest achievement — the creation of a patriotic militia force, made up of members of their former underground networks, which was proving to be more powerful than the regular police force. Its activities extended over the entire country. The government moved to abolish such militia groups, but the Communists, in defiance of the order, kept them active, operating outside the margin of the law. De Gaulle was powerless to act.

This is when he decided to make a treaty of alliance with Moscow.

127

At first, the Russians were cool to the idea, and de Gaulle had to pressure Bogomolov, the Soviet Ambassador in Paris. Finally, Stalin agreed to the offered alliance, but under one condition: the General Secretary of the French Communist Party, Maurice Thorez, in exile in Moscow, would be granted permission to return to France. On November 25, 1939, Thorez had been sentenced in absentia by a French military tribunal for desertion. Subsequently, he had forfeited his French citizenship in February 1940, and had spent the war years in Russia. De Gaulle did not hesitate and granted Thorez a full pardon.

De Gaulle left for Moscow the day Thorez's return to France was announced. Trading favor for favor, Stalin agreed to see him and to sign the Franco-Soviet pact for mutual defense. True to his word, Thorez ordered the dissolution of the patriotic militia groups, succeeding where de Gaulle had failed.

Still convinced that his dreams of grandeur could only be hampered by the Communists, de Gaulle was determined to continue his flirtation with the Reds. We saw Thorez boosted into the position of Vice-President of the government, while four Communists were given secretarial positions in the administration. Billoux, responsible for the Communist penetration of the Social Security while he was Secretary of Health, was now appointed Secretary of National Education. Croizat was offered the Department of Labor, Marcel Paul the Industrial Production, and Tillon the Armament.

All the channels of French production were controlled by Moscow's representatives. Nationalization of the electric power and the gas was enacted, followed by the nationalization of the banks, coal mines, railroads, and even the insurance companies.

In addition to his position as Vice-President of the government, Thorez was in charge of reorganizing the civil service and establishing the requirements for applicants for government jobs. How many government employees, dreaming of a promotion or of a favor, enlisted then in the Communist Party? It may be difficult to give an accurate number, but they no doubt were legion.

The leaders of the Communist underground group, Francs-Tireur et Partisans (FTP), were confirmed in the ranks they had given themselves and were incorporated into regular military units. A great number became officers of the *Compagnies Républicaines de*

Sécurité (CRS), units made up of career men, with functions similar to the National Guard. So in case of riots in France, the troops called to restore order would be composed mostly of Communists, under the command of Communist officers.

In the scientific field, Joliot-Curie, recipient of the 1935 Nobel Prize for chemistry and inventor of the first atomic pile, became Director of Scientific Research. A hard-core Communist, he surrounded himself with many party members, giving the French Communist Party a strong base in France's scientific community.

While the Allies were making every effort to enlist the services of German scientists, Joliot-Curie and the French Center, instead of recruiting them, were advising them to wait until the USSR was ready to make the most of their work. When German scientists insisted on dealing with the Allies, the Joliot-Curie team created many difficulties for them under the pretext of denazification. This is how members of the "Cellastic" group, specializing in atomic research, were dispersed through the four zones of Germany and Austria.

Another notorious Communist scientist, Genevoix, from the Bordeaux University, was in charge of disarmament problems in the French occupation zone in Germany. To complete the picture, the head of scientific section of DGER, Captain Clement, made no secret about his ties with the Communist Party.

No organization could avoid this skillful penetration by the Soviets, and the government didn't even try to prevent it. Fearing that the Communists would take the power away from him, de Gaulle was handing it to them.

If de Gaulle had received good intelligence, he would have known that the Russians, always realistic, did not want the French Communists or the Italian Communists to take advantage of the liberation to make a revolution. Stalin knew the USSR was drained by the war and had to digest Central Europe before adding further to the Communist bloc. Furthermore, he wanted to avoid conflict with the United States . . . and American troops were still in Europe.

It was through the efficiency of his secret services that de Gaulle had been able to seize power, and he could have spared France further trouble if only he had turned to them once more. But de Gaulle, believing he was God-chosen, had an aversion to anyone who had helped him. He hated his partisans and flattered his enemies. Abandoned to its own corruption, the DGER was dying of scandal.

Colonel Passy, founder of the BCRA, had become Director-General of the DGER. Disgusted by the poor performance of his agency, he had left for the Far East to assume direction of operations there with de Langlade's help. In his absence, his deputy, Manuel, tried to restore order in Paris and to come up with a formula for the reorganization of the service.

As for me, disappointed in the behavior of the staff of the Far East section, I had taken the first opportunity to get away. The government had decided to participate in the search for war criminals, and a special division had been created within the DGER. This division, specializing in hunting German and Austrian war criminals, was headed by Major Mantou, a former BCRA member whose fairness and integrity were well known. A lawyer by profession, Mantou insisted on respect for the law. No scandal ever touched his service.

De Gaulle, eager to imitate the Americans and the British, had ordered the creation of a service for the tracing of war criminals in the Far East. I was put in charge.

For several months, I studied in detail the methods employed against Nazi war criminals. It was a repelling yet fascinating experience. Day after day I was confronted with the strangest and most despicable specimens of humanity. All murderers, they did not seem to comprehend how their acts could be repugnant in the eyes of the world.

I recall one case which particularly impressed me. The service for the investigation of war criminals was located near the Avenue Victor Hugo in a town house formerly occupied by the Gestapo. The servants' quarters in the attic had been made into cells by the former tenants and were now occupied by Germans who had been arrested in the French zone of occupation or who had been transferred to us by the Allies. When I visited the installations I was surprised to see a young boy of sixteen or seventeen in one of the cells. I questioned the officer accompanying me about his particular case.

"I can't go into details now," he said, "but the prisoner is due for interrogation this morning and you might like to be present."

The interrogating officer was a lawyer. He had just finished going through the dossier when I was introduced to him.

"The case of this young boy is one of the most contemptible I have studied. I am the father of five and one is the same age as this boy. This is why I feel so strongly the horror of what a system can do to its youth. But you will be able to judge for yourself."

Two guards brought the youngster into the office. Blond and blue-eyed, with a babyish face, he was tall and skinny, as if he had grown up too fast. With his open-collared shirt, sweater, and wrinkled pants, he looked like any college student. He stood stiffly at attention before the officer. An interpreter was next to me. After the usual identification routine, the officer asked his age.

"Seventeen," he answered.

"Are you a Nazi party member?"

"No, I was too young, but my father was. I was a member of the Jungvolk, then a member of the Hitler Youth."

"You are accused of killing ten French prisoners in the camp where they were held. Is this true?"

"Yes," answered the boy, looking straight ahead.

"Can you explain why?" asked the officer.

"It was a game," the boy half-smiled.

"A game?"

"Yes," his face became serious again. "I was with a group of friends outside the camp. German soldiers were on duty. They were SS. One of them spoke to us. He showed me his rifle and asked me if I had ever shot one. I said I hadn't."

The boy became animated reliving the story. His eyes were fixed as if looking back at the scene and he started automatically to mime the gesture he had made at the time. "He handed me his rifle. It was heavy — I never thought a rifle weighed so much. Then the SS asked me if I would enjoy killing a Frenchman. I said yes. Then he showed me how to bring the gun to my shoulder and how to aim. My hands shook because of the weight, and the SS laughed at me. There was a group of about twenty prisoners standing and talking together. The SS asked me if I could see the

131

tallest one through the sights. I said I could. 'Then pull the trigger,' he said. I did. The sound was deafening, and the recoil threw me down. The SS and my friends were laughing. The prisoner had fallen to the ground screaming, and his comrades bent over him were looking in our direction. Then I picked up the gun and started shooting into the group. This time I stayed on my feet, and when the rifle stopped more of the prisoners were lying on the ground. Another guard gave me his gun and I aimed at a group further away. They also fell. The soldiers told me I would make a good SS and to come back to shoot Frenchmen whenever I felt like it. But when I went back there were other guards on duty who wouldn't let me use their guns."

The boy went through all the motions while telling his story, and the sight was horrifying.

The officer went on with more questions. "Why did you want to kill men who had done nothing to you?"

"They were Jews," said the boy, as if it were sufficient explanation.

Later, after the prisoner had left, the officer said to me, "You have heard and seen the attitude of this young Nazi, and your reaction was no doubt the same as ours at the beginning. The prisoners when being interrogated seem to be in a state of hypnosis or some kind of mental disarrangement. In fact, I believe the majority are mentally disturbed. Every day we are confronted with similar cases, and we really don't know how to handle them. Our duty is to prepare cases for trial, but most of them would be more suited for psychiatric hospitals. This boy was turned in by one of his friends who witnessed the killings. This is the elite, the cream of the German youth. What can we do with him? One day we will put him in a denazification camp, and a year from now he will be free. Ten years from now you might meet him — he will be a successful businessman. The murder of ten French prisoners will be forgotten. Tell me, what are we to do? Unlike them, we simply cannot exterminate young people. We hope the Germans will realize and take care of their own criminals."

In the following months, while studying the methods used by the service for the investigation of war criminals in Germany, I organized a small group for the same purpose in the Far East. We established files based on the declarations of French and Indochinese prisoners tortured by the Japanese and were able to make some identifications. I was ready to leave for the Far East with some of my men when we learned that General MacArthur was against French participation in the search for war criminals. So we packed up all the files and sent them to the Department of Justice, which later was supposed to take over the job.

Our section was disbanded. At the same time I was finally given my discharge from the army. With the feeling of abandoning an unfinished job, I said good-bye to the friends who had shared with me these last fascinating years. One of them closest to me was head of the section in charge of liquidating important installations in England inherited from the BCRA and also of liaison with the British services. He asked me to come and work as his assistant with the idea that I would soon take over his position, since he had received another assignment. Deep in my heart I did not want to leave and jumped at the opportunity he offered me.

The director of DGER, Colonel Dewavrin, known during the war as Passy, had initiated a reorganization of the service. First he rid the agency of its more unprincipled members, then proceeded to thin out the overstaffed departments. He set out to restore order in the administrative branch and in the treasury. Based on what he had learned from the British and his own observations while visiting the OSS headquarters in Washington, Dewavrin set up two main divisions within the DGER. One was in charge of administration and the other dealt with the research and exploitation of intelligence. The latter division included three sections — intelligence, counterintelligence, and studies. The intelligence and counterintelligence sections hunted information according to their own methods, and the section for studies was in charge of analyzing and synthesizing this intelligence, then distributing it to the government agencies concerned. The organization was conventional in form and had the potential of performing for the French government the same services that British intelligence rendered to the Crown.

In order to silence the critics of DGER, who claimed that the new organization was a political police force, it was clearly stated in the law creating the service that "it will carry no power on French territory, but operate only in foreign countries. Any counterintelligence operation in France will rest with a special division of the Department of the Interior — the Territorial Security Agency (Sûreté)."

The initials DGER being too often associated with past scandals, it was decided to name the new agency *Service de Documentation Extérieure et de Contre-Espionage* (SDECE). An official budget of twelve million dollars was voted for SDECE. Since it would have to seek intelligence in foreign countries, Colonel Dewavrin's idea, logically enough, was to have it linked with the Ministry for Foreign Affairs (our State Department), but the cautious diplomats declined to be in charge of a secret service. It was finally decided to have the agency directly under the Prime Minister.

Most of the senior members of BCRA, disgusted at seeing all the latecomers rewarded with important jobs, had given up government service to resume their prewar occupations. This delighted the military and the former members of Giraud's service, who rushed to fill the now vacant positions.

The SDECE was left with career officers heading most of its departments, even though Colonel Dewavrin had made a point of taking a leave of absence from the Army to emphasize the essentially civilian character of his service.

The intelligence division was referred to as the "geographic division." It consisted of bureaus, each specializing in a given country or a specific part of the world. I was one of its few civilians. Being a senior in the French secret services, having served successively with first the BCRA, then DGSS and DGER, and finally the present SDECE, gave me a certain advantage and probably spared me many difficulties. However, I was not blind to the latent hostility on the part of career officers who judged the presence of a civilian among them as an encroachment on their private territory.

The military because of their numbers were able to impose their own system. Therefore, they tried to make the secret service what it had been in the past. During the war we had resorted to improvisation and to methods which may have been empiric but were nevertheless successful. Now we were forced to go back to the old traditional practices which had probably caused France to lose the war.

The intelligence division was kept entirely separated from counterintelligence. The only task of intelligence was the collection of positive intelligence, meaning information on other countries' military potential, battle orders, political or economic problems. The need for a particular type of intelligence was determined by computations of questionnaires received from various departments of the government. It involved exclusively secret information.

For example, the fall of the Iraqi government would be of no concern to the secret services. This would be considered as "open information" and likely to be handled by the embassy. But the secret maneuvers of an oil concern aimed at bringing about the fall of the government would be a matter calling for close investigation and research.

To conduct thorough and quiet inquiries, the secret services set up "stations" in countries in which they were interested. The stations usually functioned under diplomatic covers and most of the time were linked to the assistant military attaché. This "diplomat" controlled a certain number of agents and tried to establish networks to operate in specific fields. Back at headquarters, the heads of the "geographic division" supervised and channeled instructions to the stations within their jurisdiction. They also dealt through networks of H.C.'s (Honorable Correspondents).

Counterintelligence's objective was to protect the nation against interference from foreign secret services. This meant the unlawful collecting of intelligence, as well as any kind of activity considered a threat to national security. In order to carry out its missions, counterintelligence set out to secure information on the structure and the organization of foreign intelligence services, on their members and the operations they conducted. The counterintelligence division controlled its own separate stations, also operating under diplomatic cover in foreign countries. After the example of the British, the French counterintelligence stations were headed by officers operating under the title of vice-consul, chief of the passport control division.

The SDECE was therefore represented in the same city by two posts entirely independent of each other. Usually located on the same premises (in the embassy), the two SDECE representatives had no activity in common. The promoters of this system advocated it for security reasons as well as because of the dissimilarity of the techniques utilized. For my part, I was never totally convinced by these reasons. In a country as poor as France was at the time, the existence of two parallel organizations for the research of intelligence in foreign countries seemed to me a waste of money and other resources. During the following years I fought earnestly against this system, and my efforts contributed to many of the changes that came later. In the meantime, I had to endure it.

The section for studies, as a rule, received information from the intelligence section. After being evaluated and analyzed, it was included in the condensed reports sent to the various branches of the government. Soon the Minister for Foreign Affairs began to resent these reports. He considered the interpretation of intelligence dealing with foreign countries as a political matter and claimed a monopoly for his department. As a result, the section for studies was transformed into an instrument of liaison, passing raw intelligence on to the Minister for Foreign Affairs just as it was received. The section's useful purpose continued to diminish as the geographic divisions established direct contact with ministries for which they were doing research.

Another important service called Action was created to carry out operations labeled "special." Made up of former resistance members, the service parachuted agents or provided other help to the Maquis or paramilitary movements supported by the government. Its exact role was not clearly defined, and many years went by before it became the sadly notorious organization that now exists.

In spite of its faults, the SDECE as it was set up several months after the end of the war was a definite improvement over the disorder of the DGER. I nursed the hope of seeing new reforms improve the existing conditions and did my best to adjust to the new organization. My section covering England had the task of keeping the government informed on the intentions of our great ally. A chain of events soon involved me in an unusual and interesting operation.

At the end of 1945, de Gaulle was disaffected with England. Although he had found with the British the financial and moral support he needed to carry out his great venture, he showed no gratitude whatsoever. On the contrary, he was nursing a grudge because of England's policy in Lebanon and Syria and waiting for the chance to pay them back in their own coin.

The opportunity soon presented itself: the Jews recently freed from German concentration camps wanted to emigrate to Palestine. England, in charge of administering the country, had imposed a severe quota on the emigration in an effort to win the friendship of the Arabs. The Jewish Agency had requested during several meetings in London that this quota be increased from 75,000 to 100,000 a year. Anxious not to antagonize Syria or Lebanon, where they had finally succeeded in supplanting the French, the British had refused to ease the quota.

Tens of thousands of Jews living in camps for displaced persons in Germany had an existence little better than they had known under the Nazis, except for now being spared the brutality. First the young, then the elderly began to leave the camps. With no identification and, for the most part, no money, they were forced to travel secretly to escape road and border checks. After crossing Germany they followed mountain paths to get to either Italy or France. Jewish organizations aided them all along the way, and clandestine camps had been installed on the Alpine slopes. One of the centers in France for their congregation was in Grenoble, the other in Marseille. Here the unfortunate refugees embarked aboard old hulks bound for what would later become Israel.

The representative of the Jewish Agency in Paris was a former French officer named Fisher. At the beginning of the war, he had been a member of our Deuxième Bureau and had many friends among the secret service members. Due to his contacts with us, Fisher was regularly informed about British interference with the refugee embarkations for Palestine. All the agents of the British CID in charge of observing French ports were themselves under close watch, and their names and descriptions were given to Fisher as soon as they were identified. Naturally the customs officials and gendarmes were under orders to look the other way when the ships which were supposed to pick up the refugees entered the Mediterranean ports. We did everything we could to help their clandestine sailing.

I could not say exactly how many Jewish emigrants transited through France, but there were many thousands. I am sure that few of them had any idea that their steps along their arduous route were being followed by us and that we were trying our best to protect them from British agents. Every time a refugee ship succeeded in getting through the British blockades and landing its passengers safely in Palestine, we felt a great joy. My modest part in this new exodus was among the greatest satisfactions of my career.

Life is seldom monotonous for an intelligence officer. All the same, I found, early in 1946, that I had fallen into a certain routine, until one day a friend entered my office. He was an old-timer from BCRA days who had undertaken many dangerous missions during the war. Now he was assistant to Colonel Dewavrin, our director, one of the hand-picked, reliable men he had gathered around him.

"I came to return your H.C. cards," he said, handing me a file of large index cards.

I didn't expect this. I remembered that it had taken quite a bit of persuasion on his part to get me to agree to hand them over in the first place. It must be emphasized that the H.C.'s (Honorable Correspondents) represent one of the greatest assets of the intelligence officer. They are his stock in trade, so to speak.

Unlike the agents, H.C.'s do not receive money for their services, and this probably explains the term "honorable." They supposedly cooperate with the secret services in the best public interest and without compensation. This statement is not completely correct, however, for while it is true that the H.C.'s do not accept money, they will not refuse and even will expect a certain recognition for their services in the form of decorations or very special favors. Often, even their professional future depends on maintaining good relations with the secret services.

Let us consider the example of journalist Jean Planchais, an authority on questions dealing with the military. As a newspaperman he had need of access to certain information, which although withheld from the news media was gathered as a matter of routine by the SDECE. So an agreement was concluded between SDECE and Jean Planchais to provide him with accurate tips. As compensation, Mr. Planchais might, during the course of an interview with a foreign military attaché, ask questions dealing with subjects of particular interest to the SDECE. Or he might, occasionally, be able to point out to them a foreign officer made vulnerable by a precarious financial position and likely to be contacted as a possible agent.

This exchange of small favors between the SDECE and Jean Planchais was profitable to everyone. No pressure was put on him and he entertained the best of relations socially with his officer friend from SDECE, without realizing that his name was listed as an H.C., with a special number to identify him. Every piece of information or favor done for the SDECE was entered on his card kept by the officer who made the contact. If worse came to worst, this officer could use it as a means of pressure should Jean Planchais show any reluctance in doing a requested service.

The number and quality of the Honorable Correspondents on the roster of an intelligence officer is very often decisive as to how successful he is in his line of work. As a rule, the individual H.C. cards were handled exclusively by the officer who established them. However, because of the difficulties experienced by the SDECE at the time of its creation and its lack of specialized personnel and funds, Colonel Dewavrin decided to establish a central card index listing all possible sources of intelligence. The friend who was visiting me that day had been in charge of this job.

"I am bringing your cards back," he said, "as I promised I would when you gave them to me. Colonel Dewavrin is leaving the service soon. His successor will most probably be a politician, and God knows the use he could make of the cards if they came into his possession."

"Who will succeed Dewavrin?" I immediately pressed.

"I don't know. He has just left for Switzerland on his honeymoon and is so fed up with the service he doesn't even have the desire to come back and put things in order."

In the beginning of 1945, General de Gaulle, unable to gain parliamentary control, had resigned. He was convinced that the political parties stemming from the resistance would not be able to get along and would soon beg him to take lead of the government no matter what his conditions. But de Gaulle's expectations had not materialized. A government had been formed by a socialist without too much difficulty, with the collaboration of the Communists and the new Christian Democratic Party (Mouvement Républicain Populaire — MRP).

The three parties had divided among themselves the various departments of the government, and it seemed natural for them to want one of their men at the head of the secret services. Although we had certain ties of sentiment with de Gaulle, whose cause we had supported during the war, we considered the SDECE as nonpolitical and resented being labeled as favoring an authoritarian government with him as chief. On the other hand, Dewavrin seemed much more preoccupied by his personal affairs than by his service. We had the feeling of being abandoned. So the nomination of a new director was anticipated with high expectations and the hope that he wouldn't owe allegiance to one of the political parties we were unfamiliar with and apprenhensive about in terms of security.

At the end of February 1946, a memo impersonally informed us of the nomination of Henri Ribière, congressman from Allier, as new director of SDECE. Ribière was generally well known. Before the war he had acted as the right arm of Max Dormoy, Secretary of the Interior. A convinced socialist, he had simultaneously fought the Communists and extreme rightist organizations like the Cagoule. After Max Dormoy was assassinated by the Cagoule, he had been the main organizer of the clandestine Socialist Party and was responsible for the creation of the most important French underground network — Libé-Nord. Ribière was also behind the uprising of the Paris police headquarters, which was a prelude to the liberation of Paris. He had been elected congressman of his home district, and his nomination as the head of our service seemed to guarantee that everything would function in conformity with the laws of the Republic.

In addition to the appointment of Ribière, we learned of the nomination of two deputy directors. Pierre Sudreau was to be in charge of administrative affairs. As a member of the underground he had been captured by the Germans and deported. Although his health had been impaired by a prolonged stay in the worst Nazi camps, he was a young and able administrator. His reputation of courage and integrity had preceded him and contributed to our new feeling of confidence.

The other deputy director in charge of all problems of research was to be Colonel Pierre Fourcaud. Of Slavic origin on his mother's side, he had the type of mind that relished intrigue. After the defeat of France in 1940 he had reached London and joined the BCRA. During a secret mission in occupied France, Fourcaud established contact with extreme rightist elements — former members of the Cagoule. He himself was said to have been a member of this secret organization. His ill-coordinated activities did not lead to much except for his arrest by Vichy counterintelligence services, who made his captivity relatively comfortable and did not stop him from escaping.

When Fourcaud returned to London after his flight, Dewavrin gave him the cold shoulder, considering his mission a failure. Succeeding in getting another mission, he was put in charge of an underground network. He fought courageously against the Germans, received a serious head wound, and was taken prisoner again, only to perform a dramatic escape as soon as he had regained enough strength. The liberation found him with the DGER, occupied with the liquidation of his network.

Fearless and with a great deal of personal charm, Fourcaud was the typical example of an adventurer unable to lead a normal life. He had no equal in making the easiest thing look complicated, and during the war he had acquired more than one enemy. He always resented Dewavrin for being his superior, and was angry at de Gaulle for not having picked him as head of the DGER.

An example of utter contradiction was the fact that Fourcaud, an extreme rightist, had managed during his first mission in France to make friends with several socialists and particularly with Félix

Gouin, who in the meantime had become France's Prime Minister. Fourcaud owed his present post as deputy director of SDECE to his socialist friends. However, he still was not fully satisfied with things as they stood, since his ambition was to be number one man in the SDECE. He considered himself expert in all intelligence matters and was convinced that Henri Ribière's appointment as director was due to some political necessity and that he would eventually get the post.

It took him only a few weeks to realize he had been mistaken. Henri Ribière was the boss and allowed no one besides himself to make the decisions. A good judge of men, he immediately realized Fourcaud's game and let him know he disapproved of intrigues and schemes. The situation grew tense between the two men, and Fourcaud had to set aside his dream of controlling the SDECE.

Ribière was then the victim of a very serious automobile accident. His car, driven by a police officer, was traveling at top speed when the brakes failed. He was taken to the hospital unconscious and remained in a coma for many days. An investigation made by the police failed to find the cause of the accident. Ribière and those around him were convinced it was sabotage. Colonel Fourcaud felt the need on several occasions to deny any responsibility for the accident. With Ribière in the hospital for an undetermined amount of time, Fourcaud assumed charge, hoping that the director's health would prevent him from returning permanently and enable him to take over.

At the time, the government was split on the draft of a new constitution. The Communists and socialists were in favor of it, but the MRP and the others were fighting it. A referendum to get public approval was defeated on May 5, 1946.

The next day the press announced the arrest of Colonel Dewavrin, alias Passy, for embezzlement. The news created a sensation. Dewavrin was known as the strongest of de Gaulle supporters. Any irregularity blamed on him would inevitably reflect on the former chief of the Free French, so the affair immediately became political.

Completely by chance, I was able to learn the story of what had happened. As a rule, the section heads took turns on night duty from 6 P.M. to 9 A.M. in the director's office. It happened that it was my turn to work at night when the decisions regarding

Dewavrin were made. The executive offices were located in a townhouse on the Avenue Henri Martin. The director's office overlooked the avenue, and adjacent to it was the office of his Chef de Cabinet, which I was occupying for the night.

The night officer handled all calls on the direct line that linked the director with members of the government, and decided what to do in case of receiving any urgent intelligence after office hours. Knowing that little ever happened on night duty, I was catching up on paper work. All was quiet when Colonel Fourcaud entered brusquely, in a hurry as usual. He took a seat behind the director's desk and spent some time calling the Christian Democrat ministers with whom he seemed to be on friendly terms. Alternately shouting and banging on the desk, then calming down but still vehement, he gave each one an account of what had just happened, not caring that only a few yards away, I could overhear all he said. By piecing together Fourcaud's conversations with other available information, I easily could reconstruct the Passy affair.

When the change of directors was made, many section heads closest to Dewavrin followed his example and resigned from the SDECE to return to private life. The head of the financial division had been replaced by Louis Fauvert, a protégé of the Secretary of the Treasury, André Philippe. During the war, Philippe had many differences with Colonel Dewavrin, who several times in de Gaulle's presence had reproached him for his carelessness. It is a fact that countless jokes circulated about his loss of an attaché case full of secret documents. But Philippe had been one of the first socialists to join Free France during the war, and he considered himself one of the originators of the underground movement and most knowledgeable in the field of intelligence. This is what brought him to recommend his protégé for the delicate post of administering the secret funds handled by the SDECE.

This new man, Louis Fauvert, had no fighting record. During the war he had been a civil servant in the Deeds and Records Office — a position which required little effort and none of the risks taken by members of the secret organizations fighting the enemy. Being unprepared for his new position, Fauvert entertained considerable suspicions about men whose profession required that they regard danger and risks as a matter of course. Succeeding a man who had administered the finances of the secret services throughout the war, Fauvert set out to examine closely the accounting of the services for the five war years, and in the process he discovered many irregularities. Luck served him when a representative in London accidentally came upon a sum of money which could not be explained. He reported his finding to Paris — and the affair broke out.

To understand its implications, one must remember that during the last month of 1945, a Chamber of Representatives election had clearly shown the Communists to be the strongest party in France, with more votes and thus more elected representatives than any other political party. Europe was suffering from food shortages and extreme poverty. The middle class, which had always been the backbone of Europe, had lost much of its influence for having too readily accepted authoritarian governments collaborating with the Nazis. The Soviets, at the same time, were enjoying enormous prestige for their relentless fight against the Germans, and the Communist propaganda machine knew how to exploit this popularity. The United States, for its part, seemed more concerned about converting its war economy into a peace economy and left the impression of being indifferent about the fate of Europe. Many people thought a shift toward the left was inevitable and the occupation of Europe by the Soviets only a matter of time.

Dewavrin himself was convinced that a conflict with the USSR was imminent and would once more necessitate a fight led from outside France. For a reason I could never understand, the French military always imagine the next war will be the same as the last, and Dewavrin believed that there would once more be an exiled French government in England. During the last war, he had suffered by having to depend on the British services for everything he needed to carry out his operations in France. So, in order to assure his future independence, Dewavrin decided to establish a secret war treasury in England and in several other countries where he calculated an immediate risk of war was unlikely. He planned that as soon as hostilities began, a few of his former BCRA companions would set up in London a temporary headquarters for a fight against the enemy in the usual secret service manner.

To carry out this project, money had to be found. This had been relatively easy for Dewavrin. During the war, British intelligence had entrusted the BCRA with a large amount of money in pounds sterling to be dropped by parachute to various resistance groups. Part of the money had been utilized for this purpose, but the rest had remained in the London BCRA offices at 10 Duke Street. Although it was accounted as having been spent, Dewavrin had told aides to put it aside awaiting further orders.

The Free French treasury in Algiers had also sent large quantities of French francs to be dropped to the underground. These funds had never been used and were added to the other, thereby swelling the cache. Dewavrin also thought to create fictitious missions with large budgets, and this money also reverted to the new London treasury. Finally, in this time of strict exchange laws, the SDECE had the opportunity to get foreign currency legally, and Dewavrin used a front to sell it on the black market. Part of this money piled up in postal pouches in the basement of 10 Duke Street. Another part was invested in an import-export company, which provided jobs to devoted followers of the colonel and profits for his fund.

When Colonel Dewavrin was succeeded by Henri Ribière, he neither informed him about his planning in case of war nor about the money, thus keeping for himself an opportunity to play a background role should the time come.

In addition to these various operations, a further verification of the books showed that Dewavrin had made use of the secret funds at his disposal to make a loan of ten million francs (equivalent to about $100,000) to the newspaper *France-Soir*. Since the SDECE had no jurisdiction over national territory, such a deal seemed scandalous, and the political parties drew from this the only logical conclusion — French secret services had used the funds they controlled to buy off certain newspapers and obtain support for the Gaullist cause.

While this was, in a way, true, it must be considered in its proper perspective. The French newspapers in circulation during the German occupation had all printed articles favorable to a collaboration with the Nazis. At the time of the liberation, these papers were seized. New ones had been started, but besides men of talent and ideas, money was also essential, and in this particular period, private funds to invest in publications were scarce. Because of the vital role they played for the information of the public, the French government decided to subsidize the new dailies.

In every department of the administration, the secretary had a completely free hand over certain secret funds. A large share of this money was used in the creation of the new press. The socialists helped a few. The Communists backed papers devoted to their cause with large sums. De Gaulle himself did not hesitate to provide funds for *Le Monde*, which plays the same role in French political life as the *New York Times* in the United States. Not only did de Gaulle provide financial help, but he also kept a certain number of shares which he later put into the hands of his confidant, Édouard Sablier. Dewavrin, although not holding the title of secretary, had, as head of the secret services, a considerable amount in secret funds at his disposal. So he seized the opportunity to back up his boss and granted a substantial loan to *France-Soir*, hoping the paper would show its gratitude with support for the Gaullist cause. The newspaper had long since repaid the loan, and the money had gone back to the coffers of the state.

It is a fact that neither the funds hidden in London or elsewhere nor the money loaned to *France-Soir* had, at any time, been utilized by Dewavrin for his own personal benefit. But he had kept his successor from knowing about it by resorting to accounting trickery. No doubt Dewavrin was at fault, but the commotion and publicity his financial gymnastics generated was hardly justified.

The politicians in power at the time felt themselves in an inferior position to their predecessor de Gaulle; they feared his ambition, but didn't dare attack him openly. After all, less than two years before he had been the country's liberator, and his followers were many. The administration did not rule out the possibility of de Gaulle being brought back to power by his most ardent supporters, and it seemed that a little persuasion was all it would take for him to agree.

Dewavrin looked like the best man to back such a coup. That is why it was decided to show him no mercy, in order to demonstrate the government's determination to have the law respected. President Félix Gouin had two alternatives — either to ask the judiciary for an investigation and proper sentencing, or to keep the affair at the administrative level. If it came to court, the risk of publicity would be enormous, and many politicians had reason to fear Dewavrin's revelations. He was said to possess a private card file on thousands of influential people. To avoid a scandal, the government chose to bring against him charges of an administrative nature and thus keep the investigation relatively secret.

Dewavrin was an officer, but the SDECE being a civilian agency, its director held a civilian position. When appointed to his post, Dewavrin had been given a leave of absence from the Army. Fourcaud, still nursing the old grudge against his former boss, pushed for the Army to terminate Dewavrin's leave of absence and call him to account for his acts.

Summoned to Paris while he was honeymooning on the Côte d'Azur, enjoying the first vacation he had allowed himself in many years, Dewavrin immediately admitted having hidden the existence of the funds from his successor. For that offense, the Secretary of Defense sentenced him to sixty days in a fortress. A commission of inquiry composed of SDECE members was appointed to question him and to hear all testimonies necessary to establish the truth.

Colonel Dewavrin had, in crucial times, demonstrated qualities that could not be contested. His courage, his intelligence, his organizational ability were outstanding, but he lacked a knowledge of psychology and was often caustic and hard on subordinates. When, at the end of the war, the government was granting rewards right and left, it did not occur to Colonel Dewavrin that the men who had served under him were also worthy of recognition. On the contrary, living lavishly himself, he gave no thought to the fact that his comrades in arms had to face hardships in providing for their families.

This explains why his close collaborators, when called to testify, were harshly critical and showed him the same injustice he had shown toward them. Some blamed his way of living. Others pretended he had induced them to cooperate by claiming de Gaulle's approval. They all tried to hide behind this last argument, to excuse their own behavior. Dewavrin, still devoted to the chief he had followed through difficult times, accepted the entire responsibility for his actions, claiming that de Gaulle never knew about the fund.

De Gaulle, as could be expected, abandoned Dewavrin to his fate and issued a statement publicly disavowing his former comrade.

But no one among those knowing the relationship between the two men ever doubted that de Gaulle had been kept closely informed about the plans of his former intelligence chief.

Dewavrin was jailed in the barracks of the gendarmerie in Metz and was authorized to see his wife once a week. He was regularly interrogated by the inquiry board members and readily admitted to the charges, but he offered a justification of sorts for his action. The money he had hidden did not come from the regular budget, it had not been used for personal purposes, and if the utilization he had made of it seemed improper to those in power, this was only a difference in interpretation.

Even if the motives of the director had been honorable, this could not apply to certain of his collaborators. One of them, Captain Landrieu, chief of the London bureau, could not resist temptation and had taken some of the funds in his possession for personal use. Then, panic-stricken, he tried to commit suicide. An atmosphere of drama was created around this incident, and the press even went so far as to announce Dewavrin's suicide in his jail cell.

Following the government's decision to sentence him a second time to sixty days and his transfer to the old barracks of Thionville, where conditions for the prisoner were much worse, Dewavrin suddenly became sick. His state of health quickly worsened and he was taken, near death, to the military hospital of the Val de Grace in Paris. The nature of his illness remained mysterious, and the possibility of poisoning was considered. It is true that many people would have slept better if Passy were not to recover.

During his stay in the hospital, none of his friends from better times came to see him. His only visitor besides his wife was Françoise Giroux, a journalist who has since become well known. She visited him regularly, bringing food certain to be free of poison. Her role as "007 if not Q22" in the underground seemed to have left her with a touching sense of loyalty. This is why later, remembering her attitude toward our former boss, I did my best when she came to me for help on behalf of her husband.

Passy could not stay in prison forever. At the beginning of September 1946, he was released. Mr. Teitgen, the Secretary of Justice and, by coincidence, a friend of Fourcaud, repeated in an awkward bulletin the charges against Passy, and made public the decisions made at a cabinet meeting of Communists, socialists, and MRP's:

The Cabinet has decided to take immediate steps against Colonel Dewavrin leading to his dismissal from the Army, the withdrawal of his decorations and his expulsion from the Order of the Liberation. It has also been decided that the Secretary of the Treasury will recover from his personal funds the money owed to the government. The accomplices will also receive punishment. . . .

A few days later, the same Secretary of Justice stated, at the end of a press conference: "Counterintelligence is not done by altar boys. However, the irregularities cannot go beyond certain limits. Still, Colonel Dewavrin must not be judged by the same standards as other civil servants."

Colonel Dewavrin requested that his case be heard in the civil courts and the proceedings be made public. The government showed no haste — especially now that Henri Ribière was completely recovered from his accident and had pinpointed Fourcaud's personal reasons for trying to increase the sensationalism of the affair. All the litigious money had been recovered, and the government wished to let the case die a natural death. However, Dewavrin brought his case before the Council of State to protest the measures taken against him. The high court ruled that all the proceedings had been illegal. Dewavrin was then reinstated in his rank of colonel, but he resigned from the Army at the beginning of 1948.

The fact remains that the name of the man who headed de Gaulle's secret service during all the war, who had performed numerous dangerous missions and made possible de Gaulle's takeover of the French government, had been dragged through the mud. His crime had been to plan an operation to back up financially a fight in the eventuality of a Communist move for power.

It is not without irony that one looks at what happened twelve years later, in 1960, when de Gaulle as chief of state felt his power threatened during the generals' revolt in Algiers. The military revolt in North Africa plus the activities of the pro-French Algeria element in France made him fear being overthrown by so-called rightist organizations. His Prime Minister, Michel Debré, panicked.

Complete disorder prevailed inside the government. It was decided that in the event of a coup mounted by the right, the Gaullist team would flee to a foreign country and lead the fight against the junta. But to fight a successful coup they needed money. Aides of de Gaulle and Debré asked the head of the financial division of SDECE to take steps to hide funds in Switzerland.

Louis Fauvert, the man who had with zeal and tenacity conducted the inquiry against Dewavrin, left immediately for Geneva and Bern to rent large safety deposit boxes in various banks under assumed names. Taking advantage of Swiss legislation, he also opened numbered accounts. Back in Paris he collected several million dollars in foreign currency. Then, on regular trips to Switzerland, he transported the money in postal sacks carrying official seals to look like diplomatic pouches. Secret funds kept accumulating in the Swiss banks, as did gold bars. Only Louis Fauvert and a handful of people close to de Gaulle and Debré knew which banks held the deposits and had the power to withdraw. Since then, the French government has not disturbed the funds. The Gaullists are thus certain of being able to finance revolutionary operations in any eventuality.

The Prime Minister showed his gratitude to Louis Fauvert and named him Commander of the Legion of Honor.

Because he had taken steps to fight, if necessary, an expected Communist coup, Colonel Dewavrin had the modest Cross of the Legion of Honor taken from him, while Fauvert, a petty bureaucrat, doing the same thing, but in provision for a rightist coup, was honored with one of the highest ranks of the Legion of Honor — the order rewarding bravery.

But who knows? France has laws and acts ruling public finances which could be enforced as far as the head of SDECE's financial division is concerned. And under a new regime a "Fauvert affair" even more unsavory than the "Passy-Dewavrin affair" could reveal to the French people the unsuspected utilization of their money.

The Communist members of the government were obviously kept informed of the developments in the Dewavrin affair, since they sat at the secret deliberations and helped decide the policy to adopt for the colonel and former BCRA members implicated with him. Probably not to cut themselves off from their sources of information, they decided against using the Passy affair for propaganda purposes. They left to their friends and fellow travelers the task of arousing the public against the secret services and their members.

One of these men was Emmanuel d'Astier de la Vigerie, whose wife was the daughter of former Russian Ambassador Krassine and who boasted of a friendship with Stalin. This was the same man who much later had a meeting with Stalin's daughter, Svetlana, in Switzerland and tried to persuade her to take refuge in France rather than in the United States. However, Svetlana knew with whom she was dealing and left immediately after this peculiar interview for the United States.

Emmanuel d'Astier de la Vigerie personally detested Dewavrin and was afraid of what he might reveal about his relationship with the Soviet. By denigrating Dewavrin he hoped to minimize the impact of his eventual declarations. In reality, this was much effort for nothing, since de Gaulle, using his influence over his former subordinate, asked Dewavrin to ignore the attacks of d'Astier, with whom he conferred regularly — to take advantage of his links with Moscow.

The French Communists were cautious in their attitude in order not to antagonize voters, but the Soviets considered themselves in France as in conquered territory — as in the case of the Pole known as Lapchinsky.

Lapchinsky lived in a small apartment on the Left Bank and had made a habit of visiting White Russian friends on the Rue Erlanger in Auteuil, one of the residential sections of Paris. One morning as he left the building after spending the night with his friends, several members of the Soviet Embassy got out of a car parked nearby and jumped him. They overpowered him and in spite of his screams and the protests of witnesses, forced him into their car and sped away.

No one ever heard what happened to the victim of this kidnapping. Several witnesses had gotten the license number, but the police quickly discovered the number of the tag corresponded to that of an innocent storekeeper whose car hadn't left the garage. Some of the White Russians had recognized the members of the Soviet Embassy involved in the kidnapping, and the investigation progressed when several Paris newspapers revealed that the Soviet

Embassy had no intention of denying its participation in the crime. On the contrary, it claimed the act was legal and based on an agreement signed by de Gaulle's government the year before allowing Soviet authorities to repatriate citizens from the USSR and other countries occupied by the Red Army and now living in France.

It was learned later that Lapchinsky was not a Pole after all, but a Russian named Theodore Kolissev who had been trying to escape from the Russian secret service.

The most important consequence of the French-USSR agreement was that Russian citizens who were disappointed with Stalin's system and wanting to seek refuge in the West were careful to avoid France, being unwilling to run the risk of being forced back behind the Iron Curtain. Kolissev apparently was the last Soviet citizen to seek asylum in Paris. Defectors know better and now select countries where Moscow enjoys less freedom.

Before the war the Communists controlled only five newspapers. Afterwards the number grew to thirty. This was the result of a law passed at the time of the liberation stipulating that all publishers of clandestine newspapers in circulation under the German occupation had the right to claim all installations and assets of those newspapers accused of collaboration with Pétain's government. The mere fact of having published some unknown sheet limited to several hundred stenciled copies during the war gave one the right to take possession of the printing plant and offices of important newspapers. No compensation was given to the owners or allowances made even in known instances in which papers had been forced, sometimes under threat of death, to publish.

The majority of the contemporary French press owes its origin to such spoilage.

Of course, the Communists were among the first to take advantage of the new measures, and their newspapers soon covered all the territory. With great astuteness, they published the only journals dealing solely with the problems of interest to the peasantry, which in an essentially agrarian country gave them considerable influence. Their audience was so large among the working class that they were able to take control of the CGT, the most important workers union in France.

153

Following several changes of government, five Communists held key positions. Thorez was Vice-President; Billoux, Secretary of Defense; Croizat, Secretary of Labor; Marrane, Secretary of Health; and Charles Tillon, Secretary for Reconstruction. Nothing could be done without the Communists' knowing about it and having to give their views.

For the SDECE it had become almost impossible to carry out any activity. Since the intelligence we gathered was made available to the members of the cabinet, there was no way to prevent the Communists from having access to it. Rather than running the risk of having their agents uncovered, the heads of sections chose to keep their networks dormant until better times. As a rule, everyone pretended to be busy, with the aim of being as inefficient as possible. It was difficult, however, to ignore the bulk of intelligence coming in from various sources and stressing the concern of some Western chancelleries over Communist gains in France. This intelligence was handed personally to the government members who were considered trustworthy.

On the other hand, the Sûreté was also gathering disturbing information on the restlessness of extreme rightist organizations, who were edgy about Communist progress.

The chief of the government, Paul Ramadier, recognized the danger of the situation and decided to take action. When during a roll call vote in the House of Representatives the Communist faction voted against the government, President Ramadier seized the opportunity and dismissed his Communist cabinet members. This move surprised everyone, including those directly concerned, who had not expected such an energetic action.

The departure of the Communists from the government instantly cleared the atmosphere. Hope revived in the various departments, and without minimizing the aftereffects of this measure, everyone set to work. Still, the rule was to use discretion when dealing with matters concerning national security, since so many Communists had been infiltrated into government positions, especially in the military and foreign affairs.

Proof of leaks inside the government was established in the matter of the firing of the Communist ministers. Russian Ambassador Bogomolov had left for Moscow on vacation when President

Ramadier, in complete secrecy, made the decision to get rid of the Communist members of his government. The day this decision was made, and only a few cabinet members informed, Bogomolov was hurriedly returning to Paris. It could not possibly be a mere coincidence, and we felt certain that Bogomolov knew of the decision. We were later to learn that Stalin, not wishing to aggravate an already complicated international situation, had sent his representative back to Paris with orders for the French Communist chiefs not to trigger an armed rebellion against the government.

Communist infiltration in the SDECE only added to the other difficulties it was facing. Fourcaud, infuriated by the return of the chief he had hoped to replace, was scheming with shady politicians to create difficulties for Henri Ribière and bring him to resign in disgust. But Ribière was like a rock, and all Fourcaud's intrigues were useless. The atmosphere of the service was charged with electricity, and division heads, finding themselves with conflicting orders from their director and from his deputy, did not know what to do. Some played politics, and things got worse. Confrontations between Ribière and Fourcaud were so stormy that one day, during the daily meeting of the division heads, Ribière used his walking stick to push Fourcaud out of his office. From that time they spoke to each other only in cases of absolute necessity.

Since the Passy affair, the few remaining members of the BCRA in the agency had been given low administrative positions. I was the only one in charge of an intelligence section. All my colleagues were officers, mostly former members of Giraud's service, still anxious to get even with the BCRA group. The feud between Ribière and Fourcaud delighted them. They kept hoping that the intelligence services would be reinstated under the control of the Army Chief of Staff, meaning a return to the old traditional methods, in spite of previous poor performances.

It was a depressing situation. Every attempt I made to organize contacts efficiently with our British ally was dampened. After months of fruitless effort, I had to admit I was wasting my time, and so I decided to submit my resignation. The world of the secret services I had known during the war was so different, demanding self-discipline and personal sacrifice. Our goal then was the success of an enterprise dedicated to the good of the country. I was surrounded now by men who were eager only to derive benefits from their positions and to engage in some kind of questionable traffic, or by military men who were willing to stoop to anything to obtain a decoration or a promotion.

Feeling that I was in a strong position since I had never solicited nor obtained any favor, I made up my mind to voice the reasons for my resignation. I had never met our director, Henri Ribière. The rule was that one must request an appointment through the usual channels. When all my requests went unanswered, I asked a friend of mine, who was on good terms with Ribière's Chef de Cabinet, to set up an appointment for me. I was not really surprised when I learned that none of my previous requests had been forwarded. At last I was given a specific date to meet with my boss.

There was something impressive about Henri Ribière. He was self-possessed, and he radiated strength and quiet authority. His features were classic, his eyes frank, coolly appraising his interlocutor. He was extremely courteous, and the reserve he displayed on every occasion, which was often interpreted as coldness, gave way from time to time to an infectious smile. He typified the ideal intelligence chief.

When I entered his office on the given day, he offered me his hand, saying, "Good morning, please have a seat," and waited for me to speak.

I did, for nearly one hour. Although he never interrupted, I could see I had all his attention by a special glint in his eyes and a faint smile now and then. At the end of my monologue, Ribière rose and said, "I thank you. Come back and see me in two days. Good-bye."

I left, somewhat disconcerted. Had I produced the right impression? In any case, his silence strengthened my intention to leave the agency. I had handed him my resignation and expected to get his acceptance at our next meeting.

When I arrived two days later, I received the same noncommittal welcome. I sat down and waited for him to speak.

"I have studied your file. The inquiries I made about you proved excellent. I need someone near me with intimate knowledge of what is going on in this agency. Would you accept a position on my personal staff?"

I could not believe my ears! It took me a few seconds to recover from my surprise enough to accept enthusiastically. The SDECE was deteriorating, and only the director could restore order. Nothing could please me more than to help him put it back on the right track.

I thought I would start in my new duties right away. Instead, Ribière asked me to carry out a confidential mission for him outside France. This was to be the first of many similar assignments.

Later, mission accomplished, I worked at headquarters with Ribière's Chef de Cabinet for several months. When he decided, for personal reasons, to leave the agency, I replaced him.

A startling discovery in my new position was to realize that Ribière's service heads had literally quarantined him. During the daily meetings in his office, they would bring in the administrative documents for which his signature was needed, but nothing more. In fact, during a conference prior to the daily meeting with the director, the heads of services agreed on what to show him, what to show Colonel Fourcaud, and what to keep from them altogether.

The intelligence handed to the director did not amount to much and, as a rule, was of little importance. When occasionally he voiced his surprise at the poor results obtained, he was told that nothing better could be expected under the service's present state of reorganization. Furthermore, they claimed, insufficient funds prevented the research division from recruiting good agents. In fact the only intelligence made available to the director chiefly concerned foreign troop movements and other minor military activities which, except to staff officers, were of little interest. Intelligence of a political or economic nature was scanty or nonexistent.

I knew, from personal experience, the exact volume of intelligence coming in daily, and I put pressure on the research divisions to see that everything be shown to the director. In order to exercise better control, Ribière, on my advice, ordered the head of the code section to bring him twice a day all cables sent or received. This should have been effective except for the determination of all section heads to replace names with aliases in the cables. As an example, a cable received would read: "In the afternoon of Robert, 3 units Jim coming from Dick proceeded toward Morris."

We had no choice but to demand from the section chiefs a list of all code names with their exact meaning. This raised a general outcry, for, we were told, it would endanger the security of the informers. After countless arguments it was agreed that an old tradition would be respected. The identity of the sources would not be disclosed, but enough details about the agents would be given to allow an evaluation of the intelligence received.

Intelligence reports arrived at headquarters by diplomatic pouch or through the mail. I decided to check once in a while by asking the head of the dispatch service to open some of the mail in my presence. Those sporadic verifications provided interesting results. For one thing it soon put a stop to the existing illicit traffic. In several instances, boxes of film supposedly unprocessed were found to contain gold, precious stones, or foreign currency smuggled into France under diplomatic cover by unscrupulous members of our organization.

I also discovered that, in order to bypass the director, intelligence was being mailed directly to several officers. Why was there such eagerness to hide intelligence? I finally discovered the explanation: the Ministry for Foreign Affairs, anxious to preserve its prerogative, had denied the SDECE the right to analyze intelligence and to prepare estimates, thus rendering useless the division in charge of disseminating information. As a result, the heads of the different sections distributed, in their own way, the fragmentary intelligence they collected, favoring certain departments or government officials over others, according to passing mood or political opinion. They had come to consider the intelligence as their personal property, using it as they pleased.

To stop this politicking, the director ordered all intelligence heads to meet daily with one member of his cabinet to study all incoming intelligence, to proceed with its evaluation, and to decide on the proper dissemination. With measures like these, the director was able to control the output of the various sections of SDECE, but he still had to be acquainted with their methods of operation.

As a rule, intelligence is provided by agents who are sent on missions in foreign countries by headquarters, or locally recruited by our representatives. During the war, Ribière had seen French patriots, members of the underground, hunting intelligence on their own initiative. But the techniques used by agents in foreign territory were much different. I stressed to him the existing methods, and he decided to take a close look at the way the research departments of SDECE operated. We discovered many abuses and corrected them.

For instance, many agents were unable, for security reasons, to travel under their own names. Passports and identification papers were issued under aliases by the Department of the Interior, upon submission of a request bearing the director's signature. However, no real control existed, and anyone could get a passport under an assumed name if he knew the right person in the research division and promised to supply a certain amount of information. To eliminate such improper practices, the chief of counterespionage was given full authority to decide on the necessity of issuing travel documents under aliases. Working in close liaison with the police, and with the files at his disposal, he was best qualified to make sure that identification papers established under false names were given only to bona fide agents and were really needed to carry out specific assignments.

As I was discussing his new responsibilities with the chief of counterespionage, he suggested that I pay a visit to the section in charge of counterfeiting documents.

During the war, underground agents could not, for obvious reasons, apply for the different documents requested by the Germans, and we had recruited a team of experts who were able to duplicate any handwriting and to reproduce exactly any type of printing or stamps. Our facilities were the best in the world and our experts were honest and beyond reproach. Loving their trade, they had gathered a complete sampling of documents issued anywhere in the world. They also produced their own ink, being able to match the exact chemical composition of the ink used in the originals. In most cases, a fake can best be spotted by a close inspection of the texture of the paper used, so they made their own paper.

Now the hectic war days were over and I expected to find the section idle. Much to my surprise, on the day of my unannounced visit, unusual activity was visible. I was puzzled to see that most of the experts were working not on foreign documents, as one would have expected, but on French ones. I discovered that any department head could request the forging of documents, and false birth certificates, police affidavits, diplomas of all sorts were issued as a matter of routine. The officer in charge showed me an order he had just received for forging a doctor's diploma. Then he greatly aroused my curiosity by showing me how documents could be altered. Handwritten letters had been changed to have a totally different meaning by the omission, addition, or changing of certain words. Technically the work was perfect, and the authors of such letters would have been unable to disavow, in a court, their own handwriting.

When I reported this to Henri Ribière, he was as shocked as I. He immediately sent for the head of the section and demanded that such activities be suspended at once. Then he charged the chief of counterespionage with the task of conducting an investigation to uncover the purposes for which the forged documents had been utilized. Later, strict and complicated measures were enforced to make sure that all documents fabricated by the SDECE were absolutely needed to carry out specific missions. Of course, duplication of French documents was forbidden altogether. It goes without saying that today a good many people are probably still using forged papers from the SDECE production line. It is unfortunate that during the past few years the rules established twenty years ago have been somewhat liberalized.

Besides such corrupt practices, our most serious problem was security. The SDECE had been created as a civilian administration under the control of the Prime Minister. Its members were supposed to be civilians with status similar to all other civil servants. However, considering the unusual type of work involved, certain allowances had to be made. Unfortunately, at the time of its creation all problems dealing with the status of civil servants were handled by the Communist leader Maurice Thorez in his capacity as Vice-President. It would have been preposterous to entrust the organization of SDECE to a former deserter known as the main supporter of Stalinist politics in France. So Louis Fauvert, head of the financial division, decided that until further notice, the civilian members of SDECE would be hired on a temporary basis and could be fired without severance pay as the administration pleased.

The wages were based on the same pay scale as used by the sedentary Department of Records and Deeds. This put French intelligence agents on the same level as employees of that antiquated organization. With such inadequate salaries, there were few civilian candidates for SDECE positions, except for subaltern jobs. So, to fill the vacant posts, the agency turned to the Army officers, many of whom were without commands since the end of the war. The General Staff cooperated by assigning to the SDECE any officer who requested it. Gradually, all the important positions were filled by the military, with civilians in the lesser jobs.

However, whereas the civilians were subjected to background investigation upon recruitment, the officers were accepted automatically because of their rank. This created a situation in which military officers declared openly their sympathy for the Communist cause. Some even belonged to the party. Once again the director called on the counterespionage chief to rid the services of these doubtful elements. It was a difficult task, but little by little, as derogatory evidence was discovered, officers were sent back to the Army, where their activities would be less dangerous than in the SDECE. Or, at least, so we hoped.

The chief of counterespionage was Colonel Laffont, better known under the name Verneuil. During the war he had succeeded Colonel Paillole as head of "Travaux Ruraux," the cover for a service of clandestine counterespionage which had done a magnificent job against the Nazis in occupied France. A shrewd man, he reminded one more of a horsetrader than an officer. He was completely dedicated to his task, and he understood that the survival of SDECE depended upon the success of the reforms undertaken by Henri Ribière. Although he was overloaded with work, he readily accepted all the new responsibilities given him. Not being certain of success in eliminating all the troublesome elements in the agency, he started with his own section and got excellent results.

Every evening, after most of the staff had gone home, he reported to the Director on the daily events. Progress was slow, but we were gradually approaching the day when SDECE would be able to function normally and efficiently. Very often, after Verneuil's daily report, Ribière liked to chat informally with us for a while and comment on the international situation. He had an extraordinary knowledge of world affairs and a sound judgment of people and facts. This man, who usually talked so little, could go on for hours analyzing the international scene. Standing in front of the immense map covering a wall in his office, he accurately predicted Soviet moves, political as well as military. Twenty years later his predictions still stand. Evaluating realistically the power of France and her neighbors, he thought it impossible to stop the hegemony of the Soviets over Europe without the help of the United States and was a strong believer in the North Atlantic Treaty, which was under preparation. I remember clearly his conclusions that the Soviets, before 1970, would establish themselves militarily around the Mediterranean to achieve their plan of encircling Europe. And I fear that his other predictions will eventually materialize with the same accuracy.

In the late 1940s Communist activities were steadily intensifying. In France, political strikes were taking place one after another and the fear of a coup d'état was present at all times. The activities of the extreme left matched those of the extreme right, which were also of great concern to us in the SDECE.

Besides the divisions in charge of research, we had a section called "Action," which was in charge of special operations. It was an inheritance from the resistance and originally had been created for the purpose of training agents in parachuting and sabotage. Its role now was supposed to be the secret dropping of agents into foreign territories. Such operations were not frequent, but the Army considered that in case of war a certain number of draftees should be trained for missions behind the enemy lines. "Action" was doing just that and was training only men who had volunteered for the job. James Bond was still unknown, but it was agents of his type that we were trying to mold. The trainees were taught day and night parachuting, how to handle explosives and how to paralyze a factory by destroying vital equipment. They were also taught judo and all possible ways to kill silently. The course was exhausting but the recruits seemed to take it in stride. Many, after serving their time, volunteered to come back on their own every year, in order to stay physically fit and keep up with the latest techniques.

We knew some of the volunteers were members of rightist organizations. Ribière, concerned over their real motives for undertaking the training, was anxious to find a way to suppress the "Action" division, for its practical usefulness was really questionable. But the General Staff opposed his view and put pressure on

162

the administration to keep "Action" operating, arguing that it was indispensable to national defense.

Jacques Foccart, the powerful and mysterious man behind de Gaulle, received a complete training there and kept urging the more fanatic among the general's supporters to do the same.

Quite a few among the alumni of this section have since attracted attention and played an important part behind the scenes in de Gaulle's France, probably contributing greatly to the survival of the Gaullist system.

French Intelligence was slowly emerging from a confused and chaotic era. Our efforts were beginning to pay off when two scandals, the Robineau case and the scandal of the generals, by reflecting discredit on our agency, greatly hampered our work.

On this day of November 18, 1949, the Warsaw airport was still in pitiful shape — a reminder of the terrible beating it took during the war. The terminal building had been hastily and temporarily repaired and was lacking any of the conveniences we now expect to find in most international airports. The departure room was crowded with passengers waiting to embark. Usually it was deserted, but this morning the Polish airline L.O.T. had a flight to Brussels and Paris.

Two men of average height stood in a line waiting their turn at the counter. They spoke French. The older man was Mr. Robineau, General Secretary of the French Institute in Warsaw. He had come to see his son, André, off to Paris. André Robineau held the position of French consular agent in Szczecin (formerly German, with the name of Stettin). He was leaving now for Paris to report on his activities and hoped to be able to take a few days vacation in France.

He handed his ticket to the counter agent of L.O.T., showing him his two suitcases. The employee placed the luggage on the scale, recorded the weight, and carried the two bags to the luggage room behind him. Then he returned the ticket to the passenger and motioned to the next person. The boarding announcement was barely audible as it came over the loudspeaker. André kissed his father goodbye and walked toward the gate. The father paced up and down waiting for the plane to take off. Ten minutes later, with a whining sound, it was off the ground. Mr. Robineau walked back slowly. As he passed by the luggage room, he suddenly started with surprise. His son's suitcases were being carried away by two uniformed policemen. He immediately asked an employee what was going on. With a shrug, the man said he did not know.

"But my son, André Robineau, was on that plane," insisted the alarmed father.

The airline agent quickly went over the passenger list and gave an affirmative nod. The father, still apprehensive, tried to obtain more information but soon gave up, realizing the futility of his questions. Wasting no time, he went straight to the French Embassy to report what had happened and voice his fears. The ambassador immediately dispatched one of his aides to the airport.

The Warsaw airport was under control of the military, and the French official asked the officer in charge of security to give him confirmation that André Robineau had been on board the flight to Brussels.

"I give you my word of honor," assured the officer, "that Mr. Robineau left on this flight."

However, the French ambassador was not fully satisfied with this assurance when it was reported to him. He called the French ambassador in Brussels, asking him to have someone check the plane upon its arrival in the Belgian capital and make sure that André Robineau was on board.

The ambassador had reason for concern. A few months before, several employees of the French consulate in Wroclaw had disappeared under mysterious circumstances, and since then all the members of French diplomatic or consular missions had felt an ever-present threat. In their eagerness to please Moscow, the Polish authorities would not hesitate to resort to the most drastic measures.

A few hours later the French ambassador in Brussels informed his colleague in Warsaw that André Robineau was not aboard the flight which had just landed at the Brussels airport.

The French representative in Warsaw immediately alerted the Quai d'Orsay in Paris, which in turn informed the division of the Sûreté in charge of control over foreign activities: the Direction of Territorial Security.

As soon as it landed in Paris, the Polish plane was thoroughly inspected by police, and members of the crew were detained for questioning. They were willing to cooperate, and they stated that André Robineau had actually boarded the plane, but a few minutes before departure time had been approached by a Polish official already on board. They spoke briefly and the Frenchman followed him out. The name of Robineau had soon after been crossed off the passenger list.

French authorities had to bow to the fact that a member of their consulate in Szczecin had been arrested contrary to all diplomatic customs. The French Embassy made several representations to the Polish Ministry for Foreign Affairs without any success.

On November 21, three days after the incident, the Polish Foreign Office notified the French Ambassador of André Robineau's arrest for espionage and stated that he had confessed his criminal activities. The official note added:

It is clear from the documents in our possession that espionage activities are also being conducted by the following members of the French Embassy: Mr. Aymar Brossin de Mère and Mr. Fernand Reneaux. The Polish government wishes to remind the French government that five months ago, employees of the French Consulate in Wroclaw were arrested for espionage and they will stand trial on this charge.

The Polish government demands that Mr. Aymar Brossin de Mère and Mr. Fernand Reneaux leave the territory of the Republic of Poland immediately.

The members of the Wroclaw consulate previously arrested had, in fact, been active in a French intelligence ring under the orders of de Mère and Reneaux. The confession of one of them would be incriminating enough to justify the Polish request for the deportation of the two French diplomats. It did not, however, throw any light on what led to Robineau's detention.

In the following days, a Polish government spokesman announced the destruction of a French espionage network as a direct result of Robineau's arrest. More than 100 persons had been involved. Then, to emphasize Robineau's confession, the Polish official played a recording of his voice admitting his crimes of espionage. Photocopies of agent's file cards authenticated by Robineau's signature were also shown to the journalists present.

All of us in Paris were bewildered. How in the world could the Poles get a detailed confession out of Robineau in no more than five days? His file indicated he was a courageous fighter during the war who had carried out missions at the risk of his life. He knew Poland well, having lived there since he was two years old. Naturally, he spoke the language fluently. His father was General Secretary of the French Institute in Warsaw, one of the most renowned cultural centers in Poland before the war.

When the Germans occupied Poland in 1940, Robineau and his family were arrested by the Nazis and spent several months in a concentration camp. Later, an exchange of civilian prisoners was made and the Robineaus were free to get back to France. André was then only sixteen, but this did not stop his escape from occupied France to reach London, via Portugal, and to enlist in the Free French Navy. His war services were brilliant and he had naturally been attracted by the new SDECE, which needed young men with his background and his knowledge of a country behind the Iron Curtain.

Since he had assumed his duties of consular agent in Szczecin, Robineau's work had been entirely satisfactory. He never left a request for information unanswered.

The city of Szczecin, because of its position at the mouth of the river Oder and also because of its important iron works, was of special interest as far as the surveillance of exchanges between the USSR and Poland were concerned. Robineau had been able to set up a very active intelligence network there. Because of his past record, we were unable to understand why he had confessed so rapidly unless he had been doped into an admission.

The Atlantic Pact had recently been signed in Washington, and Poland's exaggeration of the Robineau affair was certainly a token of Stalin's grim mood over the signing of the treaty by Western allies.

Poland, it seemed, should have been the last country to create difficulties for France. It was to come to her defense that France had declared war on Germany in 1939. Later, Polish intelligence, headed by Colonel Gano, had set up a number of networks in occupied France to work against the Germans, and Colonel Gano had been helped in his task by the French underground in a spirit of true collaboration.

The French now were not trying to obtain information against Poland, but were only gathering intelligence on the Russians, who ruled the country through a puppet government.

By putting Robineau in jail the Poles had broken all the traditional rules, and in spite of our desire in the SDECE to find grounds for agreement, the problem was now outside our influence. Robineau's official position as consular agent had been recognized by the Polish government and his status confirmed by a letter of accreditation from the Polish Ministry for Foreign Affairs. As a result, his arrest was a breach of diplomatic immunity and a violation of international agreements on the protection of diplomats in foreign countries. Making this a matter of principle, French Foreign Affairs Minister Robert Schuman, although he was well known for his conciliatory spirit, urged the Minister of the Interior to retaliate against the Poles.

This was easy, for while there were only a few hundred Frenchmen living in Poland, more than 400,000 Polish citizens had settled in France. This high figure was the result of an agreement with the Polish government signed by the Minister of Industrial Production, the Communist Marcel Paul, for the temporary immigration to France of jobless Polish coal miners. So, to alleviate France's shortage of manpower, the coal basins of northern France were worked by Polish laborers, mostly Communists. They were the source of many headaches for the administration of this region.

In reprisal for Robineau's arrest, the French Sûreté detained Lieutenant Myszkowski, assistant to the Polish military attaché in Paris, on grounds of espionage. Then they arrested the Polish vice-consul in Lille as he was coming back from a trip to Warsaw. He had just arrived at the railroad station when he was seized and immediately put aboard another train to Paris. The circumstances were similar to the method used by the Poles for Robineau.

Next, the Sûreté arrested twenty-six Polish residents, heads of various Communist organizations, and deported them without delay. This was the beginning of a veritable tug-of-war between France and Poland, each one trying to outdo the other. Another French vice-consul was apprehended together with two employees of the French Embassy in Warsaw, while in Gdánsk, Frenchmen were being jailed arbitrarily.

The members of the French diplomatic missions were subjected to constant harassment and they lived in fear. One night around one o'clock, Miss Loisel, a secretary in the embassy, was awakened by members of Polish security who had come to pick her up. She refused to open the door and alerted her neighbor, another embassy employee, by banging on the wall. He immediately called French Ambassador Bayens, who soon arrived and asked to see the warrant. The security officers were unable to produce one, but said they would come back with it. Miss Loisel was immediately given asylum in the French Embassy.

Each persecution by the Polish government was met by French retaliation in the way of new deportations and new restrictive measures against Polish organizations in France. Poland deported teachers of the French Institute in Warsaw. The French, in turn, deported teachers and professors in various Polish cultural centers. But while the Polish nationals jailed in France were allowed visits from lawyers and members of their families, the Polish authorities systematically refused the French diplomatic representatives permission to visit Robineau and the other French prisoners. Such an attitude on the part of the Polish government made us suspect that torture might have been used to induce confessions.

Upon their arrival in Paris, Brossin de Mère and Reneaux had been thoroughly questioned on the activities of their agents and the setup of their organization. They had conducted their network with more enthusiasm than prudence, and it certainly would have been easy for double agents to infiltrate it. The intelligence they had gathered was mostly military, regarding moves of Russian troops and military personnel stationed in Poland. It was the kind of information traditionally collected by foreign missions, and a Free Poland would have had no reason to make such an issue of it. But Poland was no longer free, and its security services under the yoke of the KGB had their obscure reasons for acting as they did. Even if we allowed for the presence in the network of double agents able to identify its members, we were still at a loss to explain how the Poles had come by certain documents displayed for the journalists during a press conference. The originals of the documents were kept in a safe in Robineau's office inside the French consulate, and had been discovered there, intact, after his arrest.

We thought we had the key to this mystery when Rivoire, the French consul in Szczecin and Robineau's superior, sent several letters to Polish newspapers disowning Robineau and criticizing his secret activities. His behavior was so odd and unexpected that the Quai d'Orsay recalled him to Paris immediately to explain his actions.

Rivoire was a war cripple. The loss of an arm had made him bitter, and he felt the promotion he received was not enough reward for his sacrifice. He favored the Communists, who, he told his superiors in Paris, wanted only peace, but had to defend themselves against the attacks of Western intelligence. For several days counterespionage experts thought he was responsible for Robineau's arrest, and they questioned him exhaustively. Rivoire's answers made less and less sense, even becoming at times incoherent. After a while he was dismissed as a mental case.

But the investigation was making no headway, and Colonel Verneuil, head of counterespionage, showed genuine concern. A copy of the incriminating documents was kept in a safe at headquarters, and the leak could have taken place in Paris as easily as in Szczecin. As long as the mystery remained unsolved, we had to assume the presence of an enemy agent among us. At the same time the "Scandal of the Generals," which I will review later, was making headlines, and the problems of leaks at all levels was very acute. We had to go about our work in a climate of suspicion, always taking into account the possibility that our activities were known to the Soviets.

All the leads in the Robineau affair had come to nothing, and we had no choice but to wait for new developments.

One month after Robineau's arrest the trial of the French consulate employees, mysteriously arrested some six months earlier, began in Wroclaw. The main defendant was Yvonne Bassaler, a young woman of twenty-nine who had acquired the intelligence fever while serving in the underground. The press saw her as a classic heroine of the resistance. However, she had been enlisted in our agency as a secretary for the French consulate in Wroclaw and her duties were to do the typing and filing like any other secretary. But Yvonne Bassaler had, it seemed, a Mata Hari complex and dreamed of being an agent. She knew a few Poles and discussed contacting them with her chief, who was inexperienced enough to agree. So she immediately felt out her contacts and obtained some intelligence which, from what came out at the trial, was of little value, if any. But she liked playing the game. She was hardly the seductive spy one imagines. Her rather plain face, emaciated and suffering as it appeared at the trial, wouldn't have seduced anyone.

As a resistance heroine, we expected her to show courage and deny all the charges. But to our surprise, she confessed to all the prosecutor's accusations. We learned later the reasons for her strange behavior.

Polish jails were quite refined. They had a cell called the "ice box," where the temperature was kept at 32 degrees. After a stay of several hours in it the prisoner was encouraged to confess. If he refused, he was put in the "devil cage." It was a kind of contraption, originally built by the Gestapo, in which the prisoner could neither stand, sit, nor lie down. Nobody was able to resist alternate stays in the "ice box" and "devil cage," and Yvonne Bassaler had confessed.

The Polish prosecutor was a Major Orlynski, who had worked with French intelligence in the past. He had been dismissed during the war because of his suspicious relationship with the Germans and had joined the Communists, somehow convincing them of his sincerity. Now he really had a chance to take revenge on some members of the French service, and it was easy to see how much he enjoyed it. The prosecutor put on exhibit letters found in Yvonne Bassaler's apartment when she was arrested. They were just personal or administrative letters and the only implicating evidence in them was the official letterhead of the SDECE. On the stand, poor Yvonne was revealing all she knew, and even more.

171

As in all trials behind the Iron Curtain, the accused not only recognized their faults, but testified against each other. Nothing was missing, not even the stool pigeon, who was so easy to spot that some Polish newspapermen complained against his crude perform- ance.

Finally Yvonne Bassaler was sentenced to twelve years in jail and her codefendants to similar sentences. We were sorry for them but hoped we would be able to somehow get them released in the near future. Working in intelligence, they were aware of the risks. To tell the truth, we were disappointed that no one had spoken up during the trial about the pressures exerted by the Poles to make them confess. But human nature is human nature, and no one knows what he might have done in their place. However, we still had no answer to one baffling question: What brought the Poles to arrest the members of our Wroclaw team in the first place? Who had tipped them? Nothing in the trial had given us any clue.

When an intelligence operation is uncovered, there is always a high price to pay. The U-2 affair, coming many years later, gave the United States a taste of what it is like. The Soviets, then infuriated over the signing of the North Atlantic Treaty, were determined to seek revenge even at their own cost. During the period preceding the Robineau trial, the Poles decided to break all trade relations with France. The most important agreement had been the exchange of Polish coal for French manufactured goods. France could easily find another supplier of coal, but the Poles were unable to buy elsewhere the goods they needed so badly. All the same, they went on with the arrests of French citizens down to the last Frenchman living in their country. We, in turn, ousted scores of Poles who held more or less official positions in France. At no time could they outdo us, but still they showed no sign of releasing Robineau. On the contrary, the date of his trial was set for February 5, 1950.

In Wroclaw, when the members of the French consulate were tried, a Polish visa was refused to a French lawyer sent by the Quai d'Orsay to attend the court proceedings. They also refused all facilities to a Western journalist who wanted to cover the trial. But when Robineau's turn came to be judged, Polish authorities showed an extreme generosity in the issuance of visas and other travel facilities. They went all out to give the trial an appearance of legality. There could be no doubt left for us that they had ample proof against Robineau and his codefendants.

On the first day of the trial, after the charges against him had been read by the prosecutor, the interrogation of Robineau began. Unlike the other accused Frenchmen in Wroclaw, Robineau appeared sure of himself. Looking straight at the judges he showed no sign of defeat. On the contrary, he stood proudly as a Frenchman who had accomplished his duty and would be ready to do it again if given the opportunity. Naturally, he recognized the charges brought against him; the evidence could not possibly be denied. The Poles had done a good job and Robineau acknowledged it. He had been caught — this was one of the accepted risks of his trade. Unafraid and unashamed, he impressed the newsmen present as rather cocky.

With Robineau on the bench was another French citizen, Gaston Druet, who also was charged with intelligence activities. Druet had been a radio repairman and had helped Robineau with the recruitment of agents. He admitted the charges, stating that he agreed to lend a hand to French intelligence in order to obtain an immigration visa for his German mistress.

The other three codefendants were Poles. One, a Jew, had been despicable enough to work for the Germans during the war. Another, a professional "spy" foreign officer in the prewar Polish army, had behaved questionably during the siege of Warsaw. The third one had been associated with the armed bands that terrorized Poland during the war and killed many "patriots." The choice of men picked to stand trial with Robineau clearly demonstrated the propaganda benefits the Poles expected to draw from it. Out of the hundreds of French intelligence agents arrested, the prosecution had chosen to indict only a few unimportant but rather repulsive individuals. The inference was clever — no respectable Pole would have been involved in helping an imperialist country such as France; only the scum of the population would be willing to conspire with a Western power.

Strangely enough, this show of propaganda paid off for the Poles most substantially in France. The Paris newspapers, without going as far as to find justification for the Polish authorities' decision to bring members of French intelligence to court, were bitterly critical of the SDECE and its representatives.

We were at the beginning of the cold war, and the newsmen failed to grasp the vital importance of certain intelligence such as the exact location of an airfield or the volume of goods located in a certain port. This was considered to be of little value to French security. We knew better, and we considered that Robineau had done a good job. The criticism against him was deeply resented by all the members of our service who could appreciate Robineau's dedication and hard work.

For a full week the trial went on. Many of Robineau's agents testified on missions assigned to them by their chief. Their testimony was complete and could not be denied. One or several of those agents had undoubtedly been used by Polish security as *provocateurs*, and Robineau, carried away by his work, had not followed the security measures in which he had been thoroughly trained. His negligence was probably the reason he was now in trouble. We did not know the exact amount of information the Poles had been able to gather on our network, but we had the feeling that the whole affair was due to the carelessness of our representative. Because of him we had lost a good intelligence network and it would take years to find new sources on the Russian build-up in Poland. Nevertheless, Robineau had conducted himself with dignity at the trial and we held him in high esteem.

Keeping in line with the usual form of judicial proceedings in Soviet-dominated countries, the prosecutor spoke at length against the member nations of the Atlantic alliance and requested heavy sentences against the defendants. When asked if he had any comment to make, Robineau, in a final statement, said: "I have done my duty as a soldier. During my stay in Poland I have been able to see its tremendous effort at rehabilitation and I see the harm I have done. I am sorry."

This was not what we expected him to say, but in totalitarian states they have ways of bringing those on trial to make this type of statement. But, alas, it was not all. To the amazement of the spectators, and to our shame, Robineau, before leaving the courtroom, addressed the public: "There are newspapermen here, and some of them are French. I wish through them to get a message to the young people of France and to ask them not to follow my example. I ask for a fair sentence."

What had happened? Had Robineau concluded an agreement with the prosecution to get a light sentence? Or was he under the influence of some kind of hallucinogen? After a week during which he had impressed us all with his dignified bearing, how could he become, in a few seconds, such a louse?

Along with Colonel Verneuil, we all wondered for days what had happened without being able to come up with a reasonable explanation. Worst of all, it did not seem that Robineau's statement had helped him any.

The court sentenced him to twelve years in jail. The other defendants received jail terms also, except for one of the Poles, who was sentenced to death.

There were so many scandals in France at the time that the uproar provoked by the Robineau affair died almost immediately after the sentencing. In a few days the public had forgotten the case. This is what Colonel Verneuil had expected.

With great patience, he had been collecting information on Polish agents in France and other friendly nations. Quietly he began to apply pressure on them. A Polish network was dismantled and its agents arrested in Marseille. In other countries, Polish diplomats, members of the Polish intelligence organization, were almost openly tailed. Polish airline offices used as centers for intelligence were under permanent surveillance. Polish workers were unable to obtain visa extensions when they expired. All economic agreements had been canceled and the Poles could neither buy nor sell anything in France. The Robineau affair may have been a triumph for Polish security, but it was becoming a liability for the country.

Three months after the end of the trial, we began to receive hints that Robineau and his French associates could be exchanged for the Polish vice-consul in Lille and other Polish agents we held prisoner. We decided not to show any hurry, but now the Poles were impatient. They wanted to forget the whole affair that was causing them such tremendous losses every day. Finally, in the summer of 1950 the exchange of prisoners took place.

The first of our liberated agents I talked with was Yvonne Bassaler. Her health was very poor. She had suffered terribly in jail and had developed ulcers on her legs. Henri Ribière, Colonel Verneuil, and I attempted to question her on how she thought the Poles had uncovered her activities, but she had no idea and her physical condition prevented us from persisting.

Later we thoroughly interrogated Robineau on his activities — the circumstances surrounding his arrest, what happened when he was in jail, and the reasons for his strange and unexpected statement. He explained that he could not possibly have denied the evidence confronting him and thought he should take the full responsibility for the operation to protect his agents. He justified his last-minute statement as having been made in exchange for the promise of light sentences for his associates. Everything he said was logical and nobody had reason to doubt his word. Yet many things remained unexplained and left us with a feeling of frustration. The inquiry went on. Pieces of information were collected and finally the counterespionage officers in charge of the case presented their conclusions: The French military attaché in Warsaw at the time of the arrests was General Georges Teyssier. He was known to have a very affectionate interest in Yvonne Bassaler. His wife, a Polish citizen, had discovered their affair and had demanded the departure of her rival from the embassy. Yvonne was transferred to Wroclaw. But the removal of the girl did not seem to appease the wrath of Mrs. Teyssier, whose grudge was deeply rooted. Our counterintelligence officers assumed that Mrs. Teyssier, knowing that her husband was still writing to Yvonne, decided to denounce her to Polish security. Being a Polish national helped her convince the suspicious Communist secret organization.

She had free access to her husband's office and could easily have handed to Polish officers documents he had received from the SDECE representative. After her arrest, Yvonne Bassaler had revealed everything she knew, and it was more than enough to induce the arrest of Robineau and his entire network.

To substantiate their conclusions, our counterespionage men had only circumstantial evidence, most of it negative. General Teyssier had died a few weeks after Robineau's arrest, and his widow had chosen to remain in Warsaw where she had family. The fact that she did not return to France was considered very incriminating.

176

Police at the border stations were under orders to alert counter-espionage in the event she ever entered French territory.

Did she ever come back? Was she later asked questions? I never knew. So many other things were happening that the case was soon forgotten. The matter was closed as far as the counterespionage officers in charge were concerned. The files went back to the archives.

The Robineau affair had demonstrated how nations behind the Iron Curtain could use the imprudence of intelligence agents for propaganda purposes. It had shown, too, the danger of escalation when the governments involved began retaliating against each other in a tug-of-war that could end in disaster. In the following years, I have no doubt, the Robineau affair was in the minds of the decision makers whenever intelligence agents were uncovered. When the United States' U-2 plane was shot down over Russia and the pilot Powers went through a trial similar to the one in Warsaw, President Eisenhower was careful not to repeat the mistakes made previously, and by his candid acceptance of the fact, he cut down the effect Soviet propagandists expected from their capture of the unfortunate American.

Because of its unique historical importance, the Robineau affair was mentioned once in a while in talk among intelligence specialists who liked to draw from it some lesson for their future projects. But the Robineau affair was not finished. . . .

In 1960, with the Castro government in full control in Cuba, persecutions, confiscations, jailings, and shootings were daily occurrences. Havana, beautiful Havana, was becoming a branch of hell. Freedom had disappeared, and the island's only links with the West were the daily flights of Pan American and KLM. It was difficult for Cubans to get clearance to board the planes, but foreign diplomats used them frequently to escape the inferno in which they had to live, to breathe the fresh air of Miami, the nearest metropolis. It was only an inexpensive one-hour flight. Many wives of foreign diplomats, discouraged by the lack of food and other goods in the Havana stores, made a habit of going to Miami to shop. Not wanting to leave Havana empty-handed, most of them took with

177

them clothing and objects of value left with them for safekeeping by Cuban friends who had fled Castro's murdering spree. Helping the refugees by bringing them a few of the cherished possessions they had been forced to leave behind was an act of humanity on the part of all Western diplomats. They had seen the atrocities of the regime and they were full of pity for its victims.

In Miami, the U.S. customs office shared their compassion. They knew the huge diplomatic bags and the heavy suitcases were not necessary for a two or three day trip, but they knew also that some starving Cuban refugee would be able to afford a few more necessities in the following days.

One diplomat's wife, however, never came to Miami with heavy suitcases, yet she was a frequent visitor. Her name was Mary Eckberg. Her husband was a member of the Swedish diplomatic staff in Cuba. She was not a beauty, but she was attractive. She dressed nicely, but it was more the way she wore her dresses than the dress itself which drew attention. She really did not try to be noticed; on the contrary, she wanted to be very unobtrusive. And she was . . . to a point.

Upon arriving in Miami, she would invariably get into a cab and go straight to the Columbus Hotel. There she would never take the first room offered her. She would, for some reason, be unhappy with it and ask to see other rooms. Then she would pick one at random. Intelligence agents are trained to never take the first or the second room offered to them for fear it may be bugged. In choosing one casually, there is a better chance to escape detection. Was Mary Eckberg an intelligence agent? Nobody knew at first, for nobody was paying any attention to her.

During the day she would walk around, looking at the store windows and doing some small errands. She was far from an extravagant spender, and one would really wonder why she came to Miami so often. As a matter of fact, she had friends in the Florida city — friends she would quietly visit during the afternoon or evening. Some of them were the type no one had any particular interest in, but others were being watched by U.S. security agents.

A person paying a visit to an espionage suspect automatically becomes a suspect. Mary Eckberg began to puzzle the U.S. security officers and they started to watch her moves. At the same time they began to search their files to see if any descriptions of foreign intelligence agents would match that of Mary Eckberg.

They found one.

Over a period of twenty years, several reports had been collected about a Polish girl who had been carrying out assignments for the KGB and Polish intelligence. The description of the girl was the exact duplicate of Mary Eckberg's. More than that, Mary Eckberg had been born a Polish citizen. The watch on her movements was tightened. During each of her trips she was closely tailed. After several months, the security officer in charge of the case, thinking he had enough circumstantial evidence, decided to interrogate her. It was a hard decision to make, as she held a Swedish diplomatic passport. Legally she was not a diplomat or a relative of a diplomat accredited to the United States, and so she had no real diplomatic immunity in the United States. Still, tradition goes that the holder of a diplomatic passport receives from the authorities especially courteous treatment unless surprised, *flagrante delicto*, in the act of violating the law. Had she been violating laws against the security of the United States? It was not positive, but she was certainly suspected of having done so. The security officer decided that the chance to make sure was worth the rebuke he might receive later.

Taking advantage of Mary's next trip to the United States, he confronted her upon her arrival at Miami Airport and asked her to follow him into his office.

Mary Eckberg was perfectly calm and did not even protest. She sat quietly and comfortably in her chair and refused to answer any questions. Hour after hour, the same questions were asked. Details of her previous activities were described to her and she did not react.

Finally it was getting late and everybody was tired. Mary Eckberg suddenly made up her mind. Looking directly at her interrogators, she said, "You are wasting your time. If you know anything about me, you should know that I never did anything to hurt the United States or Sweden. The only ones who may want me are the French. True, I hurt them badly, but why is it your business? I am not going to say any more. Do what you want with me."

The U.S. security officer knew that he could not keep her any longer. Maybe she was telling the truth. In any case, he had no proof she had ever done anything against the security of the United States. He let her go. The next day she was on her way back to Cuba and was never again seen in America.

The officer responsible for her temporary arrest was waiting for the reprimand he thought the State Department would surely convey to his headquarters. But weeks and months went by, and no mention was ever made of the incident. It was strange.

Security officers are like bankers and diplomats; they all know one another. One day the officer who had interrogated Mary Eckberg had the opportunity to discuss it with one of his Swedish colleagues. At the time Sweden was plagued with the Wennerstrom affair, and espionage was a serious government problem. Swedish security made inquiries and discovered that Mary Eckberg had never complained to the Swedish Ministry of Foreign Affairs for having been detained by U.S. security officers. Her behavior was considered strange, to say the least. She was the wife of a Swedish diplomat holding a diplomatic passport, and she should have immediately reported the Miami episode and the treatment she had received from U.S. authorities. The Swedish Foreign Affairs Secretary, not wanting to take any chances, called the Eckberg couple back to Stockholm.

Upon arrival, Mary Eckberg was interrogated by Swedish security. She denied everything, even her interrogation in the United States. All efforts to make her speak failed. Since no proof of wrongdoing could be found against her, the Swedes had to let her go. However, instead of being sent back to a foreign station, her husband received an obscure assignment.

Months went by. One morning, arriving at his office, the Swedish officer who had tried to interrogate Mary was very surprised to find her waiting for him. She had lost her composure and looked drawn and tired.

"My husband is unjustly suffering because of me. The position he has now is hopeless. I am ready to speak, but I want to be sure that my husband will get his former position back."

"I cannot promise anything," said the security officer, "but I will do my best."

"All right," said Mary, "I have to take a chance. First I want to tell you that I have not broken any law in Sweden. I love this

180

country and want to spend the rest of my life here. The only ones who may want me are the French and I don't think they ever heard of me. . . ."

And Mary told her story.

She was born in Poland. Before the war her parents migrated to France to work. She went to school and grew up there. Boys were attracted to her, but she didn't pay much attention to them at first. Then she discovered they would do anything she wanted to go to bed with her. It was a revelation. She did not care especially for boys, but she wanted many things, and she slept with the one who could provide what she wanted at the moment. When France was occupied by Germany, she followed one of her favorite boyfriends into a Polish Communist underground network. Knowing how to distribute her favors for the most benefit, she was a great help to her fellow conspirators and extracted much secret intelligence from her German bed partners.

At the end of the war, she went back to Poland and worked with her friends as an agent of the Polish secret services. She was assigned to watch the French diplomatic mission. Using her usual tactics, she had an affair with André Robineau, who was a young bachelor always bragging about his war adventures. Each day she would describe to her Polish boss the people Robineau met and what she could overhear. She would also, when Robineau was sleeping, take his keys and go into his office. Searching the drawers and safe, she would pass her find through the window to another agent waiting in the street. The same agent would bring all the documents back later and she replaced them carefully exactly where they had been. After closing the doors she would return to Robineau's room, put the key back in his pocket and join him in bed. Mary Eckberg carried on her deception until Robineau was arrested. . . .

So, twelve years after it happened, we were to learn how our complete network had been wiped out in Poland. Mary Eckberg alone had been able to uncover more than a hundred French agents. Because of her some of them were shot and others are still spending their lives in jail if they are not dead. After twelve years the problem was solved. Or was it?

I still wonder why Robineau always denied he had ever met Mary Eckberg and why French counterespionage closed the case with that phony story about the Polish widow of the French military attaché.

In 1963, Robineau was still a member of SDECE, working at headquarters.

Later, I was to learn that nobody really wanted the truth to come out.

In the 1780s, Joseph Balsamo, calling himself the Count of Cagliostro, arrived in Paris. He was a Freemason and an expert in occultism. He soon set up in the French capital a Lodge of the Egyptian Rite of which he was the Grand Master. No one ever knew who was behind him, but in a few months he became very popular.

At the time, Louis XVI was King of France. Marie Antoinette, his frivolous Austrian-born wife, was disliked by her subjects.

The high-ranking Freemasons were very liberal, although most of their members belonged to the nobility. Cagliostro, through his connections with Freemasonry, became a friend and adviser of the Cardinal de Rohan who, as the French ambassador in Vienna, had negotiated the marriage of Louis XVI and Marie Antoinette. The cardinal had no secrets from Cagliostro. He told him how he fell hopelessly in love with the future queen of France while escorting her from Austria to Paris. Aware of the possibilities this confidence opened for him, Cagliostro plotted an extraordinary deception. He arranged for the cardinal to meet a young woman impersonating the queen, who gave him reason to hope. Another woman posing as a lady in waiting told him of the great desire of the queen for a marvelous diamond necklace. In order to help his courtship and upon the advice of Cagliostro, Rohan bought the diamond necklace on credit and gave it to the so-called lady in waiting for her mistress. Naturally the necklace disappeared, and when Rohan was unable to meet the first payment, the jewelers went directly to the queen asking for their money or the necklace. The queen, knowing nothing of the plot, referred the creditors to Louis XVI, who simply ordered the arrest of Rohan and his confederates.

A great trial in the Paris Parliament followed in 1786. Cagliostro had so cleverly woven his plot that the judges and public were convinced of the queen's complicity. The case was dismissed. The cardinal, Cagliostro, and the girl who had impersonated the queen were released, and one among the conspirators was sentenced to be flogged and branded.

The queen's reputation was tarnished forever, and the monarch was never able to get over the blow to his prestige. Seven years later, the king and queen were beheaded.

France got a new constitution.

In 1950, history repeated itself. The plot and personages were different, but the dark forces behind them and the results were the same, when what we referred to as the generals' scandal came to light.

One morning at the end of May in 1949, I was discussing some documents with SDECE director Henri Ribière when the door of his office was abruptly opened. Colonel Fourcaud, the deputy director, came in, excited as usual and holding a cable.

"General Revers wants me to join him in Indochina. He is a friend of mine and I think I should go. Our service and the Army have to cooperate with each other."

Henri Ribière took the cable and quietly read it.

"You know nothing about Indochina," the director remarked.

"It is not a question of knowing about Indochina, but of arranging for special operations. General Revers has talked his plan over with me and I am convinced he needs me. You would not want to refuse my assistance to the Army Chief of Staff?"

Ribière, always very cold, gave the cable back to Fourcaud.

"If General Revers needs you, he should let me know. I have not received any request from him yet."

"All right," replied Fourcaud. "You will receive one by tomorrow. In the meantime, may I get ready for the trip?"

"Ask me when I have the general's request," answered Ribière.

Fourcaud left, closing the door brusquely.

Since the Passy case, relations between my boss and his deputy had been uneasy, but at least they were once more on speaking terms. Fourcaud's moods followed an unusual sinusoidal line. Sometimes his manners would be rude and discourteous, but he could at other times be warm and affectionate as only Slavs can be. The even-tempered and solid Henri Ribière never had any confidence in him.

Fourcaud tirelessly submitted crazy schemes, phony plans, and unworkable operations for the director's approval. His projects were sometimes so foolish that he succeeded in making Ribière smile, which seldom happened. After he had left that day, Henri Ribière smiled.

"I wonder about an Army Chief of Staff who needs Fourcaud's advice. Please ask Jacques Mary to come in. If Fourcaud goes to Indochina, I want Mary, who is familiar with the country, to accompany him. He may be able to prevent the worst."

The next day a cable arrived from General Revers requesting Fourcaud's help. He left the same night in the company of Jacques Mary, a colonial administrator who had lived in Indochina during the war. Mary was very bright and was well acquainted with the problems of the Far East. During the war he had courageously refused under torture to answer questions asked by the Kempeitai. His calmness in every situation was a guarantee that Fourcaud would have to use some restraint.

A couple of weeks later, they returned.

Fourcaud was delighted, importantly telling everyone that he was now going to help General Revers write his report. Jacques Mary reported on our station in Saigon. He had enjoyed Fourcaud's company and found him a good traveling companion. We soon forgot about the trip. Not for long . . .

Our service in Saigon, among other things, monitored all the broadcasts made by the Vietminh. At the end of August 1949, our

185

chief of station cabled us that a Vietminh commentator had read a report on the situation in Indochina which he claimed had been written by General Revers. A complete story of this monitoring was forwarded to French High Commissioner Pignon, who in turn passed it on to his superior, the Secretary for Overseas Territory. The Prime Minister and the Minister for National Defense studied the Vietminh broadcast and recognized it as an accurate reproduction of part of the Revers report which they had received personally from the general. This report consisted of two parts, one political, the other military. Only the political part had been made public.

At the time, the North Atlantic Treaty had been signed and the French government was particularly sensitive about any scandal involving the military establishment, for fear of jeopardizing the agreement. The United States had often complained about the lack of security in France, and the former U.S. naval attaché in Paris, Admiral Hillenkoeter, who had become director of the newly organized Central Intelligence Agency, was known to have little confidence in the ability of the French High Command to keep anything secret from the Communists. To avoid further difficulties with the Americans, the members of the government who knew about the Revers report leak to the Vietminh decided not to mention it. The incident would, they hoped, go unnoticed.

In the SDECE our counterespionage division had been investigating a very disturbing case since the beginning of the year. A Communist journalist, Jean Lautissier, had read several top secret documents coming from our service during one of the meetings of the French Union Assembly of which he was a member. The documents dealt with Indochina. The Minister for National Defense had asked the military justice to prosecute Lautissier, but the journalist, as a member of the French Union Assembly, was protected by parliamentary immunity. We had to wait for the end of his term.

The suspect was kept under surveillance. On August 17 he had left for Indochina in the company of a Miss Autissier, a journalist with the official French Communist Party newspaper L'Humanité. Four days after his arrival in Saigon, the Vietminh radio was broadcasting the Revers report and also a plan for the reorganization of our services of intelligence in Indochina.

Was Lautissier the courier who had leaked parts of the Revers report to the Vietminh? What were his sources? Obviously he had some in our service to have been able to get the documents. And if he had contacts in our agency, he could have sources in the offices of the Army Chief of Staff as well.

General Blaizot, who was in command of the Army in Indochina, told one of our station's officers in Saigon that he believed Lautissier had received the Revers report in Paris and had given it to the Vietminh. When questioned later, General Blaizot refused to give the source of his information. His relationship with General Revers was not the best, and we could not tell whether or not he had spoken out of spite.

The leaking of the Army Chief of Staff's report presented a problem of jurisdiction for the security services. According to the law, the agency for Territorial Security of the Sûreté was in charge of all counterespionage activities in metropolitan France, while SDECE assumed responsibility for counterespionage work in foreign countries. As in the FBI, the Sûreté had police power and could make arrests, while SDECE, like the CIA, could only search for information.

Counterespionage officers in SDECE were frustrated at not being able to follow their respective cases through to the end without having to hand them over to the Sûreté whenever legal action was needed. The members of the Sûreté, for their part, were critical of our officers, claiming that they were careless in the research of information and the collection of enough evidence to make cases legally airtight. Furthermore, the Sûreté was against SDECE's carrying on any research in France, but the SDECE officers continued to work the foreign embassies in Paris, arguing that in view of the extraterritoriality of all diplomatic installations, embassy grounds should be considered foreign soil.

The undeclared war between the two services, as far as counterespionage matters were concerned, became more acute over the issue of the leaking of the Chief of Staff's report. As civilians, Sûreté agents were suspicious of SDECE counterespionage military officers and felt they might try to cover up the mistakes made by other army officers. For that reason they did not want them to have any part in conducting the inquiries. But Indochina was completely outside the Sûreté's sphere of control, thus the SDECE was able to get involved.

Henri Ribière tried to stay out of this conflict over jurisdiction, and his standing orders were for the SDECE counterespionage division not to get entangled in the Sûreté cases. He had no reason to suspect his orders were being disobeyed. He knew the Sûreté was working on the Revers case and waited quietly to hear about their findings. But the idea of possible leaks in his service, to the benefit of Lautissier and his Communist associates, was constantly on his mind. He gave orders to Colonel Verneuil to reinforce security and to keep investigating the Lautissier case.

In the middle of the following month, the Defense Secretary, a friend of Henri Ribière, told him about a recent incident in a Paris railway station.

The Gare du Nord is like Grand Central in New York. Through it, French workers living in the crowded northern suburbs of Paris, where housing is cheaper, commute to work every day. The place is always a madhouse, with people running in all directions. The bus stops in front of the station are perhaps the most confused, filled with nervous, crowded, pushing groups of people. Office workers, often late for work, are determined not to miss the bus which is ready to pull out.

French buses have, or had at the time, a rear platform with no passenger limitation. Anyone who could squeeze on was allowed to ride. There was normally standing room for about ten people, but during rush hours, twenty-five would crowd against one another, with still more people at each stop fighting to get on. The ticket collector, in such instances, desperately pulls the bell cord, as in San Francisco cable cars, to signal the driver to keep going and bypass the next stop. But the traffic is such that the vehicle comes to a stop every twenty feet, with more people trying to hang on.

On this September day one particular bus was full. As the vehicle was pulling out, people crowded around making a last attempt to climb on. A French soldier in uniform was desperately trying to unhook the chain closing the rear platform. If someone on the bus had made a move or given him a hand, the young man could have made it. But the passengers were not concerned with anyone but themselves. Looking up, he spotted the passenger blocking the entrance. He was an Indochinese. The soldier had just returned from a two-year tour in Indochina.

"Please unhook the chain for me."

The Annamite paid no attention.

"Look," the soldier said, "did you hear me?"

Still no answer.

Tired of running behind the bus, the Frenchman flushed, saying with anger, "Look, yellow bastard, are you going to help me on, or do you want a punch on the nose?"

The Indochinese remained impassive.

Pulling himself up in a last effort, the soldier gained just enough balance to unhook the chain. He jumped on and did exactly as he had threatened — he punched the Annamite on the nose. The other man returned the blow. Losing all control, the uniformed man let go with a series of lightning blows until the conductor, desperately hanging on the bell cord, stopped the bus and called a nearby policeman for help. The two antagonists were arrested, handcuffed, pushed into a police car, and driven to the nearest precinct station. There they were frisked, booked, and locked in separate cells.

Looking through the Annamite's personal possessions, a police officer noticed several sheets of paper marked "Top Secret." Intrigued, but not knowing what to do, the officer called for his superior to come down and have a look at the suspicious documents. The Police Chief called the Sûreté. An inspector was immediately dispatched and, after a quick glance at the papers, recognized them as the top secret report written by General Revers, the French Army Chief of Staff.

The Annamite and all his belongings were transferred to the Sûreté headquarters located in rue des Saussaies. The Indochinese refused to volunteer any information, but his papers spoke for him. His name was Do Dai Phuoc. He was a Vietminh. Twice taken prisoner by the French Army in Indochina, he had been pardoned. After a short stay in London, he registered at the Sorbonne at the University of Paris to complete a Master's degree in law. He had been a delegate to the World Congress of Peace Advocates in Paris and to the Communist Youth Congress in Budapest. Actually, he was one of Ho Chi Minh's secret representatives in the French capital.

An entry in the Indochinese's address book, under the letter V, read "Van Co, 41 Rue Vaneau (General Revers)."

This was too much of a coincidence. The police inspectors, equipped with a search warrant, went directly to the Van Co address. There they found a duplicating machine and thirty-seven copies of the top secret Revers report. Van Co's residence was in a different location, and a search by the police brought the seizure of many files and accounting books.

Houang Van Co was a well-known figure in Paris, where he had lived most of his life. He was a member of the French Socialist Party and the personal representative of General Xuan, then Prime Minister of Bao-Dai (the Emperor of Vietnam). Editor of the pro-Bao-Dai newspaper *Horizon Vietnamien*, Van Co was also the head of the Bao-Dai lobby in Paris. He knew everybody important and everybody important knew him. When arrested by officers of the Sûreté, he pretended to be protected by diplomatic immunity in his capacity as Bao-Dai's representative, but it was not so. His functions were unofficial, and the case was much too important for anyone in the police to grant him a favor. He was taken into custody.

At Sûreté headquarters, Van Co was interrogated for thirty-six hours. He claimed to have received the report from a mysterious individual called Roger Peyre, who gave it to him on behalf of General Mast, President of the War College.

While one team of Sûreté inspectors were kept busy with Van Co, another team searched a house located at 14 and 16 Avenue du Parc in Vanves, a Paris suburb. It was the residence of a certain Mai Trung Tu, known as a secret representative of Ho Chi Minh. In one of his desk drawers, the police found another copy of General Revers' report. This copy was more complete than the ones found at Van Co's office. Several schedules dealing with the military situation were included. Mai Trung Tu admitted having received the document from Vinh Xa, another Vietminh agent. Both men were arrested and taken to the Sûreté.

The law officers, their hands full of documents and reports, left Vinh Xa alone in a room, waiting his turn to be called for interrogation. He seized the opportunity to write a letter to his wife and tried later to smuggle it out. The letter was intercepted by the Sûreté. In it he instructed his wife to ask Roger Peyre to retain the lawyer André le Troquer, who was also Vice-President of the French House of Representatives, for his defense.

This was the second time the name of Roger Peyre had come up in connection with the case. Police officers were sent to his home with orders to bring him back to headquarters. A search in their files had turned up a great deal of information about him. In 1938 he had declared bankruptcy and later had been sentenced to two years in jail for receiving stolen property. During the war he was a member of the PPF, a fascist organization supported by the Germans and their Vichy associates. After the hostilities, he offered his services to the DGER (French secret services) to help uncover a network of PPF brown-shirts who were trying to regroup in Paris. Working on his tips, the police were able to dismantle the network and arrest all its members. The Communist newspapers, without mentioning Peyre's part in the case, headlined the story and, for a change, lauded the police action. More than forty arrests had been made, and the ringleader, a certain Amedeo, had confessed completely.

In 1948, Peyre was prosecuted in a special court for his membership in the PPF. General Revers had testified in his favor, stating that Peyre was working for the underground when he joined the pro-Nazi organization, where he had been able to gather intelligence which was highly appreciated by the Allies. After such testimony on the part of the Army Chief of Staff, the case against Peyre had been dismissed.

Later, Peyre took a job with a textile company. His relations with French intelligence became intermittent and then stopped altogether.

There was not much in the file to help the interrogators direct their questions along the lines of the present charges. So they resorted to candid questions while their colleagues were busy studying the documents found in Peyre's home. At first, Peyre was not very cooperative, but when the inspectors were able to ask more specific questions, he knew it would be of no use to deny the truth they would inevitably discover.

191

Peyre admitted he had given the Revers report to Van Co and he explained why. His reasons were so incredible that the inspectors were absolutely amazed. He first emphasized his intimate friendship with the French Chief of Staff, whose point of view on many political problems, particularly on Indochina, he shared without reservation. General Revers did not agree with the political line followed by the government in the Far East and was in favor of replacing the actual High Commissioner, a civilian, by a military man. His candidate for this high position was General Mast, director of the Institut des Hautes Études de la Défense Nationale, the French War College. General Revers had asked Peyre to organize a campaign in favor of General Mast, and Peyre had introduced the general to many people able to support his candidacy. During several lunches and dinners, the situation in Southeast Asia was discussed and Peyre happened to mention Van Co, the Bao-Dai representative with whom he was on friendly terms. General Mast suggested that Peyre give Van Co a copy of the report written by General Revers, and try to obtain, through him, the support of Bao-Dai for the position of High Commissioner in Indochina.

Peyre's testimony showed how Van Co got the report, but Van Co was known as an enemy of the Vietminh, and the copy found in Vinh Xa's office could not possibly have come from him. Peyre was asked if he knew Vinh Xa. He denied it. The investigators knew, however, that after his arrest, Vinh Xa had directed his wife to contact Peyre immediately for help. Still Peyre denied knowing him. It was a deadlock. Then, in studying several appointment books seized in Peyre's home, the inspectors found mention of Vinh Xa's name in Peyre's handwriting. Disconcerted, Peyre then admitted General Mast had asked him to show the report to Vinh Xa and he had allowed him to keep it for twenty-four hours.

To give the report to Van Co was, in the first place, a serious offense. Still, Van Co was a friend of France. But to go as far as to turn it over to the Vietminh representative, when French soldiers were being killed every day by its members, was high treason — at least in the minds of the Sûreté inspectors. . . .

In a hurry now, they sifted the documents found in Peyre's and Van Co's homes, and questioned both men exhaustively on their findings.

Van Co's check and accounting books showed he had paid large amounts of money on several occasions to a Mr. Paul. Van Co immediately explained that Mr. Paul was an alias of Peyre, and the money was to be used to support the campaign in favor of General Mast's nomination as High Commissioner. Peyre, when separately interrogated, told exactly the same thing. He had used the alias of Mr. Paul for many years and he gave a detailed account of the money received from Van Co.

He had spent about $3,000 for a trip to Saigon in May of 1949. Then in June he made a first payment of $5,000 to General Mast and one of $5,000 to General Revers. Later, in July, General Revers received another $5,000, General Mast $7,000, and André le Troquer, the House of Representatives Vice-President, $3,000.

The case was becoming more and more intricate, and the part played by the French Army Chief of Staff and by the head of the French War College appeared shabby and despicable, to say the least.

The director of the Sûreté, Pierre Bertaux, and his deputy, Roger Wybot, who was in charge of Territorial Security, became apprehensive about what the inquiry could eventually reveal. Before going any further they called on their superior, Secretary of the Interior Jules Moch, to report their findings. The meeting took place at 6 A.M. on September 22, 1949. One hour later, at 7 A.M., they all went for a briefing to the Prime Minister and the Defense Minister. Both men had jumped out of bed after hearing Jules Moch's account of the situation. The deliberation lasted several hours. During this time the Sûreté investigators, still searching Peyre's residence, came across files containing very compromising letters from both generals to Peyre.

The Defense Minister called the head of the Military Justice Department to his office for consultation. The problem was clear — French law gave to the Secretary of Defense full power to decide whether or not a document should be classified "Secret." Should the minister rule the report "Secret," then General Revers, General Mast, and all their confederates ought to be arrested and charged with the crime of treason. If, on the other hand, the document was not classified, no crime had been committed, and Van Co, Vinh Xa, and Peyre had to be released immediately. All documents seized during the searches would have to be returned to their owners, including the copies of the Revers report.

The secretary of defense, Paul Ramadier, was faced with an agonizing decision. There was ample evidence for conviction against the generals and their accomplices. In their search of power and greed for material gain they had sullied their reputations, and the scandal from their arrest would reflect on the whole French Army. The North Atlantic Treaty was five months old, and the Allies would become suspicious of all French officers on the integrated international staff. The generals had to be punished, but was a public trial the best solution as far as the interests of the state were concerned?

Paul Ramadier, who previously as prime minister had thrown the Communists out of the government, was an honest man, completely dedicated to his country. All day he struggled with the vexatious situation. To let the generals go unpunished was unjust, but to jeopardize NATO on their account would be a calamity. After long reflection and a meeting with the prime minister, the defense secretary came to a decision. Calling the head of the Military Justice Division to his office, he ruled that the Revers report was not secret. The case was closed.

Yielding to the secretary's reasons, but unable to hide their disappointment over the fact that the culprits would go unscathed, Sûreté director Bertaux and his deputy Roger Wybot started back to headquarters to sign the release of the suspects and order the restitution of all documents and other items seized during the searches.

Meanwhile, Paul Ramadier summoned General Revers to his office and confronted him with the evidence. Later he did the same with General Mast. They could deny neither their campaign against the government's politics in Indochina, nor their endeavor to get control of the High Commissioner's post in Saigon, but both gave their word of honor that they had not received any amount of money from Peyre or Van Co.

General Revers and General Mast could be credited with many years in the service of the Army, and the Secretary of Defense chose not to insist. General Revers was fifty-nine years old. He had started out as a civil servant in the Post Office Department and

194

fought during World War I as a reserve officer. Offered the opportunity to stay in the Army as an active officer at the end of the war, he rose slowly to colonel, the rank he still held at the beginning of World War II. Following France's defeat, he became Chief of Staff for Admiral Darlan. Unlike his chief, he made friends in the underground movement and later became chief of the underground Army organization. This gave him enough push to attain later his present position as Army Chief of Staff.

In recognition of his past, Paul Ramadier asked him to submit his resignation voluntarily. General Revers agreed to do so in the immediate future.

The case of General Mast was slightly different in view of the reputation he had acquired. In 1942 he was already a major general in command of a division in Algeria. Because of his friendship with Robert Murphy, the American consul in Algiers, he had been chosen as the French Army representative to meet with General Clark during his secret trip to North Africa as General Eisenhower's envoy. General Mast's part in the American landing during the "Torch" operation had won him a certain prestige, and he held, for more than four years, the position of French Resident in Tunisia, prior to his nomination as the head of the War College. To have occupied so many high positions should have taught him to be more circumspect in his everyday life. The conspiracy he had hatched was disgusting, and Ramadier showed him no mercy. Taking his age into consideration — he was sixty-one — Ramadier decided to retire him immediately.

During the next two months, the periodic political crisis in the French government brought about the resignation of the Prime Minister and his cabinet. Georges Bidault took over. In the following days he received a letter from General Revers advising him that he was withdrawing his resignation. The government paid little attention to this late maneuver and, in the beginning of December, General Revers was replaced as Chief of Staff.

All should have been over, and the case only a sour memory in the minds of the people involved. However, it is all but impossible for a democratic government really to put a tight lid on a scandal. Eventually it comes to light.

A few days before Christmas, the government learned that the correspondent of *Time* magazine in Paris was about to publish an account of the real reason behind the departure of Generals Revers and Mast.

It happens that governments in many countries consider journalists an excellent source of information and systematically monitor their communications. In Paris, the *Time* bureau's teletype as well as all its telephones were connected to recorders, and so the French government got word of the article written by the *Time* bureau chief, Andre Laguerre, a well-known journalist. American born but with a French background, he had joined the Free French during the war and earned a good reputation as a man of courage and high intelligence. He was completely integrated into the French team and no one thought of him as being American until one day he said goodbye to his friends and returned home to the United States. Everyone on de Gaulle's staff was indignant. They had assumed he would take back the citizenship of his ancestors and keep his official position. Unable to understand his departure, they sent a confidential memorandum to all departments stating that Laguerre should be treated with the utmost discrimination by people who knew him, since he was suspected of being a member of American intelligence.

My recollection of this memorandum proved very useful when government members began hinting that Laguerre, known as a supporter of de Gaulle, had written his article at the suggestion of the Gaullist party, the RPF. I was able to locate and produce the memo against Laguerre, bearing the signature of de Gaulle's chief of staff, and no one dared to mention such a ridiculous assumption again. Andre Laguerre was just a good journalist who had come across a good story.

Still, the French government, so set in its habit of controlling the news in France, naturally thought that the U.S. government could use the same leverage with the American press. The French Ambassador, Henri Bonnet, received orders to ask the State Department to stop publication of the Laguerre article in *Time*. The French request was indignantly rejected, and the controversial article was published, raising a storm which shattered the already shaky foundation of the Fourth Republic.

In SDECE we followed with sad amusement the convulsions of

the actors in this drama. Our service was not involved, at least so we thought. Besides, we had our hands full with the Robineau case and several others, and paid little attention to an affair of no direct concern to us.

Henri Ribière, like all heads of large intelligence organizations, had to travel a great deal. NATO was being set up, and his attendance was required at many meetings of the Western intelligence community. During his absences Colonel Fourcaud was in charge, but he was also gone frequently, tending to operations of his own. When both Ribière and Fourcaud were away from Paris, a written memorandum instructed the division chiefs to report to me. I also had the responsibility of maintaining liaison with the President of the Republic and the Prime Minister.

In the middle of January 1950, Henri Ribière left for Italy on a trip that had been planned for some time. Colonel Fourcaud left for Strasbourg and Germany. The Revers-Mast case was then making headlines in all the French and foreign newspapers. Prime Minister Georges Bidault had given a speech before the French Assembly of Representatives, outlining the real story and answering questions raised by the press. In order to refute the Communists' accusation that the government had tried to hide the truth, the deputies of the majority requested a congressional investigation, which was voted for by all the deputies but the Communists.

Public opinion was particularly aroused because Peyre not only had been released but had left for an unknown destination, making the establishment of the truth almost impossible. Newspapers hinted that he had received help and money to aid his flight and pay for his silence. The Communists put the blame on the government, which was trying, they said, to hush up the scandal.

After the issue had been brought up in the Assembly of Representatives, General Mast, in a statement to the press, rejected all the accusations against him and explained his connection with Peyre by claiming he was an agent for the SDECE. The newspapers, which had been very critical of our agency in connection with the Robineau case, began wondering what part SDECE had played in the messy story.

I was feeling comfortable about the innuendos, sure that we had nothing whatsoever to do with the matter. I knew Peyre had been in contact with our Paris station in the past, but it was several years before and bore no relation to the Revers case. So when I received a telephone call from Paul Auriol, son of the President of the Republic and one of his personal assistants, asking me to come to see him with all information I had on the case, I went to Elysée Palace empty-handed.

Paul Auriol had several questions the President wanted answered. They dealt with an investigation conducted by the SDECE on the Revers report; an interrogation of Peyre by our officers; and the fact that an attorney had been present during the interrogation. I spontaneously answered I had heard of neither an investigation nor an interrogation. I was aware that Peyre had been an informer for our Paris station. His complete file had recently been forwarded to the Secretary of Defense, at his request. I told Paul Auriol he must be mistaken, since the Sûreté alone had investigated the case. He asked me to confirm this, and to send him any information I could gather.

Back in my office, I called in Colonel Verneuil and discussed with him the points raised by the head of state. Verneuil was usually very composed, but his face was flushed when I urged him to tell me everything he knew. I had great confidence in his honesty and I was right — very much abashed, he filled me in on some interesting details.

Peyre had been an agent of SDECE until 1967, when he involved his case officer in a shady deal, causing both men to be fired. Nevertheless, Peyre managed, sometime later, to make contact with Captain Girardot, another officer from SDECE.

Girardot was a bright counterespionage officer who had spent several years in German prison camps. He had worked for a long time on Central Europe and for that reason a few months before had been transferred from counterespionage to a newly created division in charge of keeping a watch on Central European immigrants in Paris.

Peyre, who knew some Yugoslav diplomats, offered his help to Girardot, who accepted gladly. On the same day he had set up an appointment for Girardot to meet a Yugoslav diplomat anxious to sell some of his government's secrets, Peyre was arrested by the Sûreté in connection with the Revers report leaks.

After Peyre's release, Colonel Verneuil, still anxious to obtain more evidence against Lautissier, who undoubtedly had passed secret documents to the Vietminh, asked Captain Girardot to see Peyre and try to establish his connections, if any, with Lautissier. Girardot paid a visit to Peyre, but nothing new came out of their conversation.

Now Colonel Verneuil had a strong feeling of guilt for not having told Henri Ribière or myself of that meeting. I was quite unhappy over the incident and suspected Colonel Verneuil knew more than he admitted. I decided to find out and summoned Captain Girardot to my office.

I had not met him before, but he gave the impression of someone carrying a heavy burden. He was hesitant in speaking about his relationship with Peyre, whom evidently he considered more as an influential acquaintance than an agent. Such an attitude was wrong, but I was not interested in Girardot's professional mistakes — he had a superior to take care of them. I wanted to hear the truth about the details of his last meeting with Peyre. With some reluctance Girardot recounted them.

After he received Colonel Verneuil's order to see Peyre, Girardot was summoned to Colonel Fourcaud's office by one of his assistants. Referring to his relationship with Peyre, Fourcaud told him it was necessary to save General Revers at any price, not only for the honor of the French Army but to resolve problems of internal politics which he (Girardot) could not understand. Fourcaud offered in exchange for Peyre's cooperation to provide him with anything he would need, such as money, support to escape, etc.

Girardot went to see Peyre and, with the help of Peyre's lawyer, Mr. Rochas, tried to convince him to change his testimony. Reluctantly, Peyre agreed. Now denying that he had given General Revers $10,000, he claimed to have used it himself for personal needs. However, he maintained his former statements about the money handed over to General Mast and André le Troquer. Peyre's new testimony, witnessed by Rochas and Girardot, was recorded in shorthand and transcribed by a secretary.

Elated, Girardot went immediately to General Revers with the news. The general was very appreciative and Girardot was gratified to have been instrumental in saving the honor of a five-star general, the Army Chief of Staff. He also reported to Colonel Fourcaud on the success of his mission and gave him Peyre's modified statement. To oblige General Revers, the colonel sent him a copy, then told Girardot to report his meeting with Peyre through regular channels. He added that he could help Peyre escape and offered to have a plane take him wherever he chose to go. Indeed, this would have been easy for Fourcaud since his brother was in command of the SDECE special wing and had a certain number of planes at his disposal. Girardot saw Peyre again the next day and gave him a copy of his statement.

A month later, Peyre and his family boarded the SS *Campana* in Marseille and discreetly sailed to Rio de Janeiro.

I asked Girardot if he had anything to do with Peyre's departure. His answer was negative and I believed him. Anyway, his account was quite a surprise to me, and I requested a copy of Peyre's testimony as well as of any other statements made the same afternoon. Girardot promised and kept his word.

In trying to save Revers, Fourcaud had involved the service, and we would have to take the consequences of his act. I discussed this at length with Colonel Verneuil, who reacted strictly in a military manner. Fourcaud outranked him and he could not openly criticize him. When I asked him to initiate an investigation on Fourcaud's attempt to whitewash General Revers, Colonel Verneuil insisted that he could not do it unless he received a direct order from Henri Ribière. I immediately placed a call to the director in Italy and briefed him on the course of events. Ribière confirmed my instructions. It was now imperative for us and for the government to know the truth.

Paul Auriol was not surprised when I reported Girardot's story. General Revers had already told the President that Peyre's testimony to the Sûreté was worthless since he was under pressure at the time and was deprived of the advice of an attorney, while his second account reflected the truth and had been witnessed by his lawyer. Revers complained to the head of state that he had been persecuted by the Secretary for Overseas Territories, who had fabricated the case against him.

I was not aware of any fabrication, but in the light of Girardot's statement, one thing was certain — if we were confronted with any kind of conspiracy, it had been led by Fourcaud to clear General Revers "at any price."

There was not much I could do except wait for the return of Henri Ribière and for the results of Colonel Verneuil's inquiry on Fourcaud's involvement. The case was complicated enough, and I had no idea that two more incidents would occur the same day to make it an enigma I would understand only much later.

First, a young man who had previously worked with me and was now assigned to the central files division came to me with a surprising report. The head of his division, Folliguet, had been visited the previous evening by General Revers, who was a member of his Masonic lodge. The general was "in tears" and begged Folliguet to help him prove his innocence. Folliguet was presently busy gathering all the files on individuals connected with the case. He was due to give a copy of them to the general the same day.

Again I told Colonel Verneuil about this new development. He told me his service had received, the day before, a request from Folliguet for forwarding all the dossiers connected with the case, especially Peyre's and Revers', in order to check "if they were complete." Furthermore, security guards at the entrance of the building acknowledged that General Revers' chauffeur had come to pick up a large envelope from . . . Folliguet. Colonel Verneuil immediately ordered the dossiers back from central files, but he had no way to be sure they were complete. I decided to speak with Folliguet. His explanation was less than enlightening and did not satisfy me. The fact that he went directly to Fourcaud's office after leaving me added one more piece to the puzzle.

Before the day was over I was burdened with another unexpected complication. The evening newspapers had reproduced a letter sent by Peyre to a friend in Tunisia. In the short message he mentioned the help he had received in escaping from "Albert and H.R." Journalists had no difficulty in identifying "Albert" as Albert Bouzanquet, head of a socialist union. The initials "H.R." they assigned to Henri Ribière. . . . The director of SDECE was now accused of facilitating the flight of Peyre, the adventurer and con man.

Two days earlier I had thought the SDECE was not involved,

and we were now at the center of the scandal. Not alone, I must say, in playing the riddle game, the Communist newspapers and naturally their cohorts, the Gaullists newspapers, began to imply that the name Paul found in Van Co's check book was not an alias for Peyre, but the first name of the son of the most important man in France — meaning Paul Auriol, the President's son.

Henri Ribière stayed imperturbed by my calls and reports. He returned a few days later, as previously planned. Upon his arrival, he summoned all the division chiefs and Colonel Fourcaud for a meeting. Questioning all those concerned, he requested that Colonel Fourcaud explain his orders to Captain Girardot. Fourcaud denied everything, became abusive, and openly accused the President of the Republic and his son of being behind the whole case and receiving graft money. Keeping cool and using as few words as possible, Ribière asked Colonel Fourcaud to leave the room. Everyone was dumbfounded. The meeting continued and Ribière gave his orders: every member of the agency involved in any way with one of the individuals under suspicion was to make a written statement. These would be sent immediately to the Sûreté.

After personally hearing Girardot's account, Henri Ribière paid a visit to Sûreté chief Bertaux and gave him a full report. Since the apparent conspiracy had been conducted on French soil, the SDECE had no jurisdiction, and the Sûreté alone could pursue the investigation.

Fourcaud, two of his assistants, and Girardot were called to the Sûreté. First they were questioned separately then confronted with one another. Captain Girardot did not waver from his original testimony. Colonel Fourcaud denied everything, accusing the socialist members of the cabinet of having covered the mistakes made by the generals. He kept contradicting himself, while Girardot's sincerity left no doubt.

The newspapers, not aware of what was happening behind the scenes, were conducting a campaign against SDECE and its director. In the National Assembly, the deputies could not agree on the composition of the Commission of Inquiry. After prolonged discussion, it was decided that all parties would be represented, and thus a Communist, Kriegel-Valrimont, was nominated. He was one of the

202

leaders of the Communist underground during the war and was now one of the high-ranking French Communists in contact with NKVD — predecessor of KGB. His appointment to the Commission of Inquiry was interpreted as proof of the Soviets' interest in the case.

The commission set to work. Witnesses testified behind closed doors. The Communist Kriegel-Valrimont gave daily accounts of the proceeds to the Communist paper *L'Humanité*. Other members of the commission, competing with him, reported to the dailies of their own parties. Soon all the newspapers published full pages on the commission's work. At least the French public could make its own judgment.

Letters sent by General Revers to Peyre were made public. They showed that, for several years, the Chief of Staff had consulted with him on all French military problems. He also had asked Peyre's help for his promotions and discussed with him assignments in the Ministry of Defense and in the Army. Testifying about Peyre, General Revers described him as "much more powerful than me." The general was asked countless questions on what made Peyre so powerful, but he pleaded ignorance.

Everyone involved in the case was heard by the commission. For six months all of France read the accounts every day for new revelations, but nothing really new was uncovered. Politicians had received graft money — they naturally denied it, but circumstantial evidence was impressive. An ugly traffic in monetary exchange existed between Vietnam and France while French soldiers were being killed. The military was using unethical ways to influence the government. It was like a sewer suddenly opened. The public was nauseated by the dishonesty of their politicians and the administration. The Communists were the only ones to enjoy the mud-slinging.

Henri Ribière and Colonel Fourcaud both testified. Ribière explained how he had been kept in ignorance, and Fourcaud unexpectedly went into a tirade against the Secretary of the Interior, Jules Moch, accusing him of forfeiture. Fourcaud was angered by the implicating Sûreté report on his endeavor to whitewash General Revers. Assuming attack would be his best defense, he accused Jules Moch of trying to put the lid on the case. The Communists were only too happy to find an ally against their worst enemy. Jules Moch was the one who had put down their strikes and foiled their attempts to take power by force.

Supporting Fourcaud's point of view against all evidence, the Commission of Inquiry neglected its main objective and began concentrating on the Sûreté and the SDECE rather than investigating Generals Revers and Mast. Peyre himself remained undisturbed in Brazil. The commission never really tried to have him questioned.

In conclusion, the commission recommended that General Revers and General Mast be punished. The government decided they would be retired. This had already been done. Later, the National Assembly, voting on the commission's conclusions, censured Jules Moch for having hushed up the case. It was the most incoherent accusation ever brought against an innocent man, who had done his best to discover the truth. The Communists had prevailed with the help of those supposed to be their adversaries.

The commission had gathered enough evidence throughout the hearings to prove that Henri Ribière and Paul Auriol had never been involved with Peyre. The initials "H.R." in Peyre's letter were, as he stated later, those of his associate Henri Rossi.

At this stage the case would have been over as far as SDECE was concerned if one day, during the commission proceedings, Henri Ribière had not received a strange visitor with an even stranger request.

The visitor's name was Michel Dumesnil de Grammont, Grand Master of the *Grande Loge de France*. He very matter-of-factly asked Henri Ribiére — whom he thought was also a Freemason — to help whitewash General Revers. When he realized Henri Ribière had never been a member of any secret society — he had mistaken him for someone with a similar name — Dumesnil de Grammont, without losing his nerve, tried to make a deal. He promised Ribière the help of the Freemasonry to prove his noninvolvement in the case if he cooperated in favor of General Revers, hinting at hidden manaces if he did not. Ribière kept calm until the visitor finished speaking, then he told him to get out.

This was the second time Freemasonry had entered the case, the first being when the chief of our files department had passed on information to General Revers, his lodge brother. Was Freemasonry's motive one of solidarity for a member in trouble, or was there more to it? With Colonel Verneuil and several police inspectors who had helped Ribière organize the Paris police uprising before the liberation, we discovered a number of new facts which threw a strange light on this already peculiar case.

It can be said that French Freemasonry is made up of very dedicated men. Yet there has always been a small minority more interested in personal material advantages than in the high ideals of the secret society. French Freemasonry is very deeply divided into several factions. Neither of the two most important factions, the *Grand Orient* and the *Grande Loge*, is recognized by the American or the British Freemasonry because of their atheistic leanings.

Before World War II, French Freemasonry was successful in its aspiration to win political power. Membership in one of the lodges was a sure way to be promoted in the Army or in the administration. Due to the positions of responsibility they occupied, Freemasons were held responsible for the defeat of France and were persecuted by the Vichy government and by the Germans. Many joined the underground and fought gallantly. Others collaborated with the Germans. A small group belonging to the Martinist Order cooperated with the Pétain government as members of the Synarchy.

After the liberation the Freemasons cleaned house, expelling from their lodges those members whose behavior during the war was considered out of line. But checking their membership was made particularly difficult by the disappearance of all their archives and members' files. The Vichy government and later the Germans had seized all the documents found at the headquarters of the lodges and stored them in the former building of the Theosophic Society, 4 Rapp Square in Paris. Toward the end of the war Göring ordered all the archives removed and sent to Germany to be kept in an estate used by his propaganda organization. The estate was later occupied by the Russians, who confiscated all the documents and sent them to Moscow. Later the Freemasons asked for the return of their property, but the Russians flatly refused. The contents of the files must have been of special interest for the Soviets, since on October 4, 1945, the political committee of the French Communist

Party decided to allow Freemasons to become members of the party, repealing a prewar decision of the same committee prohibiting Communists from membership in the Freemasonry.

It soon proved difficult to conciliate the high ideals of speculative Masonry with the Marxist materialism, and fights between democrats and fellow travelers broke out in the two great factions. Jean Baylot, who became Paris Prefect of Police, headed the anti-Communist group, while Jacques Mitterand, the future Grand Master of the *Grande Loge*, led the pro-Soviet group. Reports received at SDECE gave many details on the struggle, including attempts by the Soviets to blackmail Freemasons with knowledge obtained from their secret files. This was to be corroborated much later when defectors from KGB testified about it.

General Revers had been a Freemason since his early days with the post office department. It was through the help of the Freemasonry that he had begun his military career. However, he turned his back on the secret society when he became Admiral Darlan's Chief of Staff.

Peyre was also a Mason, and though during the resistance he had been a double, if not a triple, agent, he succeeded in keeping his good standing with his lodge brothers.

How Revers and Peyre met was not revealed. Peyre never commented on it, and Revers gave two different accounts. Revers was a general, politically minded and very shrewd, whereas Peyre was a hosiery and notions salesman. General Revers was the leader of an important resistance network, while Peyre played a shady part as a member of a pro-Nazi organization, reporting on his associates. Freemasonry was their only tie, and in the secret society Peyre was the more influential because of the help he had given during the war to Michel Dumesnil de Grammont, the Grand Master of the *Grande Loge*.

Dumesnil de Grammont had been a member of *Libération Sud*, an important resistance network led by Emmanuel d'Astier de la Vigerie, known as the "Red Baron" because of his pro-Communist leanings and his friendship with Stalin. Dumesnil de Grammont was sent to Algiers in 1943 to represent *Libération Sud* at the Consultative Assembly, which played the part of a temporary Assembly of Representatives. In the years following the liberation, Dumesnil de

Grammont and Peyre saw each other very often, and it was with de Grammont's help that Peyre was able to support Revers for his promotion and his appointment to the highest position in the French Army. The notions salesman was the go-between, keeping the Masonry informed on what the Army Chief of Staff was doing and obtaining help for him when necessary. After his reinstatement in the Masonry, General Revers discovered that he had less influence in the organization than Peyre — hence his statement to the Commission of Inquiry: "Peyre was much more powerful than me." It was Dumesnil de Grammont who several times invited Revers or Mast, or both, to have dinner with important political personages like le Troquer, the National Assembly Vice-President. Naturally, Peyre was always present.

The investigation conducted by Henri Ribière had revealed members of the Freemasonry at each stage of the scandal. Van Co, Bao-Dai's representative who gave money to the generals, was a Mason, as were Peyre's other contacts. Furthermore, the President of the Commission of Inquiry, Paul Anxionnaz, is now the Grand Master of the *Grand Orient*. For his part, Fourcaud is known to have had several meetings with Dumesnil de Grammont before ordering Girardot to whitewash Revers "at any price."

Did Peyre involve the Freemasonry in the conspiracy through some subterfuge and against the will of his fellow members? Did Dumesnil de Grammont try to restrain the scandal? We were unable to establish these facts for certain, but one thing cannot be overlooked: since the government had ruled the Revers report "not secret" Peyre was not likely to be charged with any violation of the law, and his exile to escape prosecution was absolutely unnecessary. When he sailed to Brazil, leaving behind his business, his friends, his home, and so forth, Peyre did it only for his personal benefit. One month before he had had no intention of taking up residence in South America. His hasty departure was made in order to be unavailable to the investigators, and was no doubt well rewarded by the people who bought his silence. Peyre is now President of the French Chamber of Commerce in La Paz, Bolivia. He is welcome at the French Embassy there and from time to time returns to France for a visit.

Where do his money and support come from? Certainly not from

General Revers or General Mast — neither one was rich enough. We made sure that Fourcaud could not use SDECE money, and he could not afford personally to support Peyre in Latin America. French Freemasons, however, have always maintained good relations with their Latin American brothers, who share their atheistic philosophy, and it would have been easy to help Peyre resettle successfully through influential contacts there.

Our inquiry also revealed other aspects of the case. The Vietnamese, Do Dai Phuoc, who was involved in the bus incident which started the whole affair, left France a few weeks after Peyre and took up residence in Prague, Czechoslovakia. He was reunited there with Tran Ngoc Dan, an associate of Vinh Xa, the Vietminh representative who had received the Revers report from Peyre. Tran Ngoc Dan had been trained before the war at the Stalin School in Moscow under the name of Blokov. He was a specialist in subversive activities and a KGB agent. According to several reports, he had met Peyre through Masonic friends.

Years later, several Russian defectors revealed how the Soviets, in their annoyance over NATO, had used their Masonic contacts to conduct "disinformation" activities. By coincidence, the Soviet resident of Paris was, until 1949, Ivan Agayants, chief of the Disinformation Division of the KGB. He had access to all the archives of the Freemasonry which were captured during the war, and showed great talent in using them to his advantage. Since a number of cases had been reported in which Freemasons acted as agents for Soviet intelligence, supporting the Communist fight for power, this coincidence, I think, is self-explanatory.

In giving wide publicity to the Commission of Inquiry's proceedings, the Communists succeeded in undermining the confidence of other NATO nations toward France. This aura of suspicion poisoned the atmosphere and proved very detrimental to good relations within the military alliance.

Some reports reached us, in SDECE, mentioning contacts between Fourcaud and the Communists. We did our best to verify them but were unsuccessful. While it is true that Communists were the first to benefit from his schemes, it is the Gaullist party which eventually got the most out of his endeavor to undermine the regime. Fourcaud was not quite so lucky. Not only did he fail in his efforts to secure the position of SDECE director he so long coveted, but he was fired. His departure rid the service of an atmosphere of useless intrigues which had been detrimental to the businesslike running of the agency.

The scandal of the generals was deeply felt in France. It destroyed completely the nation's faith in its Army, its police, and its government. In the same way Joseph Balsamo and his Freemason friends had 175 years before destroyed confidence in the Crown, Roger Peyre and his Freemason friends had destroyed confidence in our democratic government.

Henri Ribière, in complete disgust, had made up his mind to resign, but the Prime Minister persuaded him to remain until the end of 1950. During those six months we tried to patch up some of the damage caused to the SDECE by the succession of scandals, but our organization had lost all the support it ever had.

Conversely, in some fields SDECE was doing well. The deciphering division had broken countless codes and given us first-rate intelligence on Soviet aims and buildups. It always surprised me that the Soviets, who are so sophisticated in elaborating the most complicated conspiracies, used such poor coding devices in their communications. Things have changed now, but in the fifties we could easily get a clear picture of their intentions by reading their cables. I do not think that at the time any Western agency had better intelligence on the Soviets.

From a counterespionage standpoint, many Soviet networks were kept under close surveillance. Colonel Verneuil was careful not to bring any legal action against them, so the Russians felt secure in their deception. In spite of the scandals and difficulties we had to face, our efforts then were more productive than they would be in following years.

Confident about the quality of our work, we felt we were equal to any other NATO member, and we wanted to avoid being taken under the wing of another foreign service. The British, nevertheless, were trying to do just that.

One of the most important provisions of the North Atlantic Treaty was the exchange of intelligence among the participating nations. The way the exchanges would be handled had not been worked out yet when the British came forward with a proposal.

Since during the war they had enjoyed a special relationship with the United States and knew how to negotiate with the Americans, they would centralize all the intelligence coming from the European services and pass it on to the American services. In fact, they wanted to act as broker between the Europeans and the Americans for everything concerning NATO.

One of their arguments in favor of this proposal was that American laws did not authorize any representative of a foreign intelligence service to reside in the United States, and American intelligence authorities could not communicate intelligence to a foreigner. An exception would be made for the British because of the special relationship existing between the two countries. Furthermore, they insisted that they already had in Washington the qualified personnel to handle the exchange. Ironically enough, their representative was none other than Harold Philby, the former head of their counterespionage division, a specialist on Soviet problems—no one knew then to what extent.

We saw no reason why we could not handle the exchanges ourselves, and we refused to deal through the British. The legal objection raised by our British friends seemed preposterous. International relations are based on the principle of reciprocity, and since American security services had liaison with us in Paris, why could we not have liaison with them in Washington?

Ribière had several talks on the subject with the Prime Minister, and it was decided that after his departure at the end of 1950, I would be sent to Washington to organize the liaison with American intelligence.

An apprentice agent could have won a promotion or at least the appreciation of his chief by snapping a picture of the men who were seated at a square table in the back of the Pavillon Henri IV dining room in Saint Germain en Laye. The date was February 1951; the host, Pierre Boursicot, new director of SDECE. At his right was Major General Sir Stewart Graham Menzies, D.S.O., M.C., head of SIS, the famous British secret intelligence service. Opposite Pierre Boursicot was his assistant and my successor, Lalanne. I was seated across from General Menzies.

Nearly two months before, on the first of January, I had received Boursicot at SDECE headquarters on behalf of Henri Ribière, who wanted to avoid the chore. Pierre Boursicot, after a fine record in the resistance, had been Sûreté director for a while. I had done my best to introduce him to the inner workings of the agency, and he had been very appreciative.

British intelligence, strangely enough, had supported Colonel Fourcaud's position during the generals' case. Their interference in French politics had caused hard feelings in our agency, and liaison between the two organizations was at its lowest point since the war. General

Menzies, without waiting for a courtesy visit from Pierre Boursicot, had come to Paris to mend the traditional relationship between the two services. Eager to show there was no divorce between his policies and those of his predecessor, Boursicot had asked me to attend all their conversations and the informal luncheons following.

General Menzies' prestige was tremendous in the intelligence world. He had been head of SIS during the war, and everyone admired his leadership and the successful performance of British intelligence under his command. He had always shunned the limelight, and his officers referred to him as "the general" or "the chief," never by his name. Only initiates of the organization were said to know his identity. For him to come to Paris and lunch in a public place with his French counterpart was certainly an exceptional occurrence and demonstrated his keen desire to improve the relationship of the two services. The general spoke French easily and needed no translator.

"I was told you are going to Washington to organize the liaison with the Americans. Have you been there before?" The general directed this question to me.

"No, sir, not yet," I answered.

"We would like very much to help you," said the general, addressing Pierre Boursicot and myself at the same time. "The Americans are not always easy to deal with, and we have had our difficulties with them, but we are used to them now. I have a very good man in Washington, Mr. Philby, and will cable him that you will be there soon. Please do call him when you arrive, he will introduce you around and help you get settled."

The offer was very generous, and the director joined me in thanking the general.

"It was kind of the general," commented Boursicot later, "and I hope you took note of the name of his representative. You must contact him."

I answered affirmatively, wondering nevertheless if it would be wise to be introduced in Washington by my British colleague. I would have preferred help from General Menzies in the form of information on the organization of American intelligence and security services. I had some memories of the OSS, but it had closed shop after the war. I had heard about the newly created CIA and about the FBI, but knew nothing of the way they were organized or their jurisdiction. Our counterespionage division had been unable to provide me with any information of value. Our one long report on the subject was by some inventive officer who had based it entirely on a form he had found attached by mistake to some papers we had received from an American security service. Showing more nerve than wisdom, our man had made incredible deductions from the names of the divisions listed to receive the report. As counter-espionage did not know any better, this fabrication was considered an accurate description of the American secret organization. I was later to discover that nothing in it was correct.

I tried to question the Americans working in liaison with us, but they were very discreet and did not contribute in any way to my education. They did not seem too pleased by the establishment of an SDECE liaison in Washington, and one day even informed Pierre Boursicot that it would be against the law for their director to accept a French liaison. This obstacle was removed, however, when Boursicot stated that he would no longer tolerate an American liaison in Paris if he did not have his own in Washington.

On April 11, 1951, I landed in New York on the *Ile de France* and headed immediately for Washington. At the French Embassy my reception was polite, but there was a definite lack of enthusiasm over the presence of a permanent SDECE representative among authentic diplomats. I was to learn later from the CIA director that an embassy member had actually approached him and suggested that he discourage the liaison with French intelligence. Our diplomats apparently were worried that I would spend most of my time watching their activities and filing reports on their personal lives.

I was given an office in the consulate basement — a small room at the bottom of a staircase. A midget window opened under the steps of the consulate entrance and allowed neither natural light nor ventilation into the room. Air conditioning was a luxury I could not afford, and during the summer my office was like a Turkish bath. For almost a year I had no secretary and did everything myself, including the time-consuming coding and decoding. Later, when the embassy members realized I had better things to do than spy on them, my life became easier and I was given decent offices with all the normal amenities.

I called several times to make an appointment with General Walter Bedell Smith, director of the Central Intelligence Agency, but without any success. It took me several weeks finally to meet the man who formerly had been Chief of Staff for General Eisenhower. He had a reputation for his hot temper, but contrary to my expectations, I found him very gracious and kind. As for the delays in receiving me, I always thought they were due to the fact that his staff did not dare to ask him for an appointment for me. From then on I saw him quite often and was impressed by his great knowledge of international affairs and his affectionate feeling for France.

Allen Dulles was Smith's deputy. He had studied at the Alsatian School in Paris and spoke perfect French, but with a slight Alsatian accent. During the war he had followed France's struggles from Switzerland and had helped organize resistance networks with such people as General de Benouville, the present editor of *Jour de France*, and Paul Devinat, member of many French cabinets. Dulles understood Europe and her problems and it was due in great part to his accurate judgment of the gravity of the economic situation there that the Marshall Plan was implemented. It was always a pleasure for me to hear this man of great knowledge and imagination discuss world events, and I did my best to report his views as clearly as possible to my headquarters during the daily crises confronting us. Dulles at that time lived in Stewart Alsop's house in Georgetown, and his hospitality was valued by all the foreign statesmen who were already in the habit of visiting him during their stays in Washington. Dulles was sympathetic to the difficulties of my mission, and he introduced me to his associates; in a short time I met most of the people I needed to know for my liaison work.

Before I left France, Boursicot had reminded me of General Menzies' offer and instructed me to see his representative upon my arrival in Washington. Keeping in mind the many difficulties we had had during these last years with the British service, I was not anxious to meet this Philby. I tried to get some information about him beforehand, knowing I would have to call on him sooner or later. Without directly asking, I mentioned his name several times during conversations with my American contacts. They were always very evasive and changed the subject, which in itself was perfectly normal. I could understand why they were reluctant to speak of a member of another intelligence service with someone who would have to be considered as a competitor. Still, one day at lunch I mentioned to a friend in counterespionage that I intended to pay a courtesy call on my British colleague. My friend stared into his plate and played with an elusive piece of fried potato.

"I wouldn't if I were you," he said. "You have just arrived in this country and so far have done very well. You could not make a worse mistake than associating yourself with Philby . . . but you must know what you're doing."

I tried to question him about the meaning of his remarks, but he seemed to regret having spoken and changed the subject of the conversation. I could not bring him to elaborate.

In the following days, I was visited by a British journalist, the friend of an embassy member. After the usual small talk he asked me to lunch with him so he could introduce me to Philby, who wondered why I had not called him before. Claiming other commitments, I postponed the encounter. But the next week I was invited by the former Polish military attaché in Washington, Colonel Hilinski, to meet Philby. It was becoming embarrassing, and although I refused once more, I knew I could not postpone meeting the British representative indefinitely.

The defection of Burgess and MacLean saved me further embarrassment, and I was very grateful to my American friend whose warning had been so timely. I understood, too, that Philby had been under suspicion well before the defection of his two friends. Inquiring around, I learned that Philby had been drunk twenty-four hours a day since the announcement of Burgess' involvement with the Russians. Unable because of his intoxication to fulfill his duties, he would send his wife to deliver the top-secret documents he received from his headquarters to the American security services. People who had been in contact with him began to speak more freely, and I was told of many incidents which had made Philby quite unpopular in Washington, including his familiarity with the wives of friends.

The Philby affair had two opposing effects on my work. The

first was to make the Americans still more suspicious of the foreign intelligence representatives — a reaction I could well understand. The second was to destroy the special relationship between the British and American services and to open the way for the French to win the confidence of the Americans and gain an advantage in the discussion of European intelligence problems. Well aware of the limitations security rules would bring to our exchange of intelligence, I strove to secure for SDECE the place formerly occupied by the British.

Paris was not sending me a great deal of intelligence to pass to our allies but nevertheless was pressing me to ask American help for our operations in Indochina. The Far East was not within the framework of the NATO agreements, and no one in the United States, except the President and the Congress, had the authority to make any commitments. However, with the Korean War at its height, the United States needed information on the situation in Indochina and on the Chinese support of the rebels, so I began to negotiate an exchange of intelligence on the Asiatic theater of operations. With my headquarters' agreement, I offered intelligence reports in exchange for equipment and supplies. I had created interest, but the negotiations were dragging on. Then I received unexpected help when General de Lattre de Tassigny decided to come to Washington to explain the Indochinese situation to Pentagon officials.

The French government had made General de Lattre de Tassigny proconsul in Indochina by naming him not only Commander in Chief, but also Civilian High Commissioner. The general was a great military chief and a very clever diplomat, loving ostentation and *panache*. The part was perfect for him, and during 1951 he was able to stabilize the situation and to raise hopes for at least an honorable peace. He was the first to create Vietnamese units and to make them fight, but he faced the usual French problem of not having enough equipment for his men. Supplies could only come from the United States. They already had sent some help, but not enough. Burdened with the Korean War, the Americans did not want to become involved in Vietnam, and many people in Washington remembered with dismay the first U.S. involvement in

Southeast Asia, which had brought the Communists to power. If the French wanted to fight, it was their decision — the United States looked on them with favor, but that was all.

General de Lattre de Tassigny was well aware of this feeling and how difficult it would be to convince Washington of the necessity for more effective support. He remembered the American friends he had made during the war when he commanded the First French Army. It happened that the American liaison officer with his command had just been reelected to the U.S. Senate. His name was Henry Cabot Lodge. He knew little about Vietnam but was an expert in American politics. The general, even though burdened with work and responsibility, astutely took the time to write Lodge often on the Vietnamese situation and on his plans and projects. The U.S. senator, who had always admired this flamboyant French general, became interested in de Lattre's grand design and spoke about it in Washington. One of his most attentive listeners was General Walter Bedell Smith, who as Eisenhower's Chief of Staff had also been in close contact with de Lattre and admired him for his military judgment. With such allies in the capital, de Lattre had the best lobby in the world! President Truman heard from his intelligence chief daily about the exploits of the cocky French general to such a degree that he wanted to meet him. Furthermore, his success in diverting the Chinese Communists was indirectly helpful to the American troops fighting in Korea, and the U.S. government wanted an estimate on how long it would last.

It would not have been wise politically for the President officially to invite General de Lattre to come to Washington, and the Congress would not have approved. But it was quite normal for the Army Chief of Staff to ask his French colleague to stop on his way back from the Far East to brief him on his military endeavors.

Henry Cabot Lodge, who in the beginning knew nothing about Vietnam, was becoming an expert thanks to all the reports he received from de Lattre and the briefings he received in the Pentagon and State Department. The future campaign manager for Eisenhower organized a most efficient schedule for his friend from France, and when de Lattre arrived in Washington he was received with the pomp and ceremony usually reserved for a head of state. De Lattre demonstrated extraordinary stamina, even though his only son, Bernard, a second lieutenant in the French Army, had been killed only a few weeks before and he himself was beginning to suffer from the awful effects of the cancer which was to kill him a few months later.

Officially, de Lattre was not supposed to negotiate any agreement, but it was understood that informally he would do so. The best way to keep things informal and to avoid any official commitments was to have discussions at the secret service level. For that reason I became very much involved.

The war in Indochina was conventional when our troops fought against the rebel army, but it seldom happened, and most of the Vietminh operations were of the subversive type. The Communists could be successfully repelled only by gathering as much intelligence as possible and by setting up countersubversive operations, very different from the ones the army had been trained for.

Conventional operations required conventional armament, and France could only acquire it from the United States with the blessing of the Pentagon and adequate credit from the U.S. government. On its part, the Pentagon wanted to see the use made by the French and Vietnamese regulars of the weapons provided to them. This was not too difficult a problem and could be arranged by the military. But in regard to the equipment needed for subversive operations, French intelligence did not want to reveal to anyone the exact use they would make of it or even explain their operations. The old French intelligence agents in Vietnam were very suspicious of the American secret services, who had previously been of so much help to Ho Chi Minh, and they refused to cooperate with them. In their opinion, they were fighting Communism, the common enemy, in a place where they could do it better than anyone else because of their intimate knowledge of the land and the people involved. They needed material help from France's allies, but they did not want any strings attached.

Before coming to Washington, de Lattre had been authorized by the French government to accept certain American demands concerning the army supply, but I was to be present at any discussions involving antisubversive operations and had instructions to refer to Paris all requests made by the Americans before they could

218

be negotiated. It was quite an uncomfortable feeling squeezing myself between a very self-centered and high-handed French general like de Lattre, and a very peppery American one like Walter Bedell Smith.

Upon arriving in Washington, General de Lattre set up his headquarters in the old Wardman Park Hotel, now the Sheraton Park. He was accompanied by a full staff of experts in every field, and in a very short time these officers were hard at work in their rooms as though they had never left their Saigon headquarters. This demonstration of organization greatly impressed the general's visitors. Special communications had been set up, and de Lattre was able to follow the Vietnamese situation closely during his stay in the capital and to direct operations tens of thousands of miles away.

I met the general on the day of his arrival at a reception given by General Collins, Army Chief of Staff at Fort McNair. I had met him before, during the war, and he was kind enough to remember. He asked me to come to see him the same evening at his hotel. His Chief of Staff, General Cogny, informed me of the problems his chief was concerned with, and I prepared a brief on the feelings in Washington about Indochina and himself.

When I arrived at his quarters, the general was so concerned over what he thought was a breach of protocol that he completely ignored the questions his Chief of Staff had asked me to answer. The big Cadillac limousine assigned to him had in front a tag with only four stars. As a full French general he wore five stars and to have only four on the front of his car was terribly offensive to him. Since the car had been provided by the U.S. Army he thought he was being insulted by the American military and foresaw the worst for his mission. I explained to him that brigadiers in the U.S. Army wore only one star compared to two for the French and that four stars were appropriate to him as a full general. Five stars, I added, were only worn by a General of the Army in the United States — the equivalent of the French title of Maréchal.

Earnestly looking me in the eye, he said, "I know, I know. Still, I should have five stars on my car."

I could not change the subject. General de Lattre was only interested in the number of stars on his car tag and expected me to arrange it so he would have what he wanted. After I left him I wondered how such serious matters as war and the lives of human beings could be entrusted to such a man. As for the number of stars on his car, I did not care. The next day, however, I discovered that the French representative at the Standing Group, General Valhuy, had given him satisfaction.

General Walter Bedell Smith had arranged a dinner party that night for the general, and informal discussions were to take place before and afterwards on the help the United States could give France with her fight in Indochina. General Cogny asked me to come to see General de Lattre one hour beforehand so we could discuss the positions to take with our American allies. I had the government's instructions and reviewed them with him. We were in complete agreement, and the general was very gracious. He asked me to ride in his car to the Army and Navy club where the dinner was to take place.

Before entering the car, he walked around in front of it and motioned me to join him. He beamed as he showed me the tag with five stars. With his two hands, he grabbed mine and very gratefully said, "Thank you, thank you very much."

I tried to tell him I had nothing to do with the new tag he was so proud of, but to no avail. Policemen on fast motorbikes were all around the car opening the way in the heavy evening traffic with their sirens blaring. General de Lattre was seated erectly on the rear seat smiling happily.

"Were you here when the Prime Minister came last month?" he asked me.

"Yes, sir," I answered.

"Did he have an escort like this?" and with his hand he indicated the policemen all around.

"No, sir."

As a matter of fact, René Meyer, Prime Minister at the time, had made a very discreet visit to Washington and I didn't remember having seen him with even a single policeman around.

"You see, Vosjoli," said General de Lattre, "the Americans are giving me a better reception than the Prime Minister." And in spite of all his worries I could see that the general had reached the peak of happiness.

That evening we had some important conversations with General Smith and Senator Lodge. General de Lattre, as should have been expected, went completely contrary to the French government's orders and promised the Americans exactly the opposite of what we had agreed to before. I knew about the limitations the government had placed on General de Lattre's mission, but soon I became just a spectator at the special performance he was giving with the encouragement of Senator Lodge. I myself was astonished to witness the Americans becoming involved in Vietnam for the second time. The first time they had been responsible for supporting and training Ho Chi Minh. Now they were giving us equipment to use against the army they had trained. It was a complete reversal of position, and I had previously thought the Americans were much too practical for this type of reversal.

At any rate, the agreement was very advantageous for us. The United States would send observers and we would allow them to check our operations and to advise the South Vietnamese Army. They would support us by providing the French government in France with the hard currency necessary to carry on in Vietnam. The dollars would be paid in Paris and we would spend only francs in Vietnam. Our francs were worth very little, while dollars were the world standard. In substance, the United States would give us hard money and we would provide the manpower for the war. General de Lattre was very happy about the deal and I knew our government would be delighted to see our treasury refurbished by American generosity.

The next day as I was reminding General de Lattre that he had strayed from the government's orders, he laughed and shrugged his shoulders. "Don't worry, they will be overjoyed in Paris. Now the Americans are hooked and they will have to support us in Vietnam."

No written agreement had been signed — there was only an exchange of promises. I wondered if the American government would honor them, but de Lattre was very confident that Senator Lodge would be able to secure the necessary support. He was right.

American help began to pour in, and in my field I was able to get everything my headquarters needed to equip the special teams operating in Vietnam.

For months I had been begging for planes to drop agents behind the enemy lines. As a consequence of de Lattre de Tassigny's visit I was able to obtain U.S. credit to buy them. At this time, the type of plane we needed was very difficult to find. After contacting brokers all over the world, I finally found an English broker who had what we wanted. With American money I bought several planes from him. One of them had been used by Princess Elizabeth for her trip to Africa during which she learned of her father's death. The plane was of a type which easily could be converted to our use. The inside was luxuriously fitted with all kinds of conveniences for the traveling princess. It was delivered along with the others at the SDECE special airport at Persan-Baumont near Paris, to be equipped for dropping parachutists.

A few months later, General Smith called me to his office. There, in accordance with his irascible reputation, he gave me a dressing down which I certainly did not deserve but which I could well understand. The Queen Elizabeth plane had not been sent to Vietnam and had not been equipped for special operations. Instead it was being used by members of the French government who had appropriated its comfortable armchairs to fly to weekend resorts. General Smith had a full report and even pictures showing happy French secretaries leaving the plane in Deauville and in Cannes. That the United States had paid for planes being used for junkets by French politicians had so angered the CIA director that my position became almost impossible. For a while I considered asking my headquarters for reassignment. But eventually the plane was sent to Vietnam and General Smith quieted down.

Besides my liaison work, I followed with great interest the American political scene. I tried to send my director in Paris a realistic picture of what was happening and what the most influential politicians were thinking.

A few days after my arrival in Washington, General MacArthur had been recalled by President Truman. The controversy between MacArthur's admirers and supporters of the President was in full swing. At the various daily gatherings and cocktail parties, the politicians gave their opinions, and while they were always very discreet, each of them had a different idea of what should be kept secret and what could be revealed. After seeing enough people, one would have a complete story of what was happening. To keep his knowledge up to date, an intelligence man did not need agents or any special devices if he had the right connections and enough of them. The complexity of American politics, however, was and still is a mystery in Europe and especially in France. Many of the reports I sent on events of great significance in Washington were not uderstood in Paris if they did not have a direct and immediate influence on Franco-American relations. Very often I felt I was wasting my time and effort in reporting on some interesting political problem — the 1952 electoral campaign, for instance, in which, I must confess, I became indirectly involved.

One day I received a call from General Smith, who wanted to see me on some urgent matter. I went immediately to his office. After some small talk and a cup of coffee, he offered me one of the long Russian cigarettes he had begun smoking while he was ambassador to Moscow and told me the reason for his summons. "I have a friend you may have heard of — Joseph Kennedy, a member of our Intelligence Advisory Committee. His eldest son, Joe, was killed over France while piloting a bomber. Now his second son, John, is a candidate for the United States Senate in Massachusetts. Many people in that state are of French origin and it would be helpful to his campaign to have the French government confer the Legion of Honor posthumously on his brother Joe. I would appreciate it very much if you could arrange it."

The Legion of Honor had been created by Napoleon to reward soldiers and officers for their bravery on the field of battle. As vanity is human and as politicians must thank their supporters with something besides words, the Legion of Honor is now given to anybody with the right friends in the right places. During all the years when French Special Services had not enough money to pay their agents, the Legion of Honor was often given instead of cash to people who had worked for us. The funny thing was that many preferred to have the little red ribbon in their buttonhole than to be paid in hard cash.

When General Smith solicited the Legion of Honor posthumously for his friend's son, I foresaw no difficulty and asked him to give

223

me all the particulars so that I could fill in the necessary forms and write a recommendation. The ambassador had to sign the request before it was sent to Paris. I presented it to him as a routine matter, but when he saw the name, he almost jumped. You want me to request the Legion of Honor for a Kennedy?" he asked me. "But don't you know about Joseph Kennedy?"

I confessed my ignorance.

Henri Bonnet then explained to me. "Joseph Kennedy was the American ambassador in England at the beginning of the war and admired Hitler and the way Germany was organized. He was always very critical of France and after the defeat of 1940 made many statements derogatory to us. A great number of Americans have helped us and several committees were organized to support the resistance. Never did Kennedy belong to any of them. It is very sad that his son was killed during the war, but when it happened he was not on any specific mission to help the French. I cannot request the Legion of Honor for everybody killed in action. Why would France do some special favor for a Kennedy?"

"Because General Walter Bedell Smith asked for it," I answered, "and we are grateful to him for many reasons."

"Let me think about it," said the ambassador. "I will tell you my decision in a few days."

Days went by and then weeks and the ambassador had not signed the request and I understood he would not.

"What about the Legion of Honor?" General Smith would ask each time I saw him.

I could not tell him of the problems I was having, and time was running short before the election. I began to write to friends in the government and I asked my director, Pierre Boursicot, to help. After months of maneuvering I finally received a cable informing me of the decision to bestow on the late Joseph Kennedy the Legion of Honor. The elections were past, but still all the Kennedys went to Paris for the ceremony.

A few weeks later, I was invited to the French Embassy for a dinner party. One of the guests was John Kennedy, the new junior Senator from Massachusetts. Mrs. Bonnet introduced us, telling him what I had done about his dead brother's Legion of Honor, and he was kind enough to thank me. We chatted for a while about intelligence. He was just married, young and buoyant and very different from the traditional image of a Senator. I was thinking how strange it was for a French intelligence agent to have been involved even remotely in the election of this man. I could not foresee that eleven years later he would fall under the bullet of an assassin while I myself would be in hiding from paid killers.

10

There was no moon. The night was dark except for the reflection of the headlights on the snow-covered sidewalk. I had driven back to my Washington suburban home that evening after attending to some urgent matter at the office.

A voice came from behind as I was opening the garage door, "May I speak to you for a moment?" The man spoke French with a strong Arabic accent.

The idea of foul play flashed through my mind and I was angry with myself for not having been more careful. An intelligence officer must never allow himself to be caught off guard. Carefully I turned around to face the man.

I recognized him as a member of one of the Arab embassies I had met recently at a reception given by the Organization of American States. "Come in," I said. "It is freezing out."

"No . . . no, sir. I really would not want to meet anyone."

I instantly knew the kind of business that brought him to me and understood his concern for secrecy. Opening the car door, I invited him to get in where we could at least be comfortable.

"It is known that you are with French intelligence," he said, "and I have something that might interest you."

I mumbled a few words and let him proceed.

"I have here a microfilm of the correspondence exchanged between the North African rebels for the past several years. I need money. How much would it be worth to you?"

"Let me see it," and I held out my hand.

Reluctantly, the man produced a roll of microfilm.

"Of course, I have to examine it first," I said, "to see if we are interested. How did you get it?"

He avoided my eyes. "I must have it back before tomorrow morning. It's good, I tell you, and you will like it. The price is $5,000."

I gave him back the film.

"I said I have to have it back before six in the morning. How much would you give me?" pleaded the man.

"I must see it first, but it will not be more than $1,000. O.K.?"

He handed me the film and we arranged to meet at two in the morning at a certain street corner.

I set to work and with the help of my secretary duplicated the microfilm. It was good. The Tunisian and Moroccan rebels were apparently making use of this man's embassy to receive and forward their mail secretly. Naturally, the security officer of the embassy had photographed everything, and our man had stolen it for the night in order to sell it to me. He could very well have sold it before and probably would again. This did not bother me, as I knew my headquarters would be pleased with it. The man, I had no doubt, would be back to see me as soon as he had something else to peddle.

Some of the letters were from Habib Bourguiba. Their tone was violent and in sharp contradiction to the words of appeasement the author was currently spreading. In one letter, the postscript amused me, as Bourguiba stated confidentially that he was forwarding it through a channel he knew was safe, in order to elude counter-espionage services.

My superiors in SDECE were extremely pleased, and did as they usually do with this type of material — asked France's leading newspaper *Le Monde* to publish it. It came out in the issue of April 6, 1952, and covered one full page.

North Africa was in a state of turmoil, and the Arab rebels did nothing but aggravate a situation already deteriorated by the incessant combat in Vietnam. Open hostilities had not yet begun, but the main leaders of the independence movements were already planning the uprising and getting ready for it. They were trying to rally sympathetic nations to their cause.

Their most active center was naturally Cairo, where the League of Arab States spared no effort to keep alive the revolutionary spirit of its members. The Moroccan, Tunisian, and Algerian leaders were the recipients of important subsidies from the governments of Egypt and Saudi Arabia. The funds were used to purchase weapons as well as to finance diplomatic lobbying among the countries who were members of the United Nations.

Tunisians, Moroccans, and Algerians were provided with diplomatic passports by Arab governments, enabling them to sit among official delegations. Egypt and Syria sheltered the greatest number. These delegates were busy lobbying in the United Nations building, buying support from officials of the new nations which periodically joined the world organization.

Besides my liaison work with the various intelligence divisions in NATO, one of my duties was to keep a close watch on the anti-French activities of the nationalists. I had little difficulty in keeping up with what was going on thanks to informers such as this Arab diplomat who supplied me with information. Greedy and looking for a quick and easy way to make money, many of the members of the nationalist delegations established contact with us to report on their colleagues' activities. Such information was particularly valuable when the United Nations was in session. We knew then precisely the plans of the nationalists and the backing they were likely to get. Frequently, for one reason or another, a motion against France was brought forward to the Assembly. In such instances, the representatives of some Arab states were extremely active and would probably have succeeded in obtaining a condemnation for France if it had not been for my behind-the-scenes intervention.

In the United Nations a line could be drawn between the representatives of more advanced countries who did not depart from the political line laid down by their respective state departments, and other delegations free to make on-the-spot decisions according to subtle undercurrents, fluctuations, or timely opportunities. When a vote promised to be tight, such delegations could alter the results by their ballots, and for this reason were the objects of attention from nations interested in the outcome. Not hampered by strict orders or by political pressure, the heads of these delegations followed their personal sympathies. In order to win them over to one's side, one had to make it more attractive than the other side. There were many ways to win this support. Sometimes, sitting down and deferentially going over the reasons why their support was needed was all it took. Often snubbed or neglected by diplomats of the great nations who were too busy to devote a few minutes of their precious time to them, the delegates were flattered to be taken seriously by a member of the French Embassy. At other times, depending on their wants, the decisive vote could be influenced by the generosity of the solicitor.

I recall one particular instance in which the vote of the delegation of a small nation was needed on our side in an important issue. On previous similar occasions, the head of the delegation had sided with us because he honestly thought the position we adopted was right. The day before the vote, he and his wife joined me for lunch at one of New York's most fashionable restaurants, and I was trying diplomatically to obtain the assurance of his delegation's vote. The man was vague and remained uncommitted, changing the subject every time I brought the matter into the conversation. Finally he excused himself for a few minutes on the pretext of making a phone call.

"You are wasting your time," said his wife. "He has already been approached by the Egyptians, and their offer is very attractive. However, yesterday I saw a mink coat at Kaplan's I simply adore, and I'm sure I could convince my husband to change his mind. . . ."

The following day we got the ballot, and she got her coat.

A few weeks later, before returning to his country, the same delegate came to see me. He wanted more than anything else to take back with him an American sports car, and he was offering me his embassy's code in exchange for his racer. The code looked like child's play and was certainly already familiar to our deciphering services, so I declined the offer. I am sure that after leaving me, this diplomat, who is today one of the most influential figures in his country, made the rounds of other intelligence officers hoping to interest someone in the deal.

The psychology of intelligence organizations has undergone a radical change. Intelligence officers of foreign powers used to seek absolute secrecy, spending great time and effort to avoid being associated with their real activities. They were able, because of this excessive discretion, to set up operations which were marvelously complex but not necessarily productive.

It can be said that intelligence is a commodity of which intelligence officers are the brokers. Many people are ready to give or sell intelligence either for idealistic purposes, for revenge, or for money, but they do not always know where to go with it. I never attempted to hide my real position, and this policy paid off nicely. Secrecy, although necessary at times, is often more of a nuisance than an asset.

In French intelligence this concern for remaining undetected at all costs was so widespread and had become such a fixation with some agents that they never were able to work effectively. They actually had to resort to the faking of newspaper clippings to make it seem they had uncovered real information. In the same vein, I have always been surprised by the idiosyncracy of many so-called intelligence experts who cannot get results unless they organize some kind of plot or use deception. From my own experience I can say that in the majority of cases you can obtain the information desired simply by asking the right person the right question. I wonder why the intelligence services do not emphasize this point in their training schools. Agents would do their jobs at less cost and without resorting to complicated schemes if this very simple principle was followed. I myself was certainly too busy to waste time on old-fashioned fantasies and nonsense. Results were more important than the cloak and dagger approach.

Soviet subversive activities represented then, as they do now, the main danger we had to guard against. In the United States the

230

services in charge of security carried on a perpetual struggle against Soviet attempts to infiltrate agents into the government and strategic installations. The FBI's efficient work forced the Soviets to look incessantly for new avenues of penetration. Central America offered them one, with tremendous possibilities which they were quick to develop. Their most active centers were Cuba, Mexico, and Guatemala.

In 1953, Batista, tired of the subversive activities of the USSR Embassy in Havana, ordered his police to confiscate two Soviet diplomatic pouches. Their contents gave valuable indications about Soviet intentions in Central America and the Caribbean. Naturally, the Soviets broke diplomatic relations with Cuba, and their embassy in Mexico City soon replaced the one in Havana as the center of their subversive activities in North and Central America.

In matters of intelligence, gathering information is one thing, but making sure that it gets safely to the party concerned is something else. Communications is an ever-present problem, and for Soviet agents working in the United States, the difficulties are multiplied enormously because of the effective work of the FBI. The Mexican government, however, is most liberal with diplomatic representations accredited to it, insofar as they do not interfere with internal Mexican affairs. The Soviets, taking advantage of this permissiveness, set up in Mexico a huge embassy far out of proportion to their relations with this country. The roof of the building, covered with antennas of all kinds, clearly marks it as a center of communications. From there agents operate in Central America, the Caribbean, and the United States. They receive orders through the Russian Embassy, and their production reaches Moscow through the same channels.

Soviet activities as such were of enough interest and certainly a good reason for me to recruit informers in various Central American and Caribbean countries. But another reason prompted the French to seek information on Communist maneuvers in those areas.

Several intelligence reports and message interceptions indicated that the Kominform had put the French Communist Party in charge of passing on orders and acting as liaison with Latin Communist parties. Their communications system was rather complex. We were already familiar with some of it, but many details escaped us.

231

Luckily I still had contacts in Latin America — from my war days in BCRA when I dealt with problems in this hemisphere — and without too much effort I secured the cooperation of enough people to keep me posted on Soviet and French Communist activities.

In addition to the usual load of work in Washington, part of my time had to be devoted to those correspondents, who, not receiving any remuneration, had to be handled with a certain amount of consideration. They worked well and I was not surprised later on when the Mexican government, feeling uneasy about the agitation created among student groups by French Communists, acted to deport Jacques Denis, General Secretary of the World Federation of Democratic Youth. In all the places he visited, Jacques Denis' activities had been watched by my informers, and I knew about his contacts in Peru and Panama.

From Haiti I had received information about the work of agitators from Guadeloupe, all members of the French Communist Party. The same group was also active in Cuba, spreading propaganda among the colored population.

The support I always received from SDECE director Pierre Boursicot and from Colonel Verneuil was a determining factor in the creation of intelligence networks in this area. Colonel Verneuil was certainly the master of anti-Communist counterespionage in Europe at the time. Aware of the problems I had to cope with, he would send me long handwritten letters of advice suggesting certain maneuvers and guiding me, with great intuition, on the recruitment of agents. His premature death deprived the free world of one of its most ardent defenders, and I lost his substantial assistance in the hunt for Soviet spies.

Still, during my first three years in Washington I was able to set up a system of surveillance which allowed me, in collaboration with local intelligence, to follow the activities of many Soviet agents in the Caribbean and Central America. This operation yielded excellent results until the end of 1962, when it was dismantled by my own headquarters in keeping with de Gaulle's soft line toward Moscow.

Reasons other than Communist activities required me to travel to Central America frequently. The Arab nationalists were trying to establish contacts there with important Syrian and Lebanese colonies. These settlements went back several generations, and the Arabs hoped, through them, to win the support of the local authorities. Using more or less regular channels, I succeeded in providing the governments involved with accurate reports on the motivation of such groups. The Latin governments acted on these reports and in almost every instance supported France's position.

It was not uncommon for one of our diplomatic representations to seek my help, through headquarters, in resolving an especially intricate problem. The missions entrusted to me under such circumstances were often full of surprises, sometimes taking a humorous turn, as the one in January 1955 which took me to Costa Rica in the midst of the pseudo-war between that nation and neighboring Nicaragua.

The conflict was being carried out in a typically Latin vein. A group of five or six hundred supporters of the former Costa Rican President Rafael Calderón Guardia had sought refuge in Nicaragua and had pledged to overthrow ruling President José Figueres, who had gained office through perfectly democratic processes, in a part of the world where such practices were not the custom.

The people of Costa Rica, in an impressive demonstration of unity, had rallied around President Figueres and were striving to hold out against attacks launched by the rebels and supported by some elements of the Nicaraguan army and air force. At the same time our ambassador in San José was disturbed over the fact that the seals of our diplomatic pouches had been broken repeatedly. He had reported this to Paris and I was asked to go there and investigate the matter.

Landing facilities in San José were rudimentary — there was no such thing as a concrete air strip. Planes landed on the grass. To get there one had to transfer at Managua and take a small aircraft to the Costa Rican capital. Connections were not immediately available, and I had no choice but to spend the night in Managua, where a hotel room had been booked in advance. At the airport my diplomatic passport seemed to make little difference, and I reluctantly submitted to a thousand formalities. Outside, while stoically waiting for a cab, I was hailed by a hefty fellow who told me the hotel had sent him to pick me up.

We walked to his car, and to make room for me in front, he casually lifted a machine gun, a revolver, a rifle, and a heap of ammunition belts, throwing everything onto a back seat already littered with grenades and several other machine guns. The arsenal carried by my driver did very little to ease my suspicious nature, and I frankly wondered what I had walked into. Realizing my surprise, the man wiped his hand on his dirty pants and stuck it out.

"Colonel R—— at your service." Then, glancing indifferently over the army supply, he said, "I just got back from a raid on Figueres' bastards."

On our drive into the city, I learned from my talkative driver that he was the leader of a group of Costa Rican rebels. He spared me no detail about his exploits, past and future. Everything about the man was overdone, and I felt like a first-row spectator in a bad movie, but he was for real, and deadly serious about his job.

I told him I was due to board the plane for Costa Rica in the morning, and this presented no conflict. He was preparing another attack against a mountain outpost for the evening but would have plenty of time to drive me to the airport next morning.

He kept his word and showed up on time to take me first to the Ministry for Foreign Affairs, since an exit visa was required. I was received by the Deputy Minister, impeccable and dignified in a white suit. Very conscientiously he took from his pocket a set of ornate seals and stamped my passport with a flourish.

I left Managua knowing all future campaign plans of the Costa Rican rebels, and I was grateful to the god of secret agents for having made my path cross with that of the unusual chauffeur.

Once in the Costa Rican capital of San José, it took me no more than a day, with the help of local authorities, to find out who was responsible for breaking up the French diplomatic pouches. He was an employee of the airline carrying the mail. Although our pouches to Central America contained no top-secret material, the employee had been used by a Western intelligence service to perform his unscrupulous — but certainly rewarding — job. With this matter closed I was free to return to Washington immediately, but the Costa Ricans detained me a little longer asking my advice on the guerrilla war they were waging against their neighbors. With my convenient foreknowledge of the plans of their adversaries, I think I was able to give them a few useful tips.

The Costa Ricans are an extraordinary people, and their will to defend their democratic government set an example for other Latin American countries. The Organization of American States had condemned the Nicaraguan action, and the United States, in an effort to help Costa Rica defend herself, had sold to Figueres' government two bombers for one dollar each. Unfortunately, no bombs were delivered, and so they were of very little use. But the resourceful President, a former M.I.T. student, decided that since they could not afford to buy bombs, they would have to make their own.

One day, some highway patrol officers who were in command of a makeshift militia, since the country had no regular army, took me to visit their headquarters. The building, with its thick walls and battlements, looked like a fortified castle dominating the entire city of San José; it now served as a prison. Inside were a succession of courtyards separating the different wings. First I was given a tour of the section housing prisoners who had been arrested in the recent encounters and agents of the fifth column. Then I was shown into one of the courtyards in the middle of which stood a bizarre metal contraption.

"Our bomb," announced the highest-ranking officer with pride.

Walking up to the device, he climbed on a stepladder and from his perch explained to me that I was looking at a handmade product, the work of the local blacksmiths. There was no doubt that they had done a magnificent job. It stood about eight feet high and six feet in diameter. On top of the bomb were several butane tanks welded together and a long iron rod. He pointed out to me that the rod was moving freely in the upper butane tank. "And this is the detonator. We simply filled the tanks with TNT and dynamite. When the bomb falls on the rod it will detonate the blasting caps under it. This will generate a very powerful explosion."

Of this I had no doubt. I wondered why the entire city of San José had not yet been blown up by the novice pyrotechnicians when I suddenly realized that what I had taken for dog piles lying around the yard were wet dynamite sticks. Delighted with their creation, the guides were smoking and throwing their butts away with total unconcern for the explosives around them. I was introduced to the local pharmacist, the inventor of the device, and congratulated him warmly for his patriotic dedication as well as his personal courage for attending to the loading of the bomb.

They had no rigs to transport it or to secure it on the bombers but they would, they explained, simply throw it overboard in the target area.

God always protects the brave and the fearless. Two days later the war was settled and the bomb was never used — otherwise the enemy would surely have won.

I have since often wondered whatever happened to that unique bomb.

Episodes with a light side were unfortunately an exception in the difficult period France was going through. Only a few months before we had been shockingly defeated at Dien Bien Phu. This tragedy was due as much to the hopelessness of winning this kind of war with conventional means as to the faulty organization of our military intelligence, which proved unable to use efficiently and purposefully the material gathered by SDECE.

Our soldiers and young officers were fighting with remarkable courage and dedication, but back in the General Staff, a majority of field officers were interested only in personal gain. They engaged in illicit traffic in foreign currencies and other commodities and their behavior threw undeserved discredit on the commendable elements of the French Army. Seeking excuses for their incompetence, they blamed the Americans, whom they despised even more than the Vietminh. First they reproached them for inducing Ho Chi Minh to revolt against France, then for not supplying the French Army with enough equipment, arms, and helicopters.

Yet I had witnessed the tremendous effort on the part of the United States to help us in our former colony. Each month an aircraft carrier such as the *Dixmude* or the *Bois Belleau* or some other arrived in Norfolk and loaded prodigious quantities of material of all kinds — planes, artillery, and bombs, not to mention the material needed for special missions, the loading of which I personally supervised.

Not only did the United States supply France with war materials, but they made substantial contributions to the war expenses, and the U.S. dollars so acquired practically made up the totality of hard currency in the French treasury. To put an end to the war in Vietnam would have meant bankruptcy for France. Never in world history has a conflict been kept going for such contemptible financial reasons. American experts had few illusions left as to why the fighting had been prolonged.

At the time of Dien Bien Phu several proposals were discussed that are of interest now. Successive French military defeats and the shortage of men trained for special missions were beginning to be felt. The Korean War was over and a great number of specially trained American units were to be withdrawn from that theater of operations. The Pentagon tried then to work out a way to transfer these troops to Vietnam to assist with the training of the Vietnamese Army which was then being formed and to help the French with their special operations. But the French command refused to permit Americans in uniform in Indochina. A few days before the surrender of the French garrison at Dien Bien Phu the question was brought up and the representatives of the French Army declared that should the United States want to send troops to help in Vietnam, American soldiers would have to wear French uniforms and place themselves under the command of French officers. It would be as though each American soldiers had enlisted in the French Foreign Legion. Of course this French demand, which was contrary to American law, was rejected by the Pentagon. Otherwise we would have seen American troops in Vietnam as early as the end of 1953.

The French defeat was considered in Washington to be the result of the incompetence of the French command and its lack of political intuition. The absence of confidence toward France was felt in all fields but especially in defense. Besides the French defeat in Vietnam several other occurrences had created in the U.S. intelligence community grave suspicions about France's government and French intelligence.

One such instance, which was well known in Europe, implicated not only Jean Mons, General Secretary for National Defense, whose position was quite similar to that of the Executive Secretary of the National Security Council, but also two of his deputies — Labrusse and Turpin. They were charged with passing to the Communists the transcripts of secret meetings on Vietnam of the National Defense Committee at the time of Dien Bien Phu. Later Mons was found not guilty, but his two deputies were given jail sentences. All were Freemasons, and Labrusse was a known friend of Emmanuel d'Astier.

Before their arrest U.S. security agencies had been told that the real author of the leaks to the Soviet might be the Minister of the Interior himself, François Mitterand. No evidence of his implication could be uncovered, however, and the rumor was considered part of a political machination against him. The episode would not have gone any further if another incident had not come up at the same time.

Nicholas Khokhlov, the famous MVD captain who chose to defect to the West rather than to carry out the assassination of a Russian anti-Communist leader in exile, had a friend in the Soviet Embassy in Paris. Several months after his defection, he expressed his wish to speak to his friend, hoping to convince him to join him. The SDECE and the Sécurité du Territoire were informed by American security services of Khokhlov's wish. An investigation confirmed the presence of his friend, Volokitine, inside the Soviet Embassy in Paris. He was tailed on several occasions when he took walks in Paris, and apparently he enjoyed the same relative freedom as the other embassy members. He seemed to be under no special Russian surveillance. His telephone was monitored, and it was established that he immediately answered all the calls directed to him, meaning that the Soviet switchboard never tried to interfere.

It was decided that Khokhlov would come to Paris, call Volokitine on the phone, and try to set up a meeting with him. Khokhlov's visit to Paris and the reasons behind it were known only to a very limited number of people in the SDECE and the Ministry of the Interior. One morning Khokhlov, under the supervision of the Sécurité du Territoire, called Volokitine. The USSR switchboard, which until then had always put Volokitine's calls through immediately, answered briefly that he was not there. A second call brought the same answer and the operator disconnected. It was decided that Khokhlov would try again the following day.

That same afternoon, however, agents keeping watch on the

Russian Embassy saw a car speeding away in which they thought they recognized one of the passengers as Volokitine. Another embassy car was following. The Sûreté's car was, of course, the last in the caravan.

At Orly Airport, which proved to be the destination, a Russian Aeroflot plane was waiting. The first car drove straight through, right to the airplane, without bothering to stop or ask the police for a clearance. A diplomat from the embassy first got out of the car, then Volokitine, followed by another Russian official. The Russian Ambassador occupied the front seat and was the last one out. From the second car, four Russians emerged and surrounded Volokitine. They pushed him toward the steps. The men from Sûreté jumped out of their car and stopped everyone, asking Volokitine if he was leaving of his free will.

"Yes," he answered.

The French agents reminded him that he would receive protection if his desire was to remain in France, but the Russians around him started to argue and to protest vehemently, making such a noise that Volokitine's answer was never heard. Ignoring the French security officers, the Russians proceeded firmly to escort Volokitine up the steps and inside the plane, acting as if they were on Russian soil.

By that time, French police reinforcements had arrived at the scene. The officers made their way inside the plane and, once more, asked Volokitine if he was leaving voluntarily. Again his answer was yes. The French had no choice but to leave the plane. The engines were immediately started and the plane was soon on its way to Russia. Volokitine was never heard from again.

Helpless, several American security officers had watched the entire scene. Back in Washington they complained about the way the whole operation had been handled. Since I was not familiar with all the details, I asked my headquarters to brief me on the facts.

The SDECE's story was very involved. They claimed that Khokhlov had spoken with an American accent when he called the Russian Embassy and asked for Volokitine. This in itself alarmed the switchboard operator, who preferred not to transfer the call to Volokitine as she normally did. To prove their point, SDECE officers said that they had taped the conversation as a matter of routine when they were monitoring the Russian Embassy phone calls. When American security asked to have the tape played back, SDECE apologized that it had been erased and no longer existed. However, the Americans knew from the Russian interpreter who had been present when Khokhlov made his calls that he had not spoken with an American accent, especially since he spoke little or no English.

Why did SDECE officers invent that story? American security got the impression they were trying to hide something or protect someone.

In the meantime, French Sûreté officers attributed the failure of the operation to the French Minister of the Interior, François Mitterand, who was one of the few people let into the secret. They claimed he had tipped the Soviet Embassy about the forthcoming telephone call from Khokhlov.

By doing this, they were denouncing their own boss. The suspicious behavior of the Sûreté, added to the uneasiness created by SDECE, produced immediate results. After four years of effort to build up confidence between French and American intelligence, I saw the collapse of all my endeavors. And who could blame the Americans for being distrustful in the aftermath of their bitter experience with Philby?

Security was never considered extremely important in France. Daily happenings in the French Embassy in Washington were a demonstration of the contempt French civil servants showed toward secrecy.

One day the chief of the embassy code room came to see me, seeking my advice on a peculiar situation. He had noticed that the secretary in charge of typing the incoming deciphered cables was making an extra copy of each cable concerning Vietnam. At the end of the day she was seen carefully folding the copies into her purse. The head of the ciphering division called her and asked for an explanation.

"Well," she admitted, "my boyfriend, an American colonel, is in charge of Vietnam in the G2 Division. Very often we go to visit some of his friends and the conversation always ends up about the situation in Vietnam. I was feeling kind of left out at first and in order to make an impression, I began studying the cables. Now

240

I have something to talk about and everyone is surprised that I know so much. I've become very popular."

The girl was fired. But she was certainly innocent of any wrongdoing. The responsibility lay with the people who hired her. One can be stupid without being a traitor.

More serious was another case in which a Vietnam official who had been with me during the war and was temporarily in Washington in an official position came to see me. He showed me a copy of a cable addressed to the French ambassador in Washington by the French Secretary for Foreign Affairs. The cable sharply criticized the ambassador and relayed stern orders. I asked my informant who supplied him with the cable, but he refused to answer. He said that he only wanted to warn me of obvious leaks in our embassy and this for old time's sake, but he would not say anything else.

I immediately went to the ambassador with the cable. He was, of course, flabbergasted. He had personally given orders to the head of the ciphering division to keep the cable in his safe and not show it to anyone — not even the First Counselor. Two other persons besides the ambassador had seen the cable, the head of the ciphering division and the secretary who typed it. Both seemed above suspicion. Still, the fact that I was holding a copy of it proved that someone had passed it out. Security measures were tightened for a while in the code room, but to my surprise no further investigation was made, and when I suggested that a request be sent to the Sûreté to dispatch an agent to Washington, the proposal was ruled out. It seemed that our diplomats preferred the idea of a security leak to the prospect of a thorough investigation.

Added to the uncomfortable feeling of knowing that someone in the embassy was passing documents to a foreign representation was the fact that I met with the disapproval of my embassy colleagues by trying to look more deeply into the case. A girl, I found out later, was responsible for the offense, but this one had protection and was not dismissed. She was simply transferred to another department for appearance's sake — her new position being as sensitive as the former one.

The embassy clerks and secretaries were hired without prior investigation as to their backgrounds, and such a check, if suggested, would have been considered an infringement on their rights. Security problems were many, and I noted to what extent my colleagues were deliberately ignoring the rules of security. I was relieved when occasionally someone besides myself would bring up the question. From time to time a State Department official would approach the subject with the ambassador by criticizing the behavior of a certain member of his embassy. The ambassador would immediately call me and report the disturbing remarks.

This was the case when an embassy employee befriended a member of the Soviet Embassy and attracted attention. He frequently invited the Soviet diplomat to his home and was seen with him regularly in various Washington restaurants and nightclubs. The Russian was known as a member of his country's secret services, which immediately cast suspicion on their relationship. The French diplomat never tried to conceal their association, so the idea of foul play on his part could be discarded. I decided one day to have a talk with him on the subject.

Perfectly at ease, he told me how he had made the acquaintance of the Russian during an international meeting on one commodity or another. The Russian was seated on his right and their conversation progressed easily. The Frenchman had in front of him several documents issued by the Government Printing Office that were freely sold to the public. The Russian asked him if he could have a look at one since Soviet citizens, he explained, were not authorized to buy the publications of the Government Printing Office. The Frenchman was shocked by such a restriction and toward the end of the meeting proposed that the Russian follow him to his office where he would, as a friendly gesture, make available all the official publications of the U.S. government he had. The Soviet was delighted at such a golden opportunity and from then on was regularly provided with all new publications. He was also invited to all the parties given by his new friend. Of course, this was an ideal setting to make contacts with members of other foreign embassies and to identify them. As a perfect guest the Russian never failed to bring with him some of their famous caviar and a bottle of vodka.

The Frenchman probably meant no wrong, but he was one of those who were disgusted by the excesses of McCarthyism and willing to go out of their way to make friends with the Soviets as a compensatory gesture for what they considered unfair persecution. Unfortunately such an attitude is all it takes to make a Soviet agent out of a well-meaning idealist. The switch from harmless publications to secret documents is only a small step. The ambassador put an end to this relationship, and I hope the Frenchman gained some wisdom from the experience.

Differences of opinion prevailed between French counterespionage and other NATO divisions regarding the evaluation of the problems of security created by the Soviets. The French services argued that members of the Communist Party were never used by the Soviets as secret agents, while the NATO services maintained that the pragmatic Soviets were making use of every contact they possibly could for this purpose. Obviously the opportunities for recruitment among members of the different Communist parties were enormous.

To the French, a registered member of the party was above suspicion as far as espionage activities for the Soviets were concerned. This puerile conception led France to become, as it turned out later, the launching site for Communist espionage in the world.

The lack of security inside the French secret services proved to be costly. In collaboration with our NATO allies, the SDECE supported various movements composed of exiles from countries behind the Iron Curtain. Implantation of intelligence networks was a necessity in those countries but was made difficult by the tight control at border crossings. Agents had to be smuggled in, and parachuting was still the best means. Experts in SDECE were in charge of the training of agents and the planning of their missions. On clear nights the men were parachuted into carefully selected areas. Although the operation seemed to be a success, none of the unfortunate men was ever heard from after their first contact with alien soil.

We learned only much later that our missions encountered the same fate as the missions in Albania about which Philby boasted with impunity, when Communist police were right on the scene to pick up our agents. Who was feeding the Soviets precise information on our secret operations? French intelligence officers in charge of the program put the blame on the immigrants whose indiscretions were supposedly the cause of our misfortunes. It would have been a valid explanation had the immigrants known the date and exact place of the drops.

These problems with very serious overtones were not making my liaison work with NATO any easier. But being stationed in Washington involved me in other activities not directly related to intelligence.

In order to promote a better understanding of the organization of NATO command and of the capabilities of the Americans for retaliation in the event of a Soviet attack, the State Department frequently extended invitations to high-ranking European officials to visit the United States. Seldom did a week go by without a French prefect or a congressman showing up in Washington to attend a meeting at the Pentagon or be escorted on a guided tour of a particular factory or some American defense installation. Transportation bills were taken care of by the U.S. government, as well as expenses for the trip, which were covered by weekly checks on the U.S. treasury.

Many of the French officials who in recent years have followed the fashionable trend of de Gaulle's anti-American position did not complain then, when they cashed their State Department checks. Going through the photocopies of all the checks I was asked to endorse as a favor to the recipients, I cannot help but smile at the thought of their publication next to the anti-NATO or anti-American declarations now made by the same persons.

Most of those who were unfortunate enough to sample the American generosity were recommended to me either by headquarters or by a member of the government. I was always pleased to welcome them and try to make their stay enjoyable. These visitors were not picked at random by the American representation in Paris, but were selected after consultation with the French government. A French official would list the names of all the persons singled out to be invited and hand the list to a member of the U.S. Embassy along with his suggestions on which military installations or civilian plants would be of interest to the visitors. A special detailed schedule for the VIP was worked out. The man in the French government in charge of this program was Georges Paques, who, some may remember, was later arrested as a Soviet agent and sentenced to jail for life.

He had been working for the Soviets since 1943. With the help, in all good faith, of the many visitors to the United States who reported to him, Paques probably passed on to the Russians many valuable pieces of intelligence on U.S. defense plants and on American intentions and potential.

I myself received Paques in Washington when he came to attend top-secret meetings in the Pentagon. He had been warmly recommended by members of my agency, the SDECE, with whom he had a close relationship. A lot has been written about British Soviet agent Philby and his life of deception, but nothing has been said about Georges Paques' twenty years as a Russian agent. Paques' activities were certainly of as much value to the Soviets as his British counterpart. I wonder if after such a sequence of aggravating incidents, the United States' confidence in her European allies will ever be completely restored.

In Washington our well-liked French Ambassador, Henri Bonnet, had been replaced by Maurice Couve de Murville, who later became de Gaulle's Prime Minister. The cheerful atmosphere of the embassy immediately disappeared into an era of gloom. The melancholy and skepticism of the new ambassador soon rubbed off on his collaborators. Couve de Murville's first move in his new post was to have his office doors padded in order to cut himself off from the noise and most likely the problems of his embassy.

The ambassador had, at the beginning of the war, been a trusted servant of the Pétain regime. He then showed up in North Africa to become a member of the short-lived Giraud pseudo-government until President Roosevelt and some of his assistants decided that his past association with Pétain made him unfit to serve Giraud. Couve de Murville never forgave the Americans for having pushed him out and for interfering with French governmental affairs that should have been none of their business. He distrusted Washington and was angered at the weakness of the French government, which he criticized for being unable to set up a policy of its own and preferring instead to follow blindly the State Department's line.

I reported to him weekly on my activities. Although he was always extremely courteous, he never hid his skepticism about the usefulness of my efforts to promote a closer collaboration between French and American intelligence. The fact that I continually received orders requesting material or financial support from American intelligence particularly infuriated him, and his desire was to see the French government act with more pride and independence from its allies.

Before representing France in Washington, D.C., Couve de Murville had been our Ambassador in Cairo. His stay in Egypt left him with a great fondness for the Arabs, and he was never too enthusiastic about defending the French position against attacks from Algerian nationalists who were conducting a violent campaign against France in Washington and the United Nations.

Our soldiers were fighting in Algeria and our Minister for Foreign Affairs, Christian Pineau, was left practically alone to assume the defense of our interests on the diplomatic front. Unable to obtain from de Murville the support he needed, he recalled him after eighteen months and named Hervé Alphand as his successor.

Difficulties between French and Allied intelligence were increasing. France seemed to consider NATO as a defense treaty with no limitations. Whoever the aggressor was, the French government expected help from its allies. In the United States, NATO was viewed as a treaty of alliance against direct aggression from the Soviets, and although proof of Communist support to Algerian nationalists had been established, the State Department and American intelligence categorically refused to help the French. The gap was widening steadily and I was doing all I could to keep the communications channels open with my American friends.

For some time I had been suggesting a meeting in Paris at which each side could express its views and a solution could be worked out to everyone's satisfaction. Boursicot raised no objection and was willing to go along with such an attempt to iron out differences, but in Washington those involved were much too busy for this conciliatory dialogue. I had almost given up the idea when in the middle of October 1956 one of my good friends, Frank Wisner, who was Director for Plan in the CIA, told me of his plans to go to Europe in the coming days; he was willing to sit down with my director, Pierre Boursicot, and discuss the problems that existed between the two agencies. I immediately cabled my headquarters and was given the green light.

So I flew to Paris and on October 29, 1956, was on hand to receive Frank Wisner. During the few days I spent in Paris prior to the American official's arrival, the climate of mystery surrounding Boursicot and his close associates did not escape me. Several of my friends, when I questioned them, did not provide me with an answer. I sensed something unusual was going on but was unable to pin it down.

I welcomed Wisner at the airport. He was coming from London and immediately inquired about the Israeli attack in the Sinai which had been announced the same morning. I had read about it in the papers, but knew nothing more. We drove directly to Pierre Boursicot's residence, where a luncheon was scheduled.

During the meal Boursicot evaded all Wisner's direct questions, but asked his guest to join him for dinner the same evening, since Guy Mollet, France's Prime Minister, was supposed to make an important announcement. The lunch did not last as long as usual, for everyone was obviously preoccupied.

In the afternoon I accompanied Wisner on a Paris shopping excursion and happened to run into a friend who was a member of a ministerial cabinet. After the introduction and other amenities, the French official knowingly said to Frank, "So you are here in connection with the landing."

My surprise was genuine.

"Yes," he insisted, "the Prime Minister's announcement of our landing in Suez is scheduled for tonight, is it not?"

Wisner's mischievous smile told me he knew perfectly well. I asked him point-blank and the smile never faded. "I may have heard hints about it in London."

It was 2:30 P.M. in Paris, or 8:30 A.M. in Washington. He left me to go directly to the American Embassy. I am certain that President Eisenhower got confirmation a few moments later of an event he already was fully informed on. The version of Washington being taken completely by surprise is therefore a myth.

In France, Frank Wisner's visit on this very same day was regarded as a carefully planned "coincidence" and was received among government members as a tacit endorsement of the French policy.

The same evening, after SDECE director Boursicot had made a toast to the United States, his guest's answer was careful.

"As an American," he said, "I can only regret the action under-

247

taken by France, but as a friend of France, I wish her a prompt success. I hope your military understand that rapidity is the key factor in the operation you have initiated."

The director asked me to return to Washington the following day. Boarding the Air France plane with me at Orly was an American intelligence officer I knew. He was coming back from the Middle East to report to Washington. He commented that unless results were felt immediately the whole thing would turn out to be a catastrophe. Although I told him our views concurred with his, he showed a certain amount of skepticism.

After flying for six hours, our plane developed engine trouble in the middle of the Atlantic. One engine stopped and the other showed signs of being overheated. The captain decided to turn the plane back. My arrival in Washington was thus delayed for twenty-four hours.

One hour after reaching Washington, I received a call from Allen Dulles, who had succeeded General Walter Bedell Smith as head of CIA. He asked me to come to see him as soon as possible. In his official capacity he was angered and told me so, mentioning President Eisenhower's irritation over the fact he had not been informed. Following the rules, I assured him I would report our conversation to headquarters.

As soon as I got home, Dulles was on the phone again to invite me to come out and have a drink with him. When I arrived he was as I always had known him, kind and extremely courteous. He was once more the great friend of France, eager in time of crisis to show his affection for my country.

"Tell Paris to act quickly," he warned also, "with your paratroopers you should be able to occupy Cairo tomorrow, and that would change everything."

He inquired about our needs in equipment and our problems of communications and offered to help — provided that it was kept secret. Contrasted with his attitude a few hours earlier he was now offering all the help he could. I immediately informed Paris, but no reply was ever made to the offer.

At any rate, it must be acknowledged that if for obvious political reasons the U.S. officially condemned the Franco-English action in Egypt, they did not abandon their allies, but privately and discreetly offered their support. If the military in charge of the Suez operation had shown more determination and eagerness, we could have come out victorious, and this with the blessing, discreet but sincere, of Washington.

American intelligence had been looked down upon by the French secret services up to this point. They were criticized for being too young, inexperienced, and too eager to make up for their shortcomings with excessive material and financial resources. But during the Suez crisis their grasp of the situation was evident. Thoroughly grounded in French and British intentions, they were able to detect the inadequacy of the military command and the dilatory conduct of the operation. The quality of their intelligence could no longer be disputed.

Soon after the Suez imbroglio, Pierre Boursicot was replaced at the head of SDECE. He had served six years as chief of French intelligence and among other things had obtained for the civilian members of his service the status of civil servants. Intelligence officers had now joined company with all other civil servants, sharing their worries about promotions and retirement pay. Was this a good thing? It is hard to say, but this measure, by giving official status to civilians in French intelligence, resulted in antagonizing the military, who had hoped to take over completely. The military were leading the fight in Algeria and enjoyed a strong position in France. To placate them to a certain extent without alienating the civilians, the government appointed a military man as head of SDECE. General Grossin had been military assistant to Vincent Auriol, President of the French Republic, for seven years and was very knowledgeable in the field of politics. Furthermore, the new director had been in the underground during the war and was born in Algeria; at the time this was considered a guaranty to keep Algeria French.

In May 1958, following a tradition now established, General Grossin came to Washington to pay a visit to CIA director Allen Dulles, who received him with his legendary courtesy. On the other hand, for a reason unknown to me, J. Edgar Hoover, director of the FBI, refused to see him. General Grossin showed no sign of disappointment and remained undisturbed, as he did when learning of the events which had taken an unexpected turn in France.

Confronted with the incoherent behavior of the Paris government, the Army had decided to take over the secession movement in Algeria and demanded a new government. Jacques Soustelle, my superior during the war, easily could have become chief of the government, but his deep and sentimental loyalty to de Gaulle made him step aside, boosting de Gaulle in his return to power.

General Grossin, who knew well the opinions of the former leader of the Free French, had no qualms about expressing his personal views to Frank Wisner during the course of a luncheon. "De Gaulle taking power in France means the victory of Communism within the next twenty years."

One guest later reported this statement in Paris, and General Grossin was often taken to task for it. The future proved how close he was to the truth.

The following month I was grieved by the news of my father's sudden death. Before leaving for Paris to attend the funeral, I received a call from Allen Dulles expressing his sympathy and asking me to drop by his office for a short conversation.

"President Eisenhower," he said, "holds General de Gaulle in high esteem and hopes that their excellent relations will continue after he assumes the highest office in France. It is a fact that some difficulties have arisen between France and the United States, but nothing that can't be worked out. President Eisenhower will do everything in his power to improve relations between the two countries. It is considered here that an informal approach gives generally much better results.

"The President has in mind to ask his old comrade General Bradley to fly to Paris for a meeting with General de Gaulle in order to examine the current problems and work out a satisfactory solution. General Bradley invariably during the war was on General de Gaulle's side and he seems to be the ideal envoy. However, before taking a definite step, the President would like to know de Gaulle's reaction to this proposal. Could you, while in Paris, approach him unofficially?

This was part of my purpose in Washington, to act as intermediary between my government and the United States government. I promised Dulles to convey his suggestion to the people directly concerned.

The day of my father's funeral I received a telephone call and

250

was informed that Georges Pompidou, General de Gaulle's director of cabinet, would see me the next morning at Hôtel Matignon. This was the first time I had heard his name, but this was understandable since he had played no part in the underground or Free French Forces.

The Hôtel Matignon was a familiar place — I used to go there regularly to brief the Prime Minister and director of cabinets. The morning was buzzing with activity. General de Gaulle was expecting British Prime Minister Macmillan, and the courtyard was filled with the elite regiment of the *Gardes Républicains* in full uniform, waiting to present arms.

The journalists, some of them familiar, were getting ready for the flow of high-ranking officials. I stopped and chatted with several in the group, asking about the personality of Mr. Pompidou. No one was able to say much about him. They knew of his connection for several years with the Rothschild Bank and that he was now General de Gaulle's choice for his cabinet — nothing more.

French officials subscribe to the unfortunate custom of leaving visitors to cool their heels in the waiting room. This is meant to produce the impression that they are overburdened with work. Mr. Pompidou, however, did not keep me waiting. He received me immediately and with great courtesy. His office, located on the second floor, had a pleasant view, overlooking the portico of the traditional residence of French prime ministers.

After offering me a cigarette he walked away from his desk and took a chair next to me, then proceeded to ask questions about myself and my activities in the United States. I explained succinctly, giving him a rundown on the situation on the other side of the Atlantic, then related my last conversation with Allen Dulles. When I mentioned the possibility of a visit by General Bradley, he told me right away that it was unnecessary.

"The Americans," he said, "have little regard for us and wish to make France one of their satellites. They actually enjoy a position of strength since they are in possession of the atomic bomb. If they want a dialogue with us, let them assist us first with the building of our own atomic bomb. Then we will be able to talk on an equal footing. Talks with Washington would lead nowhere since Americans are in competition with European countries."

At one point I mentioned the necessity of cooperation within NATO and he exploded, "NATO is nothing more than an excuse for the United States to stick its nose into European affairs, and General de Gaulle intends to do something about it soon.

"We do not need the Americans," he said toward the end of the conversation. "They can stay home and mind their own business."

He had worked himself into such a fit of anger that I did not think it was the proper time to remind him how the same Americans had some fourteen years before landed on French soil to rid our country, for the second time, of the German oppressor.

Pompidou invited me to return to see him next time I came to Paris. Once more I asked him if an informal meeting between General Bradley and General de Gaulle, at which certain questions could be tackled, would not prove useful.

"No," he said flatly.

Walking downstairs on my way out, I wondered how Mr. Pompidou could so categorically have answered my question without first consulting General de Gaulle. Either he had taken it upon himself to answer for his superior without the latter's authorization, in which case de Gaulle had not been very wise in the choice of his assistant, or the views expressed reflected de Gaulle's own ideas and were an indication that France was indeed in trouble.

Before leaving the Hôtel Matignon I headed for the office of a certain Jacques Foccart who had been calling my friends insisting that I come to see him. I did not know him any more than I had known Pompidou. I had only been told he was once with "Action" in SDECE and was now in charge of questions dealing with intelligence for de Gaulle.

His office was located on the first floor left of the entrance and overlooked the gardens. In each corner of the room a desk was occupied by a busy young man. Jacques Foccart's desk was different from the others in that an impressive switchboard stood on the right side, as in a police station. From time to time a light went on, and lifting the receiver, Foccart listened silently while taking notes. I had the unpleasant feeling that he was purely and simply listening to conversations not meant for him. Contrary to Pompidou, his manners were not the least courteous and he acted like a reenlisted noncommissioned officer. Only one thing seemed to interest him, the way CIA operated, and he asked me countless questions about it. He told me he had been put in charge by de Gaulle of the reorganization of SDECE and asked me to prepare for him a diagram showing the organization of American intelligence. Stressing the urgency of his request, he insisted on having the information within forty-eight hours.

Two days later I handed him a hastily written report on the American conception of intelligence. He went through it quickly and voiced his surprise that no service like "Action" was mentioned.

"But how do the Americans get rid of people?"

I answered that assassination was not, to my knowledge, a common practice in the United States.

He gave me a grim look and asked for my personal address to enable him to contact me directly without having to go through official channels. Then coming back to the same subject, he insisted, "But there must be a special section in charge of eliminating certain individuals. Try to find out and let me know. I would like to know also if there is a way to make contact with the Mafia. The services of a few thugs could be useful at times."

I never contacted Jacques Foccart again, nor did I write him. It had suddenly dawned on me that intelligence, for those in power, had been relegated to the background. The era of political assassinations had now begun.

Autumn days can be dreary in the region of the Rhine river, and on this morning in November 1958 the beautiful landscape was shrouded in mist. The peaks of the Siebengebirge barely stood out against menacing black clouds, and the health resort of Bad Godesberg seemed to be in a state of lethargy. The population of the well-known spa had, however, grown considerably larger, since the foreign diplomats accredited to the West German government preferred it to Bonn only four miles away.

In the living room of a small isolated house overlooking the river, a man of short stature nonchalantly released the breech of a submachine gun he had been cleaning with great care. Several cartridge clips lay on the table next to him. Another man with dark complexion stood smoking a cigarette, an absent look on his face. When the telephone rang the first man put the gun down and lifted the receiver without a word.

"Paul," said a sharp voice on the other end.

"Jacques," was the short answer.

"The orders are to be carried out this morning."

"O.K."

He hung up and turned to his comrade. "They said to do it this morning."

His French bore the typical accent of persons coming from North Africa. He put two cartridge clips in his pocket, then loaded the gun and walked toward the garage door, carrying his weapon under his arm.

The shiny black Mercedes was ready to go. The man took the seat next to the driver and waited for his companion to open the garage door and join him. Slowly the car edged out. The iron gate was already open. The driver then stopped his vehicle and closed it behind them.

They drove along the deserted country road, heading at moderate speed toward the center of the town, then proceeding through the residential section to a busy street where the car slowed down and came to a stop. A moment later a second Mercedes with two men in the front seat appeared and parked right behind it.

It was around 8:30 A.M. when a man bundled up in a topcoat came out of one of the buildings accompanied by a young woman. They got into a black 203 Peugeot parked at the curb and drove off, heading for the *Autobahn* going to Bonn. Once on the highway the Peugeot accelerated to its maximum speed. Not too far behind, the two Mercedes followed. After about two miles one of the following cars began a maneuver to pass, then, getting back in line in front of the Peugeot, reduced its speed, forcing the other driver to slow down. The second Mercedes immediately came up alongside as if it was also going to pass. Only the tip of a submachine gun barrel was showing through the open window. It fired. The Peugeot, out of control, swerved wildly then turned over and came to rest in the ditch alongside the road. In a fraction of a second the two Mercedes had sped away and were out of sight.

As in any accident, motorists gathered around offering help. The driver was seriously hurt and unconscious. His lady companion came out miraculously uninjured. She was able to talk to the police when the emergency vehicles rushed to the scene. Her friend's name was Ait Ahcene, a representative of the Algerian revolutionaries in West Germany, where he lived under a cover provided by the Embassy of Tunisia. He had on several occasions received threatening letters, showing in place of the signature an imprint of a red hand.

Ait Ahcene eventually was flown to a Tunisian hospital, where he died from his injuries a few months later.

The following year, 1959, in the beginning of March, the action took place in Frankfurt.

At around 10 P.M. a tall, loose-limbed individual walked into one of Frankfurt's well known cafés and went directly to the telephone. He dialed a number. "Pierre," he said shortly.

"Georges," was the reply, then after a pause the sharp voice continued rapidly in French: "The Mercedes known to you is presently parked at Guiolettstrasse. Proceed immediately with Operation No. 5."

"All right," answered the man, and he crossed the room rapidly on his way out.

A taxi responded to his signal, pulled right in front of him, and started off to the address given by the passenger. After paying the fare the man lingered a while, and as soon as the cab had driven away, walked briskly into a narrow street and into a building. Rushing up the stairs, his knock at the door of an apartment was answered immediately by a man of typically North African appearance.

"Operation No. 5," the visitor said at once. Familiar with the place, he opened a closet and took out a carton containing a small metal box about five inches long, two or two and a half inches high, and three inches wide. Unscrewing the top, he proceeded to adjust something inside, then closed it and put it back in its cardboard container. Carrying his precious load, he motioned to his companion to open the door. Both men walked down the stairs and got into a late-model Porsche which was parked just outside. The distance to Guiolettstrasse in a fast car was covered in no time at all. The Mercedes in question was immediately spotted. They drove up to it. The tall man got out while the driver kept the engine running. A quick look around told him the coast was clear. Swiftly he raised the hood, inserted the metal box, securing it carefully,

256

closed the hood, and got right back into the Porsche, which took off at high speed.

The next morning the owner of the Mercedes, Georg Puchert, a dealer in ammunitions, well known in the trade, got into his car. He started it and drove a few yards before a violent explosion blew up the entire front of the vehicle, killing the driver instantly. Inside the car investigators were later to discover the imprint of a red hand. Georg Puchert had been doing business with Algerian nationalists.

The mysterious high-pitched voice contacting the killers and ordering the execution of Ait Ahcene and Georg Puchert belonged to Colonel Marcel Mercier, SDECE representative working in liaison with BND, or Bundesnachrichtendienst, the West German secret services headed by the famous General Reinhard von Gehlen.

Marcel Mercier was better known as *le petit Mercier*, to differentiate him from one of his colleagues, another Mercier who was a career officer. He had been assigned to counterespionage, and was taken prisoner at the beginning of the war by the Germans; he saw the end of his captivity in 1945. Colonel Verneuil, the chief of counterespionage, showed no particular eagerness in welcoming him back to his section and switched him to the intelligence division, which sent him to Switzerland as head of the station, with the cover of commercial attaché. Of course this title was a facade only for people not in the know, since Mercier immediately reported to Swiss intelligence and police with whom he was supposed to act as liaison. All cases and problems of common interest were discussed with SDECE through its representative Mercier.

General von Gehlen was then in Switzerland, where he had taken refuge, and Mercier had been instructed by SDECE director Henri Ribière to contact him. Ribière made a special trip to Switzerland to have a meeting with von Gehlen and sound him out on his intentions. He returned from Switzerland impressed with the knowledge displayed by the former chief of the anti-Soviet intelligence division in the ABWER, the famous Fremde Heere Ost, and authorized Mercier to facilitate things for him to a certain extent. Later, when von Gehlen went back to Germany to assume the direction of BND, he always remembered the man who played Santa Claus on behalf of SDECE.

In 1957 the main concern of French intelligence was the activities outside France of North African nationalists. Mercier's orders were to concentrate on the doings of Algerians and their partisans in Switzerland. In order to get better results he asked the cooperation of Swiss security, which as a matter of routine kept a close watch on the entry and exit of foreign nationals. The Attorney General of the Confederation, René Dubois, a friend of France, did not raise any objection when one of his assistants, Inspector Ulrich, told him of Mercier's request. To him, the identity and activities of Algerians entering Switzerland were not that important, and after all, they were French citizens. Mercier got what he wanted and developed a friendship with Mr. and Mrs. Dubois. To express his thanks to the Attorney General and to compromise him at the same time, Mercier invited him and his wife to France, and Dubois was foolish enough to accept. They thought it perfectly natural to be treated to lunch and dinner in Paris or Lyons by their friend Mercier, but back in Switzerland it was more difficult for them to refuse him anything.

Algerians and Egyptians had been watching Mercier and were intrigued by his frequent contacts with the Attorney General. While he was in France, the Swiss official was followed, and proof of his close relationship with French intelligence was established.

The fact that he was from the French part of Switzerland did not make the Attorney General very popular with his fellow citizens from the German-speaking section of his country. The publisher of a confidential sheet in German was too ready to pass on to the President of the Confederation the information he was getting first-hand from the Arabs.

Attorney General Dubois, panic-stricken and realizing he had fallen into Mercier's trap, committed suicide. Mercier did not wait to be deported and left immediately for Paris.

Sanctions are usually severe for an intelligence officer who allows himself to become involved in such an enormous and well-publicized affair. Surprisingly, Mercier was not dismissed; he only laid low for a while with no new assignment. But when the decision was made to set up a special force in charge of getting rid of Algerian nationalists and the like, Mercier's name came up naturally, since everybody remembered his good relationship with General von

258

Gehlen when both were in Switzerland. To pull strings of the dread "Red Hand" organization, Mercier was sent to Germany as SDECE representative and liaison with the head of BND. Before leaving he had been warned that he had better make up for his past errors, especially Dubois' suicide due to his imprudence. He was expected to provide the special team of "executioners" with accurate information on the individuals who were entered on the government's blacklist.

Mercier's zeal did not weaken during the time he spent in Germany. Dozens of assassinations were carried out upon the information he readily supplied. In each case, so that no complicity charges would be brought against him, an alibi was always set up, and on a specific day and hour, when the Red Hand was striking, Mercier was either with a member of BND or a police official who, if need be, could vouch for him.

Mercier received no assistance or cooperation with his gruesome enterprise from General von Gehlen's services and had to get the information he needed through his own agents. These agents were, for the most part, former Nazis who were now working either for the police or in German intelligence and were recruited by Mercier through blackmail.

Orders to do away with a given individual came either from the Prime Minister himself or from a member of his cabinet. De Gaulle's direct entourage showed little interest in military actions aimed at winning the war in Algeria, but wanted above all to be informed about special operations being carried out. The decisions of Prime Minister Michel Debré were passed on to "Action," whose responsibility was to retain the hatchet men and to decide on the murder weapon and other details of the execution.

Besides the use of guns or knives, more sophisticated methods had been perfected. Carbon dioxide guns ejecting small syringes had been purchased in the United States, where they were used to capture animals alive—but the SDECE people substituted the tranquilizing drug with a lethal poison. The victim showed all the symptoms of having suffered from a heart attack. The only problem with this near-perfect method was that an accomplice was needed on the scene of the accident — supposedly rushing to the aid of the victim but actually removing such incriminating evidence as the needle, syringe, etc. At first, several different poisons were tested with more or less satisfactory results until "Action" came out with a final product of which no trace could be detected in the victim's body.

Bombs had also been perfected. Magnetic bombs were built with specific uses in mind. A device designed to destroy an automobile was different from a bomb to be planted in an airplane, and studies had been conducted to show the exact spot where the explosive would go off with maximum results. The best methods were developed for sabotaging a plane or an automobile so that no abnormal cause for the accident could be discovered.

"Action" was composed of career and reserve officers and non-commissioned officers. One unit was stationed in Toulouse, another in Perpignan. Its members were trained in hand-to-hand fighting, but with a few exceptions they loathed the idea of killing an unarmed man. To avoid difficulties, "Action" set out to recruit volunteers for this special job among Frenchmen from North Africa whose families had been maltreated or tortured by the Arabs. But experience proved these men to be too emotional. So for its special operations, "Action" had to recruit from among ex-convicts, pimps, or former members of police forces in Morocco and Tunisia who were now idle since the independence of these two countries. The men underwent thorough training either in North Africa or in isolated dwellings in certain areas in France. They were paid excellent money and were certain to receive a kind of immunity, and they excelled in performing their part in political assassinations. Getting into the act after Mercier's agents had taken care of planning and preliminary work, they carried out their operations coolly and mechanically, always leaving the scene undisturbed.

It is difficult to set an accurate figure on the number of people murdered by the Red Hand. In Germany, Belgium, and Switzerland many of the assassinations were ruled as "natural death." Only the murders which the governments wanted greatly publicized were credited to the Red Hand, as was the case of those engaged in arms traffic.

Puchert's murder was followed by a series of attempts on the lives of his colleagues. Some, like Beisner, former head of a Gestapo division, were seriously hurt. He remained partially paralyzed following the explosion of his automobile. In another instance, Schlutter, who was Puchert's business partner, walked away unhurt from his car completely destroyed by a magnetic bomb.

The arms traffickers were not the only targets of the Red Hand. The organization also hunted supporters of the Algerian nationalists. One of those was Georges Laperche, Professor of Philosophy in Liege (Belgium). A leftist intellectual, Laperche was known to have made several contacts with Algerian nationalists. One day a package arrived through the mail that obviously contained books. In fact the name of the sender was clearly printed — *Presses Universitaires de France*, one of the main publishing houses in France. Unsuspecting, the professor opened it and was blown up by a terrible explosion. He was rushed to a hospital and died in a few hours.

One of Professor Laperche's colleagues had a luckier fate. Mr. Le Grève, member of the committee for "Free Algeria," also received a package that contained a book, *Pacification*, sent by a La Gauche publishing house. When he was opening the package, Le Grève noticed a tiny wire along the wrapping string, which seemed connected to something inside the book. Made cautious by Professor Laperche's dreadful experience, he took it to the police. Inside the book, in which a cavity had been made, experts found an extremely powerful load of dynamite. If Mr. Le Grève had put a little more pressure on the string he would have been another victim of the Red Hand, or in other words, SDECE's "Action."

Even in France the Red Hand's sinister activities were felt. Algerian nationalists considered as too dangerous were disposed of, and so were their most ardent French supporters. Liquidations had become an almost daily routine.

That SDECE should be behind acts of assassins was disgusting to the old guard of intelligence specialists in the agency who wanted no part in the criminal activities. The mass murders were in fact useless in that the Algerians were still fighting the French, and even if their source of supplies in Germany were to be cut off, weapons would still be obtained through the Soviets.

On each trip to France, I would learn that one or another of my old comrades, angered by the unsavory part now played by the agency, had simply dropped out of sight. The SDECE director was trying every way to isolate "Action" from the organization, thus protecting the traditional divisions inside the secret services. "Action" ties with SDECE were loosening — the orders came now directly from the Prime Minister. And members of the President of the Republic's personal staff who once belonged to the ill-famed service kept sending new recruits to be trained without even consulting the head of SDECE.

L'Association Nationale pour Soutien de l'Action du General de Gaulle, an association to support the endeavors of General de Gaulle, had in fact been created, and its members were asked to volunteer in the service "Action" of SDECE. I was given a list of all the people in the United States who had pledged their support to the general and told to try to talk them into joining in the training. But most of them were old ladies and middle-aged gentlemen one could hardly picture signing up for voluntary training to set magnetic bombs in the neighborhood automobiles.

The recruiting of new members of this association in the United States was the responsibility of Colonel Duperier, at the time representing Boeing in France. This position gave him the opportunity to travel freely all over the country. The goal of the association was to have "correspondents" in each of the main U.S. cities to act as liaison with members within the limits of their territory. But few among the French who were approached showed great enthusiasm. George Tilge, President of the Free French, the first to be contacted, said he had to think it over carefully since he had no intention of breaking any U.S. laws. The second, Maurice Galy, President of the French Lycée, when asked by Émile Fauguenot, one of the leaders of the association, agreed to become a member but refused to become involved or to play an active part in the organization.

But if in the United States the "National Association for the Support of the Endeavors of General de Gaulle" was having difficulty in recruiting members, things were different in France. Belonging to the association meant getting quick promotions within the administration or being awarded government contracts. Young men prompt to pledge their support to de Gaulle derived from their participation both material advantages and an outlet for their excess energy. Those who seemed best qualified were asked to take the special training of SDECE's "Action" dealing with parachute jumps, handling of explosives and their many uses for sabotage purposes, and getting rid of an adversary either with guns or knives. In order words, they graduated as experienced guerrilla fighters or full-fledged gangsters. They were then organized into units, ready, through clandestine armed action if necessary, to keep de Gaulle in power. These units were known under different names, the most notorious being the Service for Civic Action, or SAC.

Jacques Foccart, who had himself gone through the "Action" training, was in indirect control of the new teams of fanatic Gaullists. Knowing de Gaulle's plans for the future of Algeria, he consequently knew he would have to call on them sometime soon. Foccart was serving de Gaulle in the capacity of General Secretary for the Community, a position created especially for him. The French Community included all the former French colonies in Africa that had gained their independence from de Gaulle in 1958. To keep a close watch on the governments of the newly independent countries, Foccart had a simple but clever idea: the new heads of states were easily convinced of the necessity to set up their own intelligence in order to control the activity of their political foes. France agreed to supply funds and equipment needed for this project. Of course, experts in the fields of intelligence were also required to brief and advise the new presidents, and soon a Foccart man holding one title or another was assigned to each African government to counsel but also to report faithfully to the Elysée on what was going on in the respective countries. This plan was ingenious and particularly profitable, and who would believe it is still being carried out?

So Foccart had the upper hand in an intelligence network in Africa and in organized groups of Gaullist fanatics. Furthermore, acting as liaison between General de Gaulle and SDECE, he virtually had control over it.

In 1960 several African territories caused the French government concern. Guinea, under the rule of Sekou Touré, had refused to join the community. As for Cameroun, the government which had de Gaulle's backing was faced with being overthrown by the extreme leftist leader Félix Moumie. SDECE's "Action" was instructed to eliminate the troublemaker, and a former officer of dual French and Swiss nationality was picked to execute the orders.

In the beginning of October 1960, Félix Moumie was in Geneva on one of his frequent visits to meet with followers of his movement, the Cameroun People's Union. Moumie received substantial financial help from Guinea and Ghana, and was always comfortably well-off, living grandly and having a good time. He had made the acquaintance, a few months before, of a young woman of Swiss nationality, Liliane Friedli, and was seen traveling with her from Gstaad to Geneva, staying in first-class hotels and patronizing the best restaurants.

Félix Moumie was spending a few days in the company of his Swiss girlfriend when, on October 13, he told her about a dinner invitation he thought it best to attend alone, saying, "We are going to talk about politics and you would be bored."

He was supposed to have dinner that night with a journalist he had met some time before and had seen frequently since. Moumie took along his secretary, who was also acting as a kind of bodyguard. He considered an attempt on his life unlikely while he was in Switzerland and took rather lightly the threats he had received on several occasions from the Red Hand. His bodyguard secretary was more for show, and flattered his vanity.

Following the trend of the new generation of young Africans, Moumie was as careful of his personal appearance as of the food and wine he selected. He always ordered elaborate dishes which he thought would prove him to be a connoisseur of haute cuisine. He probably enjoyed an excellent and expensive meal that night with his journalist friend.

Back in his hotel room, where the charming Liliane was waiting, he complained of an upset stomach. However, it was not the first time that too much good wine had caused him discomfort and so he was not alarmed. He spent a restless night and for two days went about his various activities with a sickish feeling he was unable to understand. Before going into politics, Moumie had studied medicine, and he now tried to diagnose the symptoms he was experiencing.

On the evening of October 15, a sort of languor overcame him, his breathing became difficult, and he had trouble moving around. With great perspicacity he realized he had been poisoned with Tallium. Tallium is commonly used in Europe to get rid of rats.

The doctor who until then had done no more than give him injections to kill the pain asked that he be taken immediately to a hospital and called to report the case to the police. Tallium when taken internally causes a general paralysis. Before being put in an iron lung to ease his breathing, Moumie had time to answer a few questions. In his agony, he remembered having two Pernods that night he went out and that one seemed particularly bitter. Then he went into a coma that lasted until he died during the night of November 4.

The girlfriend, Liliane Friedli, had disappeared the day the African leader was admitted to the hospital, and for a while the Swiss police thought she might have played a part in the murder of her lover; but forty hours later she was reported in a Geneva hospital, where she had been taken after an overdose of sedatives. When she was well enough to talk, she said she had made a quick trip to Paris by taxi to meet with the Guinean Ambassador and give him Moumie's briefcase, as Moumie had instructed her to do when he realized he was dangerously ill.

One night during Liliane's stay in the hospital a car stopped in the courtyard and two men tried to enter the building unnoticed. But a nurse spotted them and, switching on the outside lights, called the police. When they realized they had been discovered, the men quickly got back into their car and fled. The auto had French license plates. "Action" had sent the two men to frighten Liliane and force her to silence. She knew the identity of the journalist with whom Moumie had dined the evening he had the fatal Pernod.

Two months later, at the end of December 1960, Swiss police issued an international warrant for a Frenchman, Bechtel, for the poisoning of the African leader. Bechtel, an intelligence officer, had served in Indochina and Africa and had retired from the Army. But he was still working for SDECE, where he was very useful since besides his French nationality, he was also Swiss.

Bechtel had worked for Colonel Mercier when he was stationed in Switzerland and this explained why he had been picked to carry out Moumie's murder. In preparation for the operation he had contacted Moumie sometime before in Accra and had made it a habit to invite the African to elaborate dinners. The poison he had received from SDECE had been recently developed and never tested before. Its effect was supposed to be immediate and Bechtel, who had studied chemistry, was supposed to administer a dose in proportion with

Moumie's weight. Either the drug was defective or the dose was miscalculated, and Moumie, during the two weeks his horrible agony lasted, had time to talk.

When he finished his dirty job, Bechtel returned to France. Later he made it a point to write to several friends in Switzerland denying his participation. To cover his trail, SDECE had the letters mailed from Austria. Sure of his immunity, Bechtel, who was sixty-six years old, changed names and went to live in the south of France, where he probably is still enjoying a quiet and comfortable life with the money he received in payment for his work.

Assassinations could not change the course of the war. The Arabs received all the help they needed in arms and ammunitions from the Soviet, and France was alone. The French were tired of the war and had no determination to carry it on any longer. De Gaulle, who had pledged to keep Algeria French, had completely switched his position and wanted to give it away without even trying to get a guarantee for those Frenchmen who had been living for more than a hundred years in this territory. When more than a million and a half people are asked to give up their home, their land, and all their possessions, without any compensation, when they are told to give up everything they and many generations before them have built up — they revolt. Part of the army supported them and planned the abortive revolt of the generals. They failed in their attempt, but this brought the officers and their followers to regroup into clandestine networks in order to fight not only the Algerian nationalists but the French faction that was sympathetic to their cause. Excesses were committed then which were inexcusable.

The de Gaulle government was afraid of being overthrown. Foccart and the Minister of the Interior, Roger Frey, had a long meeting in Elysée Palace during September 1961 at which they agreed on the creation of terrorist groups in Algeria to fight enemies of the Gaullist policy and of independence. During the course of their conversation, Foccart pointed out to the Minister of the Interior that the officers of "Action" could very well refuse to obey an order to fight fellow officers.

A purge was decided on, and only the unconditional Gaullists would be kept in "Action." This hard-core group would be used to officer former trainees of "Action" as well as new men who would rapidly be made into terrorists.

In order not to compromise themselves personally, Foccart and Frey decided to entrust the organization to Dominique Pontchardier, who had their full confidence. Pontchardier, a Navy officer during the war, fought courageously with the Leclerc Division in Indochina. He set up Vietnamese commando squads which acquired a reputation for their cruelty. After the war, he made himself a name in literature by writing spy stories which were quite popular.

A few days after his meeting with Foccart, Roger Frey asked Dominique Pontchardier and his wife to his home. Also present were Pierre Lemarchand and his wife, who were personal friends of the Pontchardiers. Frey's secretary, Mrs. Huguette Renaud, was also there.

Pontchardier, who had had a long exchange of views with Foccart, told Minister of the Interior Frey that he was still in contact with a group of Vietnamese who would blindly execute any orders they received. But more men were needed, and counting the Vietnamese and the officers of SDECE's "Action," about 200 more had to be found. Lemarchand was a criminal lawyer, and his clientele came mostly from what the French call *le milieu* — an unsavory group made up of prostitutes, pimps, gangsters, etc. The lawyer's circle of acquaintance among people from *le milieu* was large enough, and he offered his help to round up as many ex-convicts as necessary.

Mrs. Pontchardier was assigned to act as liaison with Jacques Foccart and SDECE under the assumed name of Mrs. Rollin, while Mrs. Lemarchand was put in charge of the financial side of the operation, at the same time doing liaison work with the Minister of the Interior. Because of the minister's busy schedule, his secretary, Mrs. Renaud, was instructed to see that Mrs. Lemarchand got whatever she needed.

In SDECE, Colonel Laurent and a former counterespionage expert were to plan the strategy of the operation. Intelligence officers inside SDECE, with the exception of those working directly for Jacques Foccart, were as a rule reluctant to carry out police work and preferred to stick to their task of collecting intelligence on foreign countries. But the same feelings did not prevail in the counterespionage division of SDECE and in the Surveillance of the Territory, where the heads of the bureaus and their assistants, to whom promotion was everything, spent most of their time gathering information on their fellow citizens who were known to be in disagreement with the government's policies.

The French secret services, instead of devoting their time and energy to exposing Russian spies in France, were concentrating all their time and efforts against members of the opposition. But this was not enough, and Jacques Foccart ordered the creation in Algeria of a "parallel intelligence service" with ample financial means and headed by a leftist known as Colonel Foyer. It would be, in fact, more accurate to refer to it as a service of informers. Every person suspected of being opposed to the Gaullist policy had his name recorded, along with other pertinent data. Copies of the card files were then passed to Foccart through Pontchardier, and to Frey through Lemarchand.

At the end of November 1961, Lemarchand's recruits arrived in Algeria by special planes. Colonel Laurent and several other group heads had already established their quarters in the most luxurious homes and had been working on the index cards provided by Foyer, lining up the first series of operations to be carried out.

The men started immediately by planting bombs in several Algiers cafés known to cater to the French. The first day of terrorism resulted in dozens of civilians killed and seriously wounded.

From then on the special teams struck daily, setting explosives on targets pinpointed in advance and destroying houses and apartments where the suspects lived. Some were forcefully abducted, or when frightened victims lived in isolated areas, horrible tortures were inflicted on the spot, supposedly in order to make them "talk." In fact most cases of torture were not to induce confessions but only to satisfy the cruelty and sadism of the persecutors. The group of Vietnamese recruited by Pontchardier were renowned for their extreme cruelty. Bodies were recovered showing signs of atrocious tortures, such as feet burned, sexual parts mutilated, eyes taken out. . . . Children and young girls were raped in front of fathers and husbands before being killed in the most savage manner.

Everything was set up to put the blame on extreme rightist

268

organizations, but through accounts given by a handful of survivors, the truth began to come out.

The horror of these acts and the fact that Frenchmen could resort to such barbaric methods caused a feeling of revulsion among government officials in Algeria. Pressures were applied in Paris to restrain the abhorrent activities of the group called *les spéciaux*. Colonel Laurent, whose sick mind invented new tortures and other cruelties daily, was recalled. In the meantime the other heads of groups went on spreading terror and leading lives of debauchery.

In Paris, Minister of Interior Frey and Jacques Foccart were having qualms about recalling the teams of assassins, fearing their indiscretion as well as their unreasonable demands. They agreed on a much simpler solution.

On January 29, a large wooden case sent by Mrs. Lemarchand was delivered to the Villa Andrea, living quarters of the group. The case was known to contain a printing machine needed for the duplication of propaganda material. From Paris, Pierre Lemarchand had instructed all the group heads to meet in the afternoon in the Villa Andrea, where new orders would be issued.

Around 5 P.M. a devastating explosion shook Algiers — long accustomed to the noise of explosives. The Villa Andrea lay in ruins. Everyone inside had been killed. The identification of most bodies was not possible, and the terrorist act was imputed as usual to an extreme right group.

At the end of February, the mayor of a small community in Seine-et-Oise, not too far from Paris, received through the prefect of the region orders coming directly from the Ministry of the Interior. He was instructed to have eight graves dug in the local cemetery and to receive eight coffins presently in the morgue at Orly Airport.

The mayor was urged to keep these instructions absolutely secret as well as the date of the burial, set for February 24. He was also informed of the visit of Mrs. Lemarchand, who was to see to every detail of the burial.

On the prearranged day the coffins were delivered in three hearses. The ceremony was promptly performed. A priest blessed each coffin individually and the boxes were lowered immediately. Each

269

bore an inscription: XN-1, XN-2, etc. Wooden crosses were then set over the graves with the same inscription as the coffins, but on the reverse side of six of the crosses were named: Cherroux, Veillard, etc. Two crosses remained nameless. The only witnesses to the semi-clandestine funerals were the mayor, the undertaker, and Mrs. Lemarchand, who was accompanied by an unknown young Oriental woman. Nothing of the strange burial would have become known if it had not been for two journalists from the weekly *L'Express* who, working on a tip, turned up to watch the proceedings. After *L'Express* related the grim story, the mayor of the town, Mr. Gauchard, received a brutal visit from two shady characters to teach him the value of silence.

The death certificates for the eight dead men were dated January 30, 1962, the day after the explosion of the Villa Andrea and were issued in El Biar, Algiers, the district of the villa.

The episode of the Villa Andrea failed to eliminate all group chiefs; a few of them were lucky enough to escape death by not showing up for the meeting. Their silence was bought for a high price and they were advised to leave France for a while and settle in Bolivia. One of their bosses, Dominique Pontchardier, was rewarded with an ambassadorship in Bolivia and was asked to give them some help. The other man in charge, Pierre Lemarchand, emerged at the end of the war as a political candidate of the Gaullist party in a district where a Gaullist was certain to be elected. But being elected a member of congress was no reason for him to give up any of his secret activities, and he later became involved in the Ben Barka scandal.

With de Gaulle's foes completely subdued, either eliminated with the help of the *barbouzes*, the "bearded ones" as they were known in France, or imprisoned and out of the way, the general decided to give Algeria her independence. His first goodwill move was to free from Fresne, the French jail outside Paris, the Algerian leader Ben Bella. The amusing story of that liberation has never been told and is worth recounting.

Ben Bella was to be escorted to the Swiss border, where he would join his supporters. Feelings were very strong against the Algerian leader in France, and Foccart became worried that he would be assassinated during his trip from the jail to the airport, where a helicopter was waiting to transport him to Geneva. To protect him, he sent to the Fresne jail de Gaulle's own bodyguards, with orders to shoot anybody making an attempt against the life of the Algerian. After the atrocities by the Arabs during these last months, the population was enraged and ready to give the Algerian leader a taste of what the French had received in Algeria. The de Gaulle guards, who were much closer to the population than their boss, knew this and feared that they might not be able to deliver Ben Bella alive to the waiting helicopter. So, upon arriving at the prison, they asked him to dress in a French gendarme's uniform. The Algerian agreed, and the car left the Fresne jail with one of de Gaulle's guards impersonating Ben Bella, while the future president of Algeria dressed like a French gendarme guarding him.

It was French grandeur at its zenith.

Solving political difficulties by assassination had become a habit in Paris, as was demonstrated by the Machiavellian plot to get rid of Enrico Mattei late in 1962.

Few people have been more successful or made more enemies than Enrico Mattei, president of the ENI (Ente Nazionale Idrocarburi), the Italian National Hydrocarbon Authority.

He was born in 1906, the son of a constable in the Italian police force. His father could not afford to pay for his children's education, and the young Enrico was obliged to go to work at the age of fourteen. His first job was in a factory painting iron beds. Later, the ambitious Mattei was hired as a delivery boy in a tannery and in a few years time had worked his way to the top to become director of the firm. This was not enough, however, to channel his exuberant energy. At twenty-five, he resigned from his position and moved to Milan, where he specialized in the sales of chemicals.

In 1936, he decided to go into business for himself and founded his own company for the manufacture of chemicals with a large staff of workers. When Italy went to war in 1940 Mattei's business was flourishing, but the hostilities soon interfered with its development. Disgusted with the Fascists, he joined the underground and was put in charge of an important network of partisans in Northern Italy, who had pledged to fight the Germans, and supporters of Mussolini. Through this he became one of the leaders of Christian

Democracy. His comrades in arms were the same men who formed the new Italian government after the war.

The war over, Mattei was asked to undertake the liquidation of AGIP (Italian Petroleum Agency), a creation of Mussolini. For more than fifteen years, the company had squandered enormous amounts of money attempting to strike oil in the Italian subsoil. Italy was impoverished and the general belief was that no prospecting on Italian soil would ever yield positive results.

Going against the current, Mattei made up his mind not only to continue the search for natural deposits but to keep AGIP going as a giant concern for prospecting and research. After thoroughly studying all material and reports available, he became convinced of the presence of methane in the Po Valley and concentrated the research in this particular area. In 1946, a vast deposit of natural gas was discovered.

For Mattei this meant success. His ENI, which stemmed from AGIP, soon occupied a prominent position not only in the exploitation of methane as low-cost energy for Italian industry but also in the construction of pipelines, the creation of new petrochemical industries and oil refineries all over the world. Diversifying, ENI became a tentacular enterprise with interests in textile, restaurants, motels, newspapers, etc.

Not only had Mattei become the number one businessman in Italy but he was one of the world leaders of the petroleum industry. He prepared to fight the big foreign companies by offering to Middle East countries 75–25% contracts against the 50–50% offered by his competitors. ENI refined the cheap raw petroleum bought from Russia and the satellite countries.

Enrico Mattei, who had never been well liked outside of Italy, now began to make enemies everywhere in his desire to build an Italian oil empire. Western newspapers launched attacks against him, and because of him the Italian government began having trouble with its allies. But Mattei, totally unconcerned, went ahead with his plans.

To oppose Standard Oil and the great Western oil companies was one thing, but to buck de Gaulle's government was something else, and this was Mattei's next move.

When de Gaulle gave the French colonies in black Africa and

later Algeria their independence, he assured the French people that France would retain economic prominence. To stimulate trade between France and her former colonies, de Gaulle gave them generous credit and enormous financial help.

Many French small private investors had put all the money they had in stocks of French companies researching oil in the Sahara and other North African territories. De Gaulle knew how essential the support of this important group was to him in such a crucial period, and his desire was to show them that France's political withdrawal from Algeria did not mean her replacement by some other nation in the exploitation of the oil. The French bourgeois could rest assured that France would keep control of the North African oil.

Mattei did not think so. He wanted a large part of the cake — or with luck, all of it. Already in Senegal, in Mali, in Cameroun, in the Ivory Coast, and even in Madagascar, his AGIP had concluded agreements with the governments to set up a distribution network for its oil and oil products. The Italians were successfully establishing themselves in former French colonies to the great wrath of de Gaulle and his fanatical assistant in charge of Africa, Jacques Foccart.

In Tunisia, Mattei had obtained authorization to search for oil and was building a refinery in Bizerte. The same situation prevailed in Morocco, where one of the ENI subsidiaries was prospecting oil and where a refinery had recently been completed.

Standing between Morocco and Tunisia was Algeria, currently at war against the French. Mattei could read the signals — very soon the country would be independent and would become one more star for his crown.

The leaders of the Algerian National Liberation Front often were in Italy to buy or arrange for the transportation of weapons and ammunition. The largest arms dealer in the world, Sam Cummings, president of Interarmco, whose corporate seat was in Alexandria, Virginia, had one of his largest warehouses in Genoa. From there he shipped weapons bought at surplus sales in Europe to rebels and revolutionaries all over the world. The Algerians were regular customers. Mattei agreed to give them all the financial and shipping assistance they needed, and intelligence received in Paris stated that the Arab leaders had promised him in exchange the right to build

273

a refinery in Algeria and to take over the search for oil in the Sahara in place of the French.

The politics of de Gaulle and his assistant in the Elysée Palace were in jeopardy. Something had to be done.

French intelligence had several agents inside the ENI. One of them, holding an influential position, kept SDECE informed and hoped that some drastic measures would soon be taken that would open the way to his ambitions. But Mattei was a man of importance, and the French wanted first to try to win him to their side — or at least convince him to stay out of Algeria, even if a high price had to be paid. A French diplomat was dispatched to Italy and through some kind of strategem arranged to have a conversation with Mattei. He told him bluntly that he was becoming a nuisance. However, if he would agree to stop his maneuvering in Algeria, the French government would be pleased to acknowledge his goodwill by giving him a very generous compensation. Mattei was a proud man, and he laughed in the face of the Quai d'Orsay representative. He, Mattei, did not need to accept any favor from the French nor did he intend to give them any. As for the threats, he was absolutely unafraid. The conversation was cut short when he asked the French diplomat to leave and not come back.

Since it was impossible to come to terms with him, it was decided that more and more pressure would be brought against him. Several messages had been sent to Mattei signed by an extreme rightist French organization and threatening him with assassination if he did not curtail his help to the Algerian rebels. It was even rumored that Mattei's airplane had been sabotaged but that the terrorist act had been discovered in time. This rumor planted the idea with the service "Action," which had been instructed several times to get rid of Mattei.

For his business trips Mattei used a fast twin reactor plane made in France by Morane Saulnier. His travel habits had a pattern. Normally he commuted between Milan, Rome, Ravenna, and Gela. The Italian tycoon autocratically refused to accept any change in his plans, or even to postpone a flight because of bad weather conditions. He was not particularly fond of flying and more than once bad weather and turbulence left him completely shaken. But he would prefer this annoyance to calling off a meeting he had promised to attend.

"Action" had made the decision to sabotage Mattei's plane. Catania airport was chosen as an ideal spot because of the rather relaxed surveillance of the planes parked on the Fontanarosa airfield, and also because of Mattei's frequent trips there to inspect the drilling around Gela. This new oilfield had become one of the most cherished projects of the ENI president, and he spent a great deal of his time there planning new developments.

During the two preceding years, SDECE had on several occasions resorted to airplane sabotage, and a simple technique had been developed. Mechanics who were fluent in the language of the country where the operation was to take place were specially and thoroughly trained on equipment and planes similar to the selected target. In Mattei's case this presented no special problem, since the man picked for the job had been working on an identical plane at the Morane Saulnier plant and was familiar with all the special equipment installed by the factory before delivery to their Italian buyer.

I do not know the real name of the saboteur, but I heard him mentioned as Laurent. Born in Corsica, Laurent spoke Italian fluently. In the fall of 1962, he went to Sicily and settled temporarily in Catania, where he was able to find work at the Fontanarosa airport.

The SDECE station in Rome, keeping in touch with its agents in the Mattei staff, followed the businessman's movements closely. Service "Action" was, for its part, receiving advance weather reports on all the locations Mattei was scheduled to visit.

On October 26, word came that Mattei's plane would leave Catania in the late afternoon of the next day, to arrive after dark in Milan. The forecast read low ceiling and heavy fog over Milan.

Laurent received orders to go ahead.

On the morning of Saturday, October 27, he went to the airport and was able to board Mattei's plane without being noticed. In less than fifteen minutes, working with the self-assurance of his long training, he disconnected and then reconnected in a different way some of the instrument wires. Opening the black box of the altimeter he swiftly replaced some of the parts with others he had brought with him. His job done, he removed all traces of his visit, looked around to make sure that everything was in order, and left inconspicuously. All had gone smoothly, and he found himself whistling.

Although three men were to die in a few hours, he felt no remorse. He had been well trained, and only one thought occupied his mind — the money he would soon receive for his services.

In the meantime, Enrico Mattei was showing an American journalist his Gela oilfield. William McHale, chief of the *Time* office in Rome, had come to interview him. He had spent some time in Iraq and was familiar with the oil problem. *Time* had always been highly critical of Mattei, who felt deeply hurt by the appraisal and was trying his best to show himself and his projects in the most favorable light. McHale had intended to go back to Rome by commercial carrier, but Mattei insisted that he go with him to Milan to see more of his pet projects. McHale, thinking it worthwhile, had accepted.

About 4:30 in the afternoon, Mattei and McHale arrived at the Fontanarosa airport in Catania and went directly to the Morane Saulnier, where Mattei's favorite pilot and trout-fishing companion was waiting. Irnerio Bertuzzi had been a pilot in the Italian Air Force during the war and a member of the famous squadron known as *Baracca*, meaning "good luck" in Arabic. His luck had been good so far, but he did not know that it had just run out.

The Morane Saulnier was built like a fighter plane. The cockpit was covered with clear plastic, and when the plane took off, around 5 P.M., Mattei was seen in the front seat next to Bertuzzi, while McHale sat in the rear, his arm on the back of Mattei's chair.

The distance between Milan and Catania is approximately 700 miles, and the Morane Saulnier cruised at about 450 mph at an altitude of 25,000 feet. At 6:45, exactly on schedule, the plane approached Linate airport in Milan. It was dark, the weather was bad, and the ceiling very low. Bertuzzi had no choice but to make an instrument landing.

Calling the control tower of Linate, he announced, "altitude 6,000 feet."

"Visibility on the runway 1400 meters. You are clear to land immediately," the voice in the control tower answered.

Bertuzzi replied, "Eventually."

It was a strange and laconic answer, not at all expected. A few

276

minutes later, however, the pilot called again saying that he was descending to two thousand feet and was circling in order to lose altitude.

"When are you going to land?" inquired the control tower.

"In one minute, one minute and a half," answered Bertuzzi.

They were the pilot's last words.

One minute later, as he believed his altitude to be several hundred feet over land, the plane suddenly went through the fog. A line of poplars loomed in front of him. The plane plunged into the ground and exploded.

In Paris, those directly involved in the operation were satisfied. The Mattei case was now closed. As for the innocent journalist who lost his life in the accident and the unlucky pilot who had no way of knowing that his altimeter and instruments had been tampered with, the instigators of the plot had no thought of them or their stricken families. Going home to their own children they felt no touch of conscience that the McHale family was mourning a father.

Assassination is part of the daily routine of the men in the service "Action" of SDECE. They dutifully carry out their orders and are proud of their skill, confident that it is equal to that of the Gestapo or the KGB. The Gaullist regime was well protected.

"Hello, operator . . . hello."

Minutes that seemed like hours went by. Finally, a voice trembling with excitement came over the receiver in Spanish.

"*Sí, señor.*"

"I placed a call to Washington more than half an hour ago and am still waiting."

"But, *señor,*" said the operator, "it is impossible get a circuit right now. I will keep trying."

"Why is it suddenly impossible to get a call through to the United States? Everyone on the island can't be calling their friends to say Happy New Year," I said.

It was January 1, 1959, and it could very well have been that happy callers had all the lines jammed exchanging greetings and jokes with friends or relatives back in the United States.

"But, sir, you don't know?" replied the girl indignantly. "It is the revolution!"

"Revolution? What revolution?" I said stupidly.

"Batista is gone. He left last night and the people of Cuba are so happy," said the girl. "Can't you hear them outside?"

I could hear. In fact this noise had been going on since early morning. The street below was unusually active and this was topped by the deafening racket of hundreds of automobile horns. Since in France the first of the year is always welcomed by drivers with a cacophony of horns, I had paid little attention to the mounting noise below. After all, it could also be a Cuban custom.

Now I opened the sliding door of the balcony overlooking the street. A group of youngsters were frantically breaking parking meters outside a funeral home. Two of them would swing on the pipe holding the meter, then use it as a sledge hammer until the meter itself broke spilling all the coins into the street. Then the boys would fight over the money. The ones who were dissatisfied with their catch would take the discarded pipes and in their rage break the windshields and dent the bodies of the nearby cars, leaving behind a pile of junk where a beautiful new car had been. It was vandalism at its worst. I took my movie camera and began filming. A pistol shot broke the glass of the door behind me and I had to step back into the room.

Two days before, on the thirtieth of December, I had arrived in Havana by car. This may not seem the usual way to get to Cuba, but taking advantage of the holiday season slowdown in work, I had driven from Washington to Key West. There I loaded my car on the SS *City of Havana*, the ferry of the West Indian Fruit and Steamship Company. I needed a vacation and wanted a car to tour the island. The crossing from Key West had been superb, with calm seas and balmy weather.

Landing in Havana, an unsuspected difficulty arose. My car, registered under the name of the French government, had diplomatic tags and I thought this would get me through without too much red tape. The customs officer, however, insisted that I produce a tourist card to be allowed into the country with my car. The automobile, he said, would simply have to be impounded until I left Cuba to return to the United States. After the usual dickering, I was permitted to enter with my car, provided that I supplied the customs office with an authorization from the Cuban Foreign Office the next day.

The lack of courtesy on the part of a Cuban official surprised me. The Cubans, as a rule, were very considerate and seemed to

279

like the French. It was my first brush with Cuban authorities, but I knew it would be settled quickly through our embassy.

France had always maintained very friendly relations with Cuba, and those relations were further improved during the war. At that time a French vice-consul in Havana named Grousset decided to join de Gaulle's Free French. The vice-consul, who had lived in Havana for many years, had befriended a sergeant in the Cuban army named Batista. When Batista became president of Cuba, vice-consul Grousset asked his friend to recognize General de Gaulle as chief of the French government. Batista was happy to please him, and Cuba became the first country in the world to recognize the Free French government as the legal government of France.

Since then, Batista, like de Gaulle, had fallen out of power but eventually had made a comeback, and his friend Grousset was no longer vice-consul but French ambassador in Havana. That evening, after having settled at the Hilton, I paid him a visit.

Ambassador Grousset was short, always faultlessly groomed, and very sprightly. He was very busy with all the festivities, cocktail parties, and receptions being given for the new year, but he took time to brief me on the situation. A few days before he had been received formally by his friend President Batista, who had assured him that all the rumors about the presence of *guerilleros* and acts of sabotage in the central region of Cuba were unfounded. Certainly there were some isolated Communist groups in the mountains stealing from the peasants, but after all there had always been malcontents and bandits in the *sierra*. The army was on hand now, taking care of the situation, and his government was in no danger. The ambassador showed me confidentially the cable he had sent to the Quai d'Orsay in which he repeated the reassuring words from Batista, and added that through his own sources of information and based on his knowledge of the island and its inhabitants, there was no risk of a revolution. The Batista government was there to stay.

The cable is still quoted in the Quai d'Orsay as a monument to the lack of vision of some of its representatives.

The next day, December 31, I went to the Cuban Foreign Office accompanied by the counselor of our embassy. The Chief of Protocol promised me that my car problem would be solved after the New Year's holiday. The Chief of Protocol walked with us from the ministry, and as we were the last ones to leave, the guard padlocked the heavy iron gates behind us. I did not know then that with the closing of the doors, an era was ended. None of the Batista diplomats was ever to go back to the ministry.

I had expected a tumultuous New Year's Eve party at the hotel. A gala supper was advertised everywhere, with Lilo, the famous French singer, performing. Lilo had made a success on Broadway with the musical *Can-Can*, and we had met several times in New York. I decided to attend the dinner and watch her show. The room was packed, but around midnight, people began to leave. By one o'clock it was all over. This surprised me greatly. Havana had always been a lively city, with parties going on until daybreak. Everyone, I thought, must have gone to another spot and I decided to drive around the city. The streets were deserted, all nightclubs were closed. I went to bed perplexed.

When the pistol shot hit the window behind me, I finally believed it was the revolution. Obviously, the ambassador's information was erroneous, and I decided to do some inquiring. I could at least try to get an accurate account of the situation through my own agents.

It took ten minutes for the elevator to get to my floor. The young operator tried to convince me not to go down to the lobby.

"It's very bad, *señor*," he insisted. "Better stay in your room."

Stepping out of the elevator, I understood his warning.

The hotel lobby was empty, but outside the door a large group of angry men with rifles, pistols and submachine guns were trying to force their way in. Inside, a man was standing alone squarely in the middle of the door, keeping the crowd back. He was dressed in white pants and a white *guayavera* shirt, the type popular among the Cubans. The group leaders were trying to push him away and guns were shoved in his belly. But he remained calm and in control. He was lecturing them in Spanish.

"Listen to me!" he said. "You are patriots, good Cubans. Do you want to hurt Cuba?"

"No," they would shout, not understanding what he meant.

"Don't you know this hotel is owned by the Cuban people? By the Social Security? And what is the Social Security but the hope for many of you! Do you want to destroy your own property?"

281

This went on for more than fifteen minutes.

Some of the men began to relent, holding their rifle stocks to the ground. Then, little by little, the crowd thinned and finally vanished.

I had watched the incredible scene, knowing that one wrong word or move would have triggered a rampage and, inevitably, bloodshed. I walked toward the man to congratulate him for his remarkable handling of an explosive situation. His name was Frank Brandstetter, the former intelligence officer for General Ridgway who during the war had discovered the German prisoners' scheme to capture London. He was now manager of the Havana Hilton. His actions during the confusing weeks that followed resulted in the continued protection of lives and property.

Police officers, not wanting to be identified with the Batista regime, had disappeared. Havana was completely in the hands of armed bands who were without organization and did not really know what they were doing in the streets. There had been no resistance. Once in a while a blast of gunfire could be heard, coming either from an inexperienced gunman or from vengeance seekers getting even with some innocent fellow.

In the lobby of the hotel I had met Guy de la Passardière, Lilo's husband, who was taking the whole thing as a lark. We listened together to the radio playing military marches interrupted every few minutes by orders to the population from the temporary Havana representative of Castro's 26 of July movement. This man called himself Commandante Diego and had established his headquarters in a radio station just a block away from the Hilton. We decided to try to see him in order to get a permit to tour the city. To insure our welcome by the revolutionaries, we emptied all the cigarette machines in the hotel, and with our pockets full and also with a large bag began the hazardous crossing of the street. We were stopped time after time, but we told the unfriendly Cubans that Commandante Diego was waiting for us. Taken by surprise and led to believe we were on some revolutionary errand, they let us go. We found the radio station in an incredible state of confusion. Through the influence of our cigarettes we were able to see the young lady who acted as secretary and first lieutenant to Commandante Diego. She introduced us to him and two minutes later, instead of a pass that might not be honored, we had a squad of men armed to the teeth with orders to protect us on our tour of the city.

With one man holding a submachine gun seated on each fender, and three men armed with grenades and pistols and rifles on the back of the car, Guy de la Passardière and I started out to see and feel the pulse of Havana. All the streets were closed by heavily guarded roadblocks, but the sight of the "26 of July" emblems on our guards' armbands opened the way immediately. The Malecon, the large avenue, along the sea was deserted. The President's Palace and the Capitol were obviously occupied by the revolutionaries, but the most revealing sight was at the chief of police headquarters.

The building looked like a fortress. The doors were heavily guarded, and one after another cars would stop and unload their cargoes of prisoners who were shoved roughly inside by armed militia. Many of the prisoners wore Cuban police uniforms, but others were elderly people or mothers with their young children. I had often seen people molested and arrested when they were in opposition to a new regime, and each time I was overcome with the same feeling of sadness and sorrow for the persecuted. People supposedly rebel in the name of liberty, but when their cause is victorious and they hold the power, their first move is to deprive those who do not share their views of that same liberty. The Cubans, I could see, were no exception.

We ended the tour with a visit to the French Ambassador. He was not as buoyant as the day before, and our arrival in the company of armed guards gave him a shock. His friendship with Batista, which the day before had been his greatest asset, had now become a deadly liability. He tried to find consolation in the fact that he had spoken by telephone with the French Foreign Office, but he knew his cable had been a blunder. We left him to his depressing thoughts and went back to our hotel.

For several days there was no transportation on or off the island, and I had ample time to speak with revolutionaries and with my many friends in Havana. All were happy about Batista's departure, but they could not really understand how it had come about. The army had remained very loyal to him, and the regiments barricaded in the Cabana, the old fortress at the harbor entrance, could have cleaned up all the rebels in two hours. Batista's panic did not seem justified.

With the first days of stupor over, one would expect the city to resume its normal life, but strangely enough, the stores stayed closed and hotels and restaurants seemed out of business. Many were beginning to make plans to leave the country on account of their past dealings with the Batista regime. The radio played the "Internationale," and Communist leaders would speak for hours on end. Otherwise, Havana was like a forgotten city. No administration had taken over. There were no police. Gangs of revolutionaries roamed the streets, making their own laws and arresting people at will. Meanwhile, Castro was touring the country in triumph getting support from the peasants and agricultural workers. He knew that Havana was not yet his own. In the capital, people were beginning to realize that the revolution could ruin them.

I could sense an undertone from the so-called socialist speeches and from Castro's attitude. It was very fashionable then to admire Castro and to insist that he was not a Communist. Still, he acted very much like one. When communications had been reestablished and I was able to return to Washington, I was candid in expressing my opinions on what to expect in the future from Cuba. But I met only with skeptical smiles.

My first impressions were further confirmed during subsequent trips to Cuba. On the road to power Castro had claimed to be a fervent advocate of anticolonialism and had pledged his support to the Algerian rebels. Now the strong traditional ties with France were shaken by an anti-French campaign initiated by the governing revolutionary group, and French renegades as well as Algerian fanatics were extended a warm welcome.

To cope with this new threat to French interests, I decided to reinforce my existing intelligence networks, and I engaged the collaboration of Cubans loyal to France. I learned that the Cubans had seized a French diplomatic pouch before it reached our embassy and opened it in the presence of the Egyptian ambassador, who was given a copy of all documents. Why the Quai d'Orsay did not issue a stern protest and why the affair was hushed up is still not clear to me.

Several French Communists who had fought side by side with Castro were striving to undermine Franco-Cuban relations. One of them, Fuertes, was killed during 1959 while leading an operation for the invasion of Haiti. Another, Lavandeyra, became one of Che Guevara's lieutenants and tried to get Che to influence Castro not to receive the new French ambassador, who was appointed to replace the unfortunate friend of Batista.

The new envoy, Ambassador Robert du Gardier, had been stationed in Guatemala when a revolution brought the downfall of Arbenz, and so he was no stranger to Latin America's revolutionary climate. Not only was he remarkably intelligent, but he had one quality seldom found among diplomats — courage. Tall and distinguished, the French ambassador impressed everyone he met with his self-possession and a certain air of contempt for personal risk. The officials of the new regime sized him up and knew immediately that they would have to use more restraint when criticizing or even insulting France, as was common practice then. A polite relationship was established. This failed, however, to deter Castro from welcoming the Algerian leaders with jubilation and treating them as conquering heroes by putting at their disposal arms, ammunitions, the use of the government-owned radio, and his channels of communication.

Naturally the Cuban diplomatic mail carried FLN (Front of National Liberation) correspondence between Paris and New York, and training camps for guerrilla warfare were set up in Cuba. Since very few Cubans knew Arabic, but all Algerians spoke French, the guerrilla training was conducted in French by Che Guevara's Cuban instructors. One day I managed to hide near one of the camps training the future Algerian guerrillas. The sight was not particularly humorous, but I was amused by the atrocious French being spoken by both sides. How in the world could they understand each other?

Stocks were getting low and the island's economic situation was rapidly deteriorating. One year after Castro's takeover, private property was virtually nonexistent. Still, some people were debating whether or not Fidel Castro was a Communist.

In the beginning of 1961, the doubters looked like fools when it was revealed that 700 Soviet technicians were operating in the Cuban government. Each department had its own contingent. The Soviets made an effort not to be too conspicuous, and their real activities were not easily detected. It took me some time to find out that they were studying the existing methods and organization of each ministerial department and teaching the Cuban civil servants how to improve efficiency and performance at each level. Programming and quotas set up and thought out in the "Soviet" manner were ill-suited to the Latin style or tropical surroundings. The instructors themselves judged them inappropriate and ridiculous and tried their best to adapt them to the situation, which resulted in many confused and incoherent measures.

The Soviets stayed in hotels that were once the favorite spots of American tourists. The Hilton Hotel, renamed Habana Libre, attracted them particularly. The population learned through official propaganda that imperialist tourists had been replaced by East European tourists who deserved their best attention and most gracious welcome. The Soviets seemed pleased with the attitude of the people and soon were enjoying the charm of Havana in the company of attractive señoritas.

Some of the young Cuban girls did not find any particular attraction in the Russian men but were able to report interesting information to their respective underground groups. It is significant that no Russian was ever seen with a black girl, and the reports I received at the time mentioned their distaste not only for the blacks but the mulattoes as well, no matter how light their skin.

Underground movements began to spring up, and on each of my trips I was approached by members of one organization or another, volunteering information. The Cubans, who are without doubt a marvelous people, have two known weaknesses. They cannot keep a secret, and they have a definite tendency to exaggerate everything. When the first Soviet technicians began to pour into Cuba, the reports I received gave estimates varying from 2,000 to 15,000 men, when the true number was about 700.

Reports reaching me almost daily mentioned the landing in coastal harbors of Russian MIGs and missiles, but in most cases when I ordered a verification, these turned out to be fairy tales. Soon it became obvious to the intelligence community that a Cuban source had to be taken cautiously. The value of a piece of information could not be determined until it had been corroborated by someone who was professionally trained.

In their strong desire to bring the United States into their fight, the Cubans circulated many false reports which unfortunately worked against their goal and destroyed faith in their statements.

In my contacts with resistance organizations I was appalled by the carelessness of their members. To seem important they would confide in me or anybody else, speaking freely about their organization, their friends, giving names and even addresses when asked. There was no doubt in my mind that Castro's secret police knew many of them but made no arrests, preferring to watch known conspirators rather than hunt secret ones. I always avoided using a member of a resistance organization as an intelligence agent, for his security and for my own. When impressed by someone, I would ask him to give up his activity with the group, then train him to work for me. This avoided unnecessary conflicts and produced greater efficiency.

In March 1961 I arrived to find Havana transformed into a military camp, with armed militiamen stationed at each street corner behind a pile of sandbags. Castro had launched a new campaign to defend the country against the imperialist invaders who, he proclaimed, were ready to land and occupy the island. This sounded like one of his fantasies. The possibility of a landing seemed very remote. The resistance organizations were fighting one another. The émigrés were arguing about who should replace Castro, and the main worry of the population of Havana was the food shortage. Nothing had been prepared psychologically or otherwise for a popular revolt, and without this no victory was possible.

Still very fresh in my memory was the reaction of the French during the resistance, and I could sense among the Cubans the same feeling of frustration, the same acute patriotism, the same desire to do something for their country. Unfortunately, they were utterly disorganized and had no training in underground methods.

Ardent young Cubans used to tell me of their plans to blow up Havana's electric plant or the tunnel under the harbor, and my advice was always to hold back, arguing that the destruction of such installations would only play against them. The people of Havana

287

had endured enough suffering and restrictions, and the sabotage of the electric plant would only alienate the population without causing real damage to Castro. Listening to the cocky young men with their fiery plans, I wondered why some of them had not been sent secretly to training schools in the United States and taught to use their energy purposefully. As a Frenchman interested only in intelligence I could not direct them in subversive activities which I was unable to support financially or otherwise. But I gave them the best advice I could, based on my own experience in the underground.

Returning to Washington, I told my American friends what I had seen in Cuba and mentioned half-jokingly the Castro propaganda about an American landing on the island. The general reaction was a hearty laugh about this highly improbable occurrence.

But my reports continued to predict a planned landing by a Cuban task force presently training in Guatemala. When questioned, my American counterparts showed no reaction. Intrigued, I decided to check into the matter personally. Taking advantage of the Easter holiday, I went to the Guatemalan capital and from there I drove to Reuthaleu, where my persistence was rewarded. A large force of Cubans were training in a hacienda owned by the Guatemalan president. When several newspapers reported it, the president ordered them moved to another hacienda nearby. So the landing force was constantly shifted from the hacienda "Helvetia" to the hacienda "La Suiza." Journalists tried in vain to locate them. I was able to, and spoke with several in the group. They did not know when they would land, but were convinced it would be soon. I had no idea it would be quite so soon.

Two days later, in Mexico City, I learned of the landing at the Bay of Pigs. Reading about it in *Excelsior*, the leading Mexican newspaper, I found it hard to believe. I knew the area of the Bay of Pigs and could not imagine any large landing force engaging the Cuban army in those marshes. Furthermore, I knew there was absolutely no chance right now for an uprising in Havana. Before heading back to Washington, I had a conversation with the head of Mexican security and discussed the topic with him. He told me that Mexican intelligence had been intrigued by the large number of unmarked planes flying to Guatemala during the last two weeks. He had suspected the planes were carrying the landing forces and felt sure that with the backing of the United States they would be in command in Cuba in the next two days. I somehow did not share his optimism.

When I arrived in Washington it was all over. American officials were dismayed by the catastrophe. Over lunch one of them asked me if I intended to return to Havana soon, mentioning that Allen Dulles would be grateful if I would. Since the disaster of the Bay of Pigs no communications had been reestablished with the island, and no one really knew what the situation was there.

I saw Dulles the same day and he told me that he would welcome news from Cuba. Pan American was resuming its flights to Cuba the next day and I could be on the first plane leaving Miami. I immediately cabled my director in Paris explaining the situation and asking his authorization to go to Havana. He agreed and a few hours later I was on my way to Miami, where I rushed to catch the first Pan Am flight to the unhappy island.

Our ambassador was waiting for me at the airport and I felt elated when he told me he had invited all the Western ambassadors for lunch the same day. It isn't very often that one has a chance to listen to the top diplomats in a foreign country commenting informally on a situation.

I did not expect their views to concur, but I was wrong. They were all disturbed by the cruelty of the Castro repressions, and thought the United States should not have launched an operation without the assurance of an uprising in Havana. This was also my belief. Most of them thought that the United States, having made a mistake, should repair it by landing the marines in Havana. I had no opinion at first, but later became convinced they were right. The marines could have landed with almost no casualties. Castro, not knowing where a landing might take place, had spread all his better troops very thinly around the island. Havana was defended only by inexperienced militiamen who, although very vicious when arresting a defenseless citizen, had not been trained to fight an organized task force of professional soldiers.

The desire expressed by many diplomats to see marines land in Havana was motivated by the wave of arrests and the barbarous treatment of prisoners. Obviously Castro had been tipped off in advance of the landing. Two days before, on April 15, the trucks due to transport the militiamen to the Bay of Pigs were assembled on a field close to the Commodore Hotel, and the next day the head of the Technical Investigation Bureau was in Colón, near the Playa Girón. He confided to friends that a landing of American troops was expected for the next morning and that he would be in charge of the interrogation of the prisoners. Forced to withdraw his best soldiers from the capital and knowing that he did not have a very firm hold on Havana's population, Castro simply ordered the arrest of all persons likely to cause or be involved in disturbances or sabotage around the city. No fewer than 35,000 persons were arrested within three days, and many others were imprisoned all over the island. The Embassy of Switzerland, representing American interests in Cuba, estimated at about 100,000 the number of persons thrown in Cuban jails.

The old prison of Principe was housing about 7,000, while the Palacio de Deportes, or Sports Palace, held more than 10,000. Although their lot was not to be envied, they still had at their disposal minimal sanitary facilities. Worst off were the unfortunate people confined in the Castillo Morro, the old fortress that was Havana's trademark, a favorite spot for amateur photographers. The ancient moldy cells within twenty-foot thick walls were full to capacity, and the prisoners were left to themselves in the moats. Four or five thousand people were there, engaged in a fight for survival. Taken from their homes in the middle of the night, with inadequate clothing, many were too tired to hang on and were left to die among others too distraught even to react.

I was able to see for myself the pitiful situation of the prisoners from an observation post on the wall of the Castillo Morro. A sea of human beings was exposed all day to the burning tropical sun with no protective shelter. At night the temperature dropped more than twenty degrees and the humidity was stifling. No blankets were available and people slept on the wet ground. I saw men and women in their sixties crawling on their knees to drink water from a dripping hose, the only source of water. A horrible stench rose from this mass of people. No sanitary facility was available and I could see several corpses in a state of decomposition in a corner of the moat. Pregnant women and young children were haggard and in a state of terror. With no human feeling, the militia guards walking back and forth were dousing the prisoners with DDT. In the evening a group of prisoners was ordered to pick up the dead and throw them into the sea. A chute built in the sixteenth century by the Spaniards to get rid of their political enemies was utilized for this purpose.

A counselor in the Swiss Embassy told me he had absolute proof that on the Sunday, April 30, 1961, the director of the Castillo Morro prison had sixty prisoners chosen at random and shot and that he personally had executed seventeen. But the Castillo Morro was not the exclusive arena of cruelty. Havana was proud of claiming that the Blanquita was the largest movie theatre in the world. Castro decided to use it as a jail, and his militia packed 4,000 persons into it who remained without food or water for four days. Many were older American citizens and Cubans from the upper classes. During those four interminable days there occurred several abortions, deaths, and births. Three prisoners went berserk, triggering a general uproar. Bloodhounds were brought onto the stage and the guards threatened to let them loose on the frightened crowd. Some among the militia were young boys in their teens, members of the organization Jovenes Rebeldes, "young rebels." One night several got scared and opened fire on the protesting prisoners, killing an undetermined number.

Among the Cubans captured at the Playa Girón were four priests —three of them of Spanish origin. So Castro immediately ordered the arrest of all priests, bishops, and other men of the church. Some were jailed, others were kept under close watch in their convents or respective churches. The Archbishop of Havana, Monseignor Boza-Masvidal, was kept prisoner in his room. Six friars from the Christian School, who were French citizens, were also put under arrest. The only ones to keep their freedom were the bishops of Cienfuegos and of Santiago.

The situation of the clergy became so disastrous that on April 26, 1961, the Pope sent a personal message to Castro through his legate. The Holy Father insisted on the release of all priests and bishops. In an unexpected move, Castro agreed to meet with the Papal Legate the next day, April 27, in the hacienda "de Cojimar" located about fifteen miles from Havana. Flattered at receiving a message from the Pope, he first denied ordering the arrests, then, confronted with the evidence, promised to free all members of the clergy.

Going into one of his long tirades, Castro told the astonished Papal Legate that he had no desire to persecute the men of God, although he was perfectly aware of the antirevolutionary activities of some of them. Contemplating the possibility of an American landing in Cuba, he expressed fear of being wiped out in less than a week should this happen.

In his own way, Castro kept his word. He had the bishops and priests released, but on the day of their liberation, the dictator's militia paraded the streets of Havana carrying dummies dressed as priests, which they later burned in effigy. On May 1, Castro announced the nationalization of all religious schools and the deportation of all foreign priests, some of whom had spent a lifetime on the island.

Besides the massive arrests of people suspected, because of their social standing, of being hostile to the Communist philosophy, the Cuban G2 began hunting members of underground movements and so-called agents of American imperialism. The G2 acted as Castro's secret police, and its chief, Ramiro Valdez, enjoyed the trusted confidence of the bearded dictator. The majority of the G2 members were either blacks or mulattoes, and Valdez encouraged a climate of racial antagonism among his subordinate that led to a feeling of hatred toward the whites.

Headquarters of the organization was located on Havana's Fifth Avenue, between Twelfth and Fourteenth streets. The building itself was painted green and was easily recognized. Other homes in the block were used as interrogation and detention centers. Prisoners were frequently locked up in groups of twenty-five or thirty in twelve by eighteen-foot rooms. Interrogations were conducted under powerful projectors, and beatings were not uncommon under the G2 roof, but no mention was ever made to me of extreme cruelty or tortures. Hunger, thirst, and sleepless nights usually broke down the resistance of most prisoners.

Sometimes Cubans on the wanted list eluded arrest after being tipped off by a friend turned Communist. Others made successful escapes when G2 men showed up at their domicile. But in the prevailing climate of terror the persecuted could not seek refuge with friends. A foreign embassy was their only hope.

In Latin America, where revolutions frequently have to be reckoned with, most of the countries have entered into an agreement concerning asylum. Under provisions of the treaty, the ambassadors of the government signatories are allowed to grant asylum in their embassies on foreign soil to people who so request it, without interference on the part of the host government. The Embassy of Venezuela in Havana opened its door to more than one hundred fifty refugees, among whom was Urrutia, the first president appointed by Castro. The Embassy of Argentina sheltered about fifty, including the Cardinal of Havana and the President of the Supreme Court. Each Latin embassy had its quota of refugees according to the space available.

The European countries were not signatories of the asylum agreement, and their ambassadors did not accept refugees unless they were citizens of that country. Nevertheless, two of the Western ambassadors showed exceptional courage, exposing themselves to criticism from their own governments and to reprisals from Castro's bullies. The two were French Ambassador Robert du Gardier and Italian Ambassador Theodoli. Neither would hesitate to pick up people who were in hiding from Castro's police and drive them to their embassies. Ambassador Theodoli, whose residence was rather small, gave his bedroom to an aged refugee and slept in his living room. Every room in the embassy was being used as a bedroom for Cuban refugees.

One day the G2 tried to arrest the Cuban chauffeur of the French Ambassador, but du Gardier arrived in time to free him by resorting to some shoving and pushing around of secret police officers. It would be difficult to say how many Cubans were saved by these two gallant ambassadors. When Cuba is once more a free nation, I am convinced that its people will remember and honor them as they deserve.

Most of the prisoners' personal property had been confiscated. The Capitol had been transformed into a sort of flea market, where the stolen goods were sold to the public. Walking through it, I felt sick at heart at the sight of baby clothing, wedding dresses, beautiful Dresden as well as cheap aluminum plates all thrown together. Rich and poor alike had lost everything.

Before I left Cuba I had a long talk with Mr. Carl Burckhardt, the Swiss Ambassador who had agreed to come out of retirement to represent American interests in Havana. He had acquired a reputation of great wisdom in the very sensitive positions he had previously occupied. Formerly High Commissioner of the *Société des Nations* in Danzig, he was the president of the International Red Cross during the war and had witnessed some of the worst situations. I accompanied him to the United States Embassy. This beautiful building on the seashore, closed since the beginning of the year, was guarded by a handful of militiamen. Inside everything was very quiet, except for the presence of a few Swiss employees. Ambassador Burckhardt took me to the former office of the U.S. Ambassador at the top of the building. We went onto the balcony in case the office had been bugged.

"These people are insane," the ambassador told me. "What they are doing now equals in cruelty what the Nazis did to the Jews. People are dying every minute. I am doing my best to save as many as I can, but it is not enough. I am a man of peace, but I feel the United States should do something to save the lives of persons whose only fault has been to like America. I do not know what can be done, but please tell everyone in Washington about what you have witnessed. A military action would be better than to let so many innocents die."

I told him frankly that the climate in Washington when I left was one of contrition and mutual reproach and that I had not detected any intention to intervene militarily.

When I arrived in Washington the next day, I reported by cable to my director on what I had seen and heard. Then I briefed Allen Dulles on the situation. He tried to look cheerful but could not convince me that there was still hope. Dulles was a professional man. He knew the politicians had ruined an operation that would have been successful had it been supported by more airpower and a better preparation. A landing now could have rid the hemisphere of the Communist presence and revolutionary activities, but the American people were no more prepared for it than the Cuban people had been for the landing of the Bay of Pigs. A tremendous opportunity was lost. Looking back now I feel that a good fight then would have been much better than to have the United States live with a hostile Communist state only miles away, its planes being hijacked and its neighbors enduring subversion and guerrilla warfare by the Cuban Communists.

As a consequence of the Bay of Pigs disaster, the Cubans felt let down by the Americans. Many, giving up hope, reluctantly joined Castro's partisans. Others refused to take any more chances, and knowing they would not be protected, declined to be involved in intelligence work. It became a very disappointing task for Western intelligence to replace the agents who were killed or imprisoned. Because I had always been careful not to compromise my agents, I was still receiving vital information. During the months following the Bay of Pigs, I took advantage of each of my trips to Havana to set up new dead drops and to improve my communications. I knew I was one of the best-informed men on what was happening on the island. At a time when French secret services were mainly concerned with assassination plots against enemies of the regime, I continued to apply myself to gathering intelligence. To a professional nothing could be more exhilarating than the excitement of leaving Cuba with an attaché case full of intelligence reports. If through some unfortunate circumstance Castro's police had stumbled upon them, my position would have been precarious, especially at those times when I carried letters from his sister, the courageous Juanita Castro.

In July of 1962 my reports started mentioning the arrival of Soviet ships in Havana and, strangely, in Mariel, a small harbor seldom appearing on maps of Cuba. Other ships were landing people and cargoes in harbors where the Soviet flag had, until now, been a rarity. We say in France that too many precautions can cause harm, and this was the case when the Mariel harbor was closed to the Cubans, and when Soviet servicemen were seen unloading the cargoes themselves. What precious goods could Khrushchev be sending to Cuba?

I had the opportunity to discuss the situation with the new director of the CIA, John McCone. Nobody knew what was really happening, and more hard intelligence was needed. I decided to fly to Havana at once. There, all the intelligence I collected showed that Russian missiles had been brought in. But it was the same old story. For years, the Cubans had flooded all the intelligence services, embassies, and newspapers with tales of *cohetes*, as they called the missiles, supposedly hidden in the numerous caves along the coast. I had already checked many of the reports but to no avail, as I am sure others did with no better results. One report, however, seemed particularly intriguing.

Soldiers were reported to be guarding a cavern where work was being conducted secretly. Photographs taken by the agent showed that a large hole was being drilled through the ceiling of the cavern to the pasture fifty feet above. This hole had the appearance of a large tube, big enough to hold a missile and oriented in the direction of the United States. The Cuban informer insisted that its function was to launch missiles. I inquired and learned that in France plans were now in progress to drill a cavern in the Jura region for the purpose of firing missiles through directional holes. Was the Cuban cavern being drilled for similar use? I did not know, but I passed on the information to my headquarters and to my American correspondent, as Paris had instructed me to do.

As for the missiles themselves, I suspected our Cuban friends of talking about something they hardly knew. While they might have seen pictures of missiles in magazines or on television, very few had actually seen the real thing. When the reports began to pour in, I tried to pin down my informants, asking them if they had ever seen a real missile before. None of them had, but they all claimed to know what one would look like. I was soon convinced that their imagination had been working again, in their secret desire to bring the United States to intervene in Cuba.

One day, however, a young man who had served in the French army in Germany as a noncommissioned officer and was now spending some time with his family in Havana reported having seen a missile transported by truck. He described the scene very accurately: a huge multiwheeled trailer transporting Russian rockets under canvas cover. They were, he swore, "bigger, much bigger" than anything the Americans had in Germany.

Again I passed the information on to Paris and shared it with American intelligence authorities. As intelligence kept coming in confirming the presence of large Russian missiles in Cuba, I reported regularly to my headquarters, filling in our American allies as I had been ordered.

I have every reason to think that the intelligence I collected was included in the bulk of information on which the President of the United States based his decision to call the Russians to account. I have had, in private, the thanks of CIA director John McCone. Words of appreciation were also conveyed to my chief in Paris and later were to be used against me by those who felt uneasy about the success of my operations against Soviet plans.

It was evident that neither de Gaulle nor my headquarters were in the mood to show much interest in my work in Cuba. The liquidation of the Algerian problem, of paramount importance to them at the moment, overshadowed everything. I had done my share in this struggle with the Arab rebels, too. But we had lost, and although I deeply regretted it, nothing could be done now. A page was turned, or at least I thought so.

In Paris, de Gaulle was now getting even with those who had opposed his politics, Algerian or other, but I never imagined I would be involved in the revenge process initiated by the old general and his entourage.

One day I received a peculiar cable from the chief of counter-espionage stating that Jean-Jacques Servan Schreiber, publisher of the weekly *L'Express*, was coming to the United States and was suspected of plotting against the security of the nation. My orders were to keep him under close surveillance and to report immediately by coded teletype message on all his moves and activities.

I had never met Jean-Jacques Servan Schreiber and did not share his ideas, but I credited him with courage and determination to fight for what he believed. With the many connections I had in the journalistic community, I already knew about his trip and the reason he was coming to New York. A journalist trying to improve his magazine is certainly not doing subversive work, and I decided to ignore the orders I had received. There is a great difference between intelligence work and the actions of the fanatics of the political secret police. I had no desire to be one of the *Barbouzes*, as de Gaulle's secret police were called.

Daily cables persistently inquired as to whether Servan Schreiber was under surveillance and what he was doing. I continued to ignore the orders, feeling very strongly, as I always have, about the freedom of the press. I resented being in any way connected with a plot to interfere with that basic freedom.

Requests of this type would certainly not have been made when General Grossin was director of SDECE, but General de Gaulle had decided upon advice from Jacques Foccart, his counselor for all security and intelligence matters, to appoint a new man, General Jacquier, head of SDECE.

General Jacquier was an Air Force pilot who had spent the war as a prisoner in a German camp for captured officers after his plane was forced to land in Cyprus in 1940. His greatest achievement had been to join the Free French Forces after the French armistice, but he had to wait until de Gaulle came back to power to receive the promotions he wanted. Along with the directorship of SDECE, de Gaulle gave him another star, making him a major general. The only way Jacquier could demonstrate his gratitude was to obey unquestioningly orders coming from the Elysée Palace, and this is exactly what he did. I was to learn from him later that the order to inquire about J.-J. Servan Schreiber came from Jacques Foccart, which did not surprise me.

Another cable and a memorandum from the chief of counter-espionage, Colonel Delseny, which I received at about the same time, were still more disturbing. He asked me to give to the American security services a list of more than thirty French politicians and ask that they be put under tight surveillance should they come to the United States. Furthermore, the CIA was requested to forward to SDECE any and all information they could gather about the French political figures, hinting they were suspected of activities against the security of the nation and of connections with the Soviets. On that list were such well-known names as Mendès-France, Soustelle, Pinay, and many others. It was abhorrent and once more I decided to ignore it. But Colonel Delseny would not. The messages were repeated with threats of sanctions.

I have always believed that men are entirely responsible for their acts and that claiming to be under orders is no excuse for committing a crime. The Nazis sentenced at Nürmberg and the French who persecuted their fellow citizens during the war were all under some kind of orders, and they were all judged guilty. I was firmly resolved not to follow any order contrary to my conscience and my convictions. I would not falsely denounce to American security services men whose only mistake was to disagree with the politics of Mr. de Gaulle.

A few weeks later I learned that in Paris Colonel Mareuil, who was in charge of SDECE's liaison with the foreign services, had given to the representative of the American security agencies the list I had decided not to forward to the CIA. In order to straighten things out, I went to see one of the highest-ranking officers in American intelligence and told him that my action had been motivated by my strong personal feeling that the accusations against the persons listed were absolutely groundless. Jacques Soustelle, for instance, who had been my superior during the war, was undoubtedly beyond reproach. I would vouch for him at any time and welcome him in my home. With great dignity the American told me that CIA had no intention of interfering in France's political affairs and that Paris's request was considered in bad taste. The CIA kept its word, and no action was taken in the wake of the Mareuil request.

False accusations against opponents of de Gaulle, charging they were Communists, were very disturbing to me because I had known for some time about the existence of real Soviet agents inside the French government. I had acquired this knowledge from reports and transcripts of interrogation of a Russian defector who was now in the United States.

My first clear proof of the existence and special importance of the man we came to know as Martel arrived, so to speak, through the back door. It all started in the spring of 1962.

One morning at 5 o'clock the telephone rang in my bedroom. "Mr. de Vosjoli?" a voice asked.

"Yes," I said.

"Pardon, this is . . ." The voice went on in French giving the last name of a man well known to me as one of the senior officers of SDECE. "I have just landed at Washington airport with five colleagues. Ask no questions, please, but I would be much obliged if you would send a car to pick us up and arrange for a convenient place for us to stay for a few days."

I assured my colleague — I will call him "X" — that his needs would be attended to.

"X," with five companions, descending on Washington unannounced, in the middle of the night? Something urgent must be afoot, something of the utmost gravity in Paris.

Just before noon "X" entered my office on the second floor of the French consulate. Closing the door, he strode across the room and drove immediately to the point.

"The director general," he began, "has instructed me to explain to you in the fullest detail why I am here. I beg you not to take offense over the failure to give you advance notice of our arrival. The truth is that we are no longer sure of the security of our communications. We are not even sure our codes are safe. In fact, we can't be sure of who is getting our reports."

From this ominous preface, "X" launched into the following extraordinary account: Some weeks before, a special courier had arrived in Paris from Washington, bearing a personal letter from President Kennedy to President de Gaulle. The letter informed de Gaulle that a source in which Kennedy had confidence had stated that the French intelligence services, and even de Gaulle's own cabinet, had been penetrated by Soviet agents. Because of the obvious implications of such a security breakdown, the American President had chosen to employ a personal courier to transmit the warning, rather than depend upon possibly vulnerable, more formal channels. Kennedy further assured de Gaulle that he would provide his representatives with whatever means or contacts they might desire in verifying the value of this information for themselves.

To make a preliminary reconnaissance, "X" continued, de Gaulle had picked General de Rougemont, an officer with excellent connections in Washington. De Rougemont was attached to the Prime Minister's office as director of the Second Division of the National Defense staff and had the responsibility of coordinating the various branches of the military intelligence.

About a week after Kennedy's letter reached de Gaulle's hand, de Rougemont had slipped into Washington — avoiding completely all his French friends, including me — and made contact directly with the American authorities. The source of President Kennedy's information, he was told, was a Russian who had been a high-ranking officer in the KGB, the huge state security apparatus through which the Soviet Union conducts its foreign espionage. De Rougemont was taken to the man, to ask such questions as he wished. He was later to say that he had begun the questioning half-convinced that the whole thing was some sort of trick by which the Americans were trying to dupe de Gaulle. But after he had put the Russian through three or four days of intensive questioning, it was de Rougemont who came out shaken by the appallingly detailed information the man had on the innermost workings of the French government and its security and intelligence systems. The general flew back to Paris to make his report directly to de Gaulle's trusted assistant, Étienne Burin des Roziers, secretary-general of the Elysée Palace, and as such the aide who manages de Gaulle's staff and organizes the presidential business. Manifestly on de Gaulle's command, Burin des Roziers summoned the heads of the two main French intelligence establishments — General Paul Jacquier, Director of SDECE, and Daniel Doustin, who ran the DST (Direction de la Sécurité du Territoire), the French equivalent of the FBI. The gist of de Rougemont's report was that the KGB man was authentic, that he was indeed as important as the Americans claimed him to be, and that his assertions about the KGB's infiltration of French services demanded further and much more exhaustive questioning of the Russian by French counterintelligence experts, together with a complete checkout of the evidence which he stood ready to give. The two services — SDECE and DST — quickly assembled from their own staffs separate and expert interrogation teams, each made up of three men. These were the men with whom "X" had arrived in Washington during the night.

After telling me all this, "X" said, "Our only business here is to question the source. We have a number to call and the meetings with him are to be arranged by our friends. I expect that we shall be at this for some time."

I was not, as a matter of fact, altogether surprised to learn that such a figure as the Russian existed. The intelligence community of Washington is a freely circulating body of professional military officers and civil servants inside the diplomatic community. A certain amount of informal and more or less honest brokerage goes on among the members. In the winter of 1961–1962 I had picked up some strong clues that the Americans had recruited, or otherwise gained custody of, two and possibly three defectors from beyond the Iron Curtain, and that one of them in particular had brought very important information out with him. Naturally, I had sought out the Americans I knew who were in the business and asked about the reports. In every quarter but one I was put off with either a profession of ignorance or a bland smile. The closest I came to the truth was a guarded disclosure by an American friend that a Russian had come over who exhibited an "amazing knowledge of the inner workings" of Western security networks, including the French, but the man was being difficult in regard to his future prospects and well-being. This meager information I passed on to SDECE in Paris and for some weeks thereafter I received daily cables pressing me to find out who the man was, where the Americans were hiding him, and what he was telling them. I met a blank wall. Then, abruptly, there arrived a jarring order from Paris: I was to cease my efforts to track down the man and to stop asking questions about him. The reason for that peremptory, almost insulting directive was now made clear by what "X" had told me. It must have been that Kennedy's letter had reached de Gaulle, a decision had been taken to send de Rougemont secretly to Washington to assess the reliability of the source, and it was thought best to order me off the scent, lest I complicate matters.

At this juncture — before the interrogation teams had begun their work — I remained somewhat skeptical of the Russian's real value. It still seemed possible to me that he might be a clever plant — a double agent — whose mission was to disrupt relations between my country and the United States. Beyond that, I was unhappy at the way the Americans had broached the affair to my government, however urgent their concern. There were at that time any number of career intelligence officers high in the SDECE and the DST known by their American counterparts to be trustworthy beyond question. The grave implications raised by the Russian could and should have been first made known at that professional level. Instead, by being passed over everyone's head to de Gaulle, Kennedy's letter unnecessarily and unfairly impugned everyone in both services and created almost impossible tensions and suspicions everywhere.

The questioning of Martel — the code name given the Russian by "X" and his colleagues — began forthwith. I was kept fully abreast of what he was saying.

One of his early and most disturbing assertions was that French KGB agents in NATO headquarters in Paris were so strategically placed and so facile in their methods that they could produce on two or three days' demand any NATO document Moscow asked for. A whole library of secret NATO documents, Martel insisted, was available for reference in Moscow. Indeed the KGB's familiarity with supposedly supersecret NATO material was so intimate that its officers, in ordering fresh material from its sources in Paris, freely used the same numbering system for documents as NATO did itself. Thinking to trap the Russian, my colleagues asked him if he himself had ever seen NATO documents.

"Oh, yes," was the confident answer. "Many."

At a later meeting, a collection of some scores of classified NATO documents, dealing with different subjects, was presented to him. Most of the papers were authentic; a number, however, had been fabricated in Paris for the occasion. The whole lot was put down before the Russian and he was asked to pick out those he had read in Moscow. He did not identify all the papers, but every paper that he claimed to have read in Moscow was authentic, and among the papers he put aside were all the bogus ones. It was, for the French teams, an unnerving experience.

Martel gave the French interrogators another turn with an exhibition of an all but encyclopedic knowledge of the secret workings of the French intelligence services. He described, for example, in rather precise detail how a thoroughgoing reorganization of the SDECE had been carried out in the beginning of 1958. He further knew how and why specific intelligence functions and objectives had been shifted from one section to another, even the names of certain officers who were running certain intelligence operations — details of a nature that could have come only from a source or sources at or close to the heart of the French intelligence organizations.

Martel did not know everything. In some areas, he had only bits and pieces of intelligence to offer. He would tell his questioners, for instance, that in a certain city in the south of France a member of the municipal court who had made a name in the resistance was really a Soviet citizen — an "illegal," as we say in the trade — who had acquired a false French identity and was under KGB discipline. But he did not know the man's name — only how he fitted in. Martel knew that a French scientist of Asiatic origin, who had attended a certain international meeting of scientists in London, had been recruited there by the KGB under particular circumstances. Again, no name — only a whiff of a treasonable association. He knew that an intelligence officer who had been posted to certain Iron Curtain countries during certain periods (periods which he *did* know) and who was then attached to a specific section in a certain security service had been a KGB agent for a certain number of years.

It was not in the least surprising that Martel did not know the names of these agents. He was not personally running the KGB networks for whom these people worked, and for purposes of evaluating the intelligence they supplied it was quite sufficient for him to know only in a general way where they were placed. Martel's work in Moscow had required him to sit in on many KGB staff meetings which reviewed or directed Soviet intelligence operations in a number of countries, including France, and he additionally was more directly involved in other operations. It was from his memory of these operations that he drew the links to France and supplied the leads which could be checked out there.

The French counterintelligence teams were thorough. They sat down with the Russian day after long day. They pressed him hard. Everything he said was recorded on tapes. The tapes were run back at the end of the day, the leads were separated out, and every night a long coded summary went out to SDECE headquarters in Paris. In the interests of security the teams had brought special

305

codes with them and did their own encoding. At the end of a fortnight the teams returned to France, taking with them all the tapes and hundreds of pages of transcript. Investigations were started on the basis of the leads Martel had supplied; and then, after further questions developed, the teams flew back to Washington to pick and test the memory of the Russian afresh. They would present a name to Martel — the name of someone who was thought to fit a certain lead he had supplied. Martel would be given certain particulars about the man's work, his position, his travels, and then would come the hard question: could this man be the one who was working for the KGB inside NATO or in the political area at, say, the ministerial level? In his careful way, Martel would answer, "He looks to be," or "Yes, he could be," or "No, there's a discrepancy."

In the course of these interrogations, Martel would open other avenues for investigation. The Ministry of the Interior, which has responsibility for internal security, the French representation in the NATO organization, the Ministry of Defense, and the Ministry of Foreign Affairs were all penetrated in the higher echelons by KGB agents.

An official who appeared to be presently a member of the de Gaulle cabinet and who had ministerial or near-ministerial rank in 1944 in de Gaulle's first government had been identified in KGB discussions as a KGB agent.

A network with the code name Sapphire, consisting of more than half a dozen French intelligence officers, all of whom had been recruited by the KGB, was operating inside the SDECE itself.

A new section for collecting scientific intelligence had been, or was being, created inside SDECE with the specific mission of spying out U.S. nuclear and other technological advances, eventually in the Soviet interest.

I myself had no way of assessing the accuracy of Martel's leads, but there was no mistaking the impact he had on my colleagues. His familiarity with France's supposedly most secret affairs first astonished, then depressed them, as it did me. I could no longer doubt that Martel was the genuine article, although I still was not convinced that everything he said was true. His assertion that French intelligence had a scheme for spying out American scientific secrets I found hard to accept at the outset. Yet the Russian had been most specific on this point. In July 1959, he insisted, he heard General Sakharovsky, who was in charge of the KGB's covert operations, analyze for his senior staff officers the implications of the reorganization of the French intelligence services. In the course of the lecture, Sakharovsky mentioned the plan for the proposed intelligence section, with its targets in the United States, and noted with satisfaction that the KGB expected to receive any reports within a day or two after SDECE got them. All this was supposed to have happened nearly three and a half years before. When Martel's account was related to me, in my office, one of the DST men asked his SDECE counterpart, "Really, are you people doing this sort of thing?" None of us had ever heard of the scheme.

As the questioning of Martel went on through the summer, the procedures being used by our people to follow up Martel's leads began to create an increasingly difficult situation for me in my own work. Our teams would do some preliminary work at home and return to Washington with a number of names, any one of which might fit into the necessarily meager network of facts Martel had offered. But Martel could never answer with absolute assurance either yes or no about any of them. The problem in this for me — and, in fact, for the whole French intelligence system — lay in the fact that each session with Martel was also attended by American representatives, and each time our people dropped a name in front of Martel, that person automatically became suspect to the Americans. Small wonder, but as the list of clouded reputations lengthened, my professional contacts with the Americans (and with other Western nations) began to dry up, even on routine matters. The word seemed to be out not to take any chances with the French. I could understand this and would probably have done the same thing in their position.

The French teams were conducting their meetings with Martel in a peculiar way. For instance, they would state that two persons were already under suspicion in General de Gaulle's entourage and name the two. One, Jacques Foccart, was suspected on account of his friendship with a Czech named Saar, who was naturalized French after the war under the name of Demichel. Demichel was involved in many business deals with the Soviets, who bought through him most of the industrial equipment they were getting from Western

Europe. The close relationship between one of de Gaulle's most trusted aides and a man of indeterminate extraction doing most of his business with Moscow certainly seemed strange. And that, in addition to this, the French security services should consider him suspect, added to the already established suspicion. Even if nothing else was proved against Foccart, the black mark would remain in his file.

Two facts, however, appeared to be inconsistent with the theory that Foccart might be the Soviet agent hunted by the Sûreté; he had not been close to de Gaulle during the war and was not known to have traveled to Moscow at any time — two conditions set for the KGB agent described by Martel.

The second suspect was Louis Joxe, who had been secretary-general of the government during the war, a position nearly ministerial. Later he had been French Ambassador in Moscow, and now was the Ministre Délégué, a position similar to vice-premier. A few years before, a Soviet agent had been arrested by the Dutch carrying in his address book Joxe's address and the mention of a rendezvous. Everything about Joxe fitted the Martel description and many reports by various NATO organizations were disturbing, but no absolute proof of wrongdoing could be offered.

Discussing the Soviet spies inside NATO, French counterespionage specialists came up with the name of an officer, head of one of the three Deuxième Bureaux. The French Deuxième Bureaux can be compared to G2, A2, or the ONI. The Army, Navy, and Air Force each has its own. This officer drew the suspicion of the Sûreté when he was acknowledged as one of the few to have handled the NATO reports now in the hands of the Russians. Inquiries into his personal life had shown him as a gambler, heavily in debt. Some aspects of his private life remained obscure.

One non-Communist member of the Chamber of Representatives was suspected by the Sûreté of being a Russian illegal (a Soviet citizen who, usurping the identity of a French citizen, is working for the KGB).

Lists showing scores of names of French officials and high-ranking military officers and also giving the reasons each was suspected were submitted to Martel and American security.

The French administration, as pictured by French counter-espionage, was shown in such a light that dealing on a mutual trust basis seemed impossible to American officials. When overwhelming proof had been accumulated against someone, French counterespionage officers were perfectly right to consult their American allies, but when no evidence could be produced, it would have been better to refrain from tarnishing a Frenchman's reputation and destroying confidence in the French administration altogether.

They should have pursued Martel's leads vigorously to a straightforward finding, for or against. They then should have been able to say, "We have investigated and found something wrong with this one and this one. But the other people are clear."

On October 5, my director, General Jacquier, arrived in Washington for the purpose of getting acquainted with the American intelligence authorities. An aura of suspense hung over the first encounter with the American intelligence people. Nearly six months had elapsed since the Kennedy letter, and nothing had changed in France. The Americans were concerned not only about the penetration of our intelligence services but specifically about the apparent invulnerability of a certain official close to de Gaulle around whom Martel had seemed to close a ring of evidence. I had in fact been impelled as early as May to warn Jacquier that rumors were circulating in Washington that Foccart and Joxe were already marked as possible Soviet agents.

A month before Jacquier's arrival in Washington, the British arrested Vassall, and other actions were imminent; the absence of action in France was disquieting. At an otherwise agreeable dinner in Jacquier's honor one evening, at the elegant 1925 F Street Club, which was attended by the most senior American intelligence officials, Jacquier was quietly but emphatically put on notice that American patience was wearing thin.

An American intelligence officer who knew what the Russian had told the investigators said bluntly to Jacquier, "Your service is infiltrated. We know that you are not at fault, because you are new in your job and new at this business. But you must take the right measures."

There was a plain warning in this that American cooperation in intelligence matters would stop unless the suspected spies were cleared or removed from the line of communications.

Jacquier and I spent hours together. In our long discussions, he referred several times to the Kennedy letter and the steps being taken by the SDECE to pursue and weigh the leads supplied by the Russian. When I saw him off to Paris, he carried under his arm a briefcase stuffed with memoranda which I had helped to prepare. But I doubt that Jacquier took any of this seriously.

Early in December, he called me to Paris for a meeting on urgent business. His greeting was disconcertingly cold. First, he said, I was to see Colonel Mareuil, whose office was on the floor below. Mareuil was in charge of coordinating SDECE's liaison with foreign intelligence. He put to me two extraordinary propositions. First, I was to supply a certain officer with the names of my principal sources in Cuba. Second, I was to organize a clandestine intelligence network in the United States for the specific purpose of collecting information about U.S. military installations and U.S. scientific research.

"The Americans," Mareuil said, "have refused to help us with our *force de frappe*. We must find how to proceed on our own. General de Gaulle is adamant."

The first suggestion I rejected indignantly and out of hand. If there is one inviolable rule in the intelligence business, it is that one never discloses the identity of a source. It is a matter of common sense.

As to the second proposition, I could not believe my ears. This was the very scheme Martel had revealed to his French interrogators months before. I told Mareuil that the idea would be difficult — impossible technically — and that it would most certainly invite the rupture of relations with America if ever it was uncovered. I doubted, in any case, that I was the man for the work.

"No matter," Mareuil said smoothly. "The adjustment can be made. The matter is to be discussed at length tomorrow."

I was confident that Jacquier would put matters to rights. But I was to discover that suddenly he seemed to be overshadowed by his staff. At a meeting next morning with the senior members of the SDECE staff, I unexpectedly found myself having to defend my actions with respect to Cuba. Out of the blue, I was accused

310

across the table by my colleagues of having acted without instructions in supplying French-gathered intelligence to the Americans. This accusation was followed by a worse one: I had misled de Gaulle into supporting the Americans, with spurious evidence that the Russians had introduced offensive missiles into Cuba. It had since been established to French satisfaction, they argued, that the missiles were merely defensive weapons of the Russian SAM type — I had been duped by the Americans. And France, consequently, had been unwittingly put into a difficult position with the Soviet Union.

It was crazy. But the dreadful argument went on past noon. When it was over, I burst into Jacquier's office.

"Look," I cried, "what is going on? What does this mean? You knew that I was authorized to work on Cuba. You gave me written orders. You wrote that you were pleased with what I did."

Jacquier was flustered and embarrassed. His response was a lame one — something to the effect that my reporting from Cuba had left de Gaulle no choice but to support the Americans against the Soviet Union and that was a mistake, a misunderstanding, that "we all have to clear up."

An unspeakable lunch followed in Jacquier's private dining room. The pressure on me never abated. I felt as if I were being put on trial. In another private session with Jacquier, the explanation for the hostility finally emerged. It was a bad time for relations between France and America. President Kennedy had met with the British in Nassau and concluded an agreement with them concerning nuclear forces and nuclear sharing that reaffirmed the special "Anglo-Saxon" relationship that de Gaulle detested. France was outraged, and word flashed through the government that de Gaulle was through with the Americans. My mistake, I was told, was in continuing to work with them when I should have caught the signals of the sharp shift in course. Jacquier finally went to the heart of the matter.

"Until now," he said, "you have been working in liaison with the Americans. That is all behind you, because we no longer consider America our ally, our friend. On the contrary, France must go it alone. France has no friends. You will get fresh orders and, remember, you will follow them, please. Just obey them, that's all."

The day before I was to take the plane back to Washington,

I was summoned to Colonel Mareuil's office to receive my new instructions. A new officer was about to be attached to the embassy staff in Washington, under my control. He was to collect information relating to American military and scientific organization.

"Good God," I said, "you are not really going through with this?"

"You are," he said.

"But surely," I said, "you've read the reports from Martel?"

"Martel?" Mareuil demanded. "Who is Martel? What does he have to do with this?"

Did Mareuil really not know? Had the Martel information been kept from him? Perhaps. It was being held very closely. I said no more.

Mareuil read aloud to me from three closely typewritten pages the operational requirements for the research against the Americans. The instructions included, among other things, a requirement for certain military particulars, such as the U.S. deployment of ICBMs that had nothing to do with scientific developments.

"France has no need for this kind of information," I said. "It would be useful only to the Russians."

"The instructions are clear," was the comment.

I said it was all wrong. It wouldn't work. There would be great risk for all concerned. The answer was that the risks had to be taken, and should I fail, ample protection would be forthcoming. I asked for a written copy of the orders. Mareuil replied that since their mere existence constituted a danger, the copy in his hand was to be destroyed.

It so happened that Pierre Masson was about to be assigned to me in Washington as my deputy. At my insistence Mareuil read the orders aloud to me in his presence. My parting word with him was that if anyone attempted to carry out the plan, and if it miscarried, France would have to be prepared to sacrifice the long American friendship.

Jacquier being unavailable, I appealed to his chief of staff, Colonel de Lannurien. "This business gets crazier and crazier," I said. "You know about the Martel affair. Somebody is out of his mind."

Lannurien answered that it was Martel who was out of his mind. "The Americans," he went on, "have thrown the apple of discord

312

in our service. Because of them, everybody is suspicious of everybody else. We can no longer worry about the niceties. The orders, for your information, came from General de Gaulle."

I returned to Washington very much disturbed, and worried about the future relations of France and America. As late as January 1963 I made an appeal to Colonel Delseny, SDECE's chief of counterintelligence, who had come to Washington to measure Martel for himself, to abandon the spying enterprise altogether. He shared my misgivings, but argued that it was too late now to cork the bottle. "We can pray," he said, "that SDECE's shortage of resources will keep the plan from ever being mounted."

I had asked Jacquier, when he was in the United States, why the government had not moved faster on the Martel evidence. He replied that the government could not stand a scandal at the time, with the nation still just getting over the giving up of Algeria. It was a ready answer, given the place and time, but after all the other things I had heard and witnessed in Paris, I was persuaded that other, possibly sinister forces were the real reason for the inaction. There was no mistaking the suspiciousness, the mistrust, even the hatred for American policies which had come to permeate the thinking of the men closest to de Gaulle.

Events in my own jurisdiction deepened my suspicions. About two months after the Paris episode, at the beginning of February, there reached me from Cuba a long and detailed report on the Soviet order of battle in Cuba after the withdrawal of the missiles. I passed the information on to SDECE and was astonished to receive a peremptory order to name the source of the report.

I refused.

Then Jacquier himself commanded me to give the name. One of my assistants, who worked with me on Cuban matters, begged me to comply.

"You are in trouble enough now," he said. "After all, Jacquier does have the authority to ask."

After considerable soul-searching, I finally sent forward the name to Paris. Not long afterward, word came from Cuba that the source had been arrested. The French Ambassador advised me in a separate message to be discreet when I returned to Cuba.

"You have a difficult name to pronounce in Spanish," he said,

313

"But friends who have attended espionage trials here believe they have heard your name mentioned several times."

I never went back.

A little later I was ordered from Paris to cease working on Cuba altogether. My inquiry as to who would take over there went unanswered. The network of faithful people who had served the West so well in the missile ordeal died on the vine. It was becoming obvious that my superiors in Paris wanted me out.

Then a very senior American intelligence officer passed on to me, as being of particular interest to French military intelligence, two documents which between them supplied a rationale of certain highly intricate administrative structures inside the Soviet defense establishment. The American warned me to be exceptionally careful in handling them. I sent them on, with special security precautions, to Jacquier. Some time later, there arrived at the consulate by ordinary diplomatic pouch, innocent of classification, a general staff critique stating that the reports were quite worthless — nothing more than extracts from the Soviet press. One day my American friend asked me what reaction I had received from Paris. I told him, and he exploded. The papers, he shouted, were among the last pieces of intelligence to reach the West from the famous Colonel Penkovsky, who had been run down, tried, and shot only a short time before.

My friend added, "That information was first-class intelligence. Because the KGB was able to prove that Penkovsky had passed this information on to us, the Soviet defense establishment was obliged to make certain drastic changes in its military planning. Now you might ask your colleagues if they still need further proof that your service has been penetrated?"

I was miserable. I was now isolated from the Americans, as well as from my own service. If I had retained any hopes, they were dispelled by a strange incident arising from the arrest in June of the Swedish Colonel Wennerstrom as a Soviet spy. Wennerstrom, from long service in Washington as the Swedish air attaché, knew a great deal about NATO defense plans. He also had a strong reputation as a fun-loving partygoer, and I recalled now that he had been a frequent social associate of several French officers then stationed in Washington. I naturally moved at once to have these relationships examined, only to be ordered by Paris, in peremptory tones, to cease my investigations.

All that I had worked for in twelve and a half years of NATO collaboration was dissolving. In July, that last summer in Washington, I was notified of a promotion. It arrived with the warm congratulations of Jacquier himself. But I knew it was intended to silence me. And I let it be known that I would not be silenced.

Over the years I had a good working relationship with my ambassador, Hervé Alphand, a highly experienced diplomat. Knowing that he was returning to France in August for a holiday, I decided to take him into my confidence. He had not been aware of Martel's existence until I told him what was going on. My point to him was that France's relationship with the United States was being imperiled by the government's dilatoriness in facing up to Martel's assertions and would be ruined if the SDECE persisted in the scheme for mounting an intelligence operation against the United States. Alphand was upset. He promised to take up the matter at the Quai d'Orsay. In a little while word came back to me, through my private channels, that the Foreign Office had also been wholly ignorant of the existence and meaning of Martel until Alphand started to ask questions, and that there was fury in several quarters over my indiscretion in divulging so sensitive a topic.

In August Georges Paques was arrested in Paris. He was a senior NATO official and undoubtedly one of the KGB's men there. But manifestly he was not the only one.

Paques was arrested red-handed as he was passing a briefcase full of NATO secret documents to a member of the Soviet Embassy in Paris. Obviously the de Gaulle government was far from happy over this arrest, which, to quote a member of de Gaulle's entourage, "could disturb the excellent relations France is now having with the Russian government." The counterintelligence officers who made the arrest received no congratulations, nor did they expect any.

After his arrest, Paques gave a complete confession in which he admitted spying for the Russians since 1943 when working in Algiers for de Gaulle's war government. He had married a girl who for many years had been a member of the Communist Party and had convinced him to work for the Soviets. During the years preceding his arrest, he had been personal assistant to nine Prime

Ministers or Secretaries. He had also been Director of Studies for the French War College. And during nineteen years in these sensitive positions, he reported weekly to the Russians. There was no possibility of suppressing the evidence against Paques.

I followed the developments of the Paques affair with the greatest interest and hope for a very special reason. A few years earlier, Paques had come to Washington to visit the Pentagon and the NATO Standing Group. During his stay in the capital he called me on behalf of a very important member of French intelligence who recommended him warmly and asked me to facilitate his trip, which I did, and which, according to the rules, I also reported to my headquarters.

I was convinced that I would be asked questions about Paques' activities in the States. I thought an inquiry on who recommended him to me would begin and be rewarding. But not a question was asked; no one wanted to know about any other Soviet agents.

On September 16 a cable was laid on my desk. My mission in the United States was to end on October 18. My relief would arrive in Washington in a fortnight. I would have two weeks to brief him on his duties. And then I was to report without further delay to headquarters in Paris. After all my years in Washington, I was being commanded to wind up all my affairs and pull up my roots in just one month.

I stayed on in my post to the last hour permitted me in my orders. On the morning of October 18, at the desk in the consulate which I yielded in the afternoon to my successor, I composed a letter to Jacquier. In it I summed up the disquieting matters and concerns which I have described here. I ended it all this way:

Considering that the questioning I was subjected to on Cuba proves that some members of the service were worried over the efficiency of my work against the Soviets;

Considering that by demanding to know the identity of my sources (although you have been informed by American intelligence services of the presence of infiltrated Soviet agents in your organization), you committed an imprudence which could only serve the agents of a foreign power;

316

Considering that your order to collect intelligence on the United States, even at the price of a rupture of diplomatic relations between the two countries, could only benefit the Soviets;

Considering that the cancellation of my mission on Cuba, although the results obtained were outstanding enough to bring the Americans to thank you, was of benefit to the Soviets;

Considering that the contemptuous criticism of the Penkovsky reports can only serve the Soviets;

Considering that the lack of support showed by the service in an inquiry on the French contacts of Wennerstrom can only protect Soviet agents;

Considering that the orders I received were technically unrealizable or could only bring a crisis beneficial to the Soviets;

Considering that the vexations I received during the past nine months do not leave any doubt as to your determination to harass me and to neutralize the representative of French intelligence in Washington, whose knowledge is considered embarrassing;

Considering that the reports received from American intelligence of the presence of Communist infiltration agents inside the service and inside the French government have been corroborated by the Paques affair;

Considering that for all reasons mentioned above, it is impossible for me to cooperate in any way with the SDECE;

I have the honor to submit by resignation as of today, October 18, 1963, reserving all my rights for future legal action.

P. L. Thyraud de Vosjoli

With this letter, Lamia — the code name given me by headquarters — closed the book on twenty years in intelligence.

Now that my resignation was a *fait accompli*, I was taking time to put my affairs in order in America before sailing to Paris. But on November 22, 1963, half an hour after the assassination of President Kennedy, I received a cable from SDECE ordering me to fly at once Paris. The airports were closed, no immediate transportation was available, and I decided to think it over until the following day.

That night a very dear friend called me from Paris, with a

317

serious warning, "You are now in a free country. The minute you get back to France you will no longer be free. Orders have been given to silence you by all means."

Another transatlantic call reached me in the morning: "Notice who signed the cable ordering you back. You will be lucky to be alive within a few hours after your arrival."

I picked up the cable.

The signature read Mareuil, Colonel Marcel Mercier's new alias.

Marcel Mercier . . . who had been directly involved in the suicide of the Attorney General of Switzerland, and who had fingered the victims for the so-called Red Hand killers. Marcel Mercier, who had changed his name to escape vengeance by the families of those he had sent to death.

Only then did I realize I was condemned to exile.

Epilogue

The diplomatic visa allowing me to live in the United States expired the day I left the French Embassy, and the only way to obtain a resident visa was to request it from a United States Embassy abroad.

Canada was just a few hours away, but I rejected the idea of going there because of the presence of so many Gaullist agents sent to organize subversive activities in the French provinces. I chose to go to Mexico, where freedom is a tradition and the persecuted can always find asylum. I knew, too, that the Mexican government refused to permit any foul play by foreigners.

During the year I waited in Mexico for my visa, I could contemplate the liberty enjoyed by the Mexican people and compare it with the oppressive system developed by the Gaullist regime. In Mexico, freedom and privacy are everyone's rights. In France, a man has only the rights the police feel in the mood to grant him.

De Gaulle had enacted a law by which the Minister of the Interior, without a warrant or having to give a reason, could put under arrest and hold in a concentration camp any man he chose, for as long as he chose. There was no trial, no appeal.

France is one of the few countries where there is no *habeas corpus.* The police are allowed to arrest a man on suspicion and to keep him incommunicado for as long as two weeks. It is called the *garde à vue,* or to keep in view, and during this time the prisoner is not authorized to consult with a lawyer. He is questioned twenty-four hours a day by teams of police officers working in shifts, and if he does not answer questions, drugs are mixed in his food. Large quantities of scopolamine, the so-called truth serum, are often used without the prisoner's knowledge.

The Court of State Security — a special court — is made up of judges appointed by the government. The chief of the service "Action" was one of its judges. Trials are usually held behind closed doors and the decisions of the court cannot be appealed.

All judges in France are appointed by the government and are under the Minister of Justice. Their promotions are based upon grades they receive for their work during the year. The State Attorneys decide on the grades. Therefore, if the government is unhappy with their decisions, they are not promoted. The magistrates complain regularly about this domination by the state, but no reforms have ever been initiated. The police force is, in its entirety, under the control of the Minister of the Interior, which means, for instance, that the mayor of a city has no right to give an order to a policeman. Only a minority of police officers are involved in law enforcement. The majority are members of a division called "general intelligence" in charge of gathering information on the activities of the various political parties and on the private lives of their members. All their reports are filed, and a up-to-date record of the activities of almost every Frenchman can be found in the Sûreté's central files.

Directly under the Prime Minister is a division in charge of monitoring private telephones. In a country where a citizen must wait at least two years to get even a party line, more than four thousand lines are used in Paris alone to monitor private conversations and teletypes used by French and foreign newspapers.

SDECE has a department in charge of special operations in France — special in that they are specialists in breaking into offices and apartments to steal or photograph documents. They also have, without the owners' consent but with the help of some of the staff, permanently bugged many rooms in hotels such as the Crillon and the George V in Paris. Photographs are taken of any extraconjugal activities of guests and used later, eventually, for blackmail. At all airports, especially at Orly, a room was equipped with the most sophisticated devices to open diplomatic pouches, suitcases, and mail. Contents are photographed and it is impossible, even to the keenest expert, to detect any signs of the indiscretion.

Through SDECE, de Gaulle's regime had not only hidden very large amounts of money in Switzerland and in other foreign countries, but tax money had been used to create corporations and to buy shares in many businesses. Trustworthy Gaullists are used as straw men and are given top positions as directors or executive officers, drawing large salaries. The profits of the corporations are used for political purposes or to add to the secret accounts. Intelligence services all over the world are known to set up corporations in foreign countries as a cover for their intelligence activities, but most of SDECE-controlled corporations are located in France, mainly for the purpose of acquiring control over important industries, such as newspapers, electronic plants, hotels, publishing houses, import-export businesses, airlines. A long list could be made, but it is not my wish to ruin the many honest people working for these companies.

When the Gaullist regime is over it will probably be impossible to produce as evidence the documents signed by the straw men recognizing that they are not the rightful owners of the stocks. This will result in nice payoff for Gaullist subversive activities.

In a nation dominated by such a dictatorial regime I was forced to acknowledge sadly how little chance there was of making myself heard or of obtaining justice. But the day has to come when the French people, fed up with all the abuses, will get rid of those who oppress them. Waiting for that day, I have followed through my many friends left in SDECE what has happened inside my former agency.

At the time of my departure General Jacquier decided to put only one person in charge of intelligence, counterintelligence, and all services of research of SDECE. He appointed to the position Colonel Leonard Houneau, who, ten years before, had performed the same

321

duties. After the nomination became known, several Western intelligence service expressed their surprise to General Jacquier and gave him their files on Colonel Houneau, pointing out several facts.

Colonel Houneau was said to have befriended, during the resistance, Demichel, alias Saar, present supplier of French and Western equipment to the Soviets, and to have given him a job inside SDECE as chief of what was called the political division. In the early 1950s Colonel Houneau, after leaving SDECE, had been sent to Prague, Czechoslovakia, as a military attaché. Allied intelligence had been puzzled by a trip he made then to Moscow to spend his vacation, and by a lady friend with whom he occasionally traveled. The lady was known as a Soviet agent. Furthermore, his recent appointment was believed to be the result of a request by Demichel to his friend Jacques Foccart. No specific accusation could be made against Colonel Houneau, but his previous association made the NATO Allies worry that such a sensitive position should be given him.

General Jacquier angrily rejected the information made available to him and reconfirmed Colonel Houneau's appointment. But his chief of staff, Colonel de Lannurien, who had no special liking for Houneau, approached several Allied agencies asking for derogatory evidence against him. He was coldly received and told bluntly that if there were some facts in Colonel Houneau's background which were questionable, he, Colonel de Lannurien, was not exactly beyond reproach. In fact, Martel's disclosures had caused him to be on the list of suspects established by French security services.

Georges de Lannurien's father, General de Lannurien, had been military aide to Vichy's Maréchal Pétain. A letter written at the end of the war by General de Lannurien to his boss stressed the necessity of continuing with the "beneficial operations of Darnan . . ." (Darnan was head of the militia responsible for the death of thousands of resistance members). In spite of his father's leanings, Georges de Lannurien, then a captain, went to Czechoslovakia at the end of the war to lead the French task force supporting the Slovak uprising. He fought with courage, and when the Slovak partisans were beaten by the Germans, he was able to escape with the help of the Soviets. After the war, as an SDECE agent, he was sent to Prague to control, under cover of military attaché, the French intelligence network there. A year after his arrival, the

Czech police arrested all the French agents, with the exception of Lannurien, who safely got back to Paris.

He explained that one night he had been to the home of a girl working for him and that, undoubtedly, Czech security had the room bugged, monitoring all his conversation. Afterwards, they made some of his contacts talk and he had been plain lucky to escape further prosecution. The explanation seemed questionable to the chief of counterespionage Colonel Verneuil, who advised Henri Ribière, the SDECE director at the time, to dismiss de Lannurien from the agency and send him back to the Army. But Ribière was a generous man and, taking into consideration de Lannurien's courageous attitude with the Slovak partisans, chose to keep him in our intelligence division.

Later, de Lannurien requested a return to the Army to get a promotion, and when General Nordstad assumed command of NATO, he was appointed as his French aide. He was careful enough to tell the American general of his previous ties with French intelligence, but kept SDECE informed on what the NATO Supreme Commander was doing. When certain problems developed and General Nordstad asked to be returned to the United States, he left without knowing the part played by his French aide in his difficulties.

According to Martel, one of KGB's sources inside NATO was a French officer occupying a high position in the organization, with access to the most important documents. This officer had been in contact with the Soviets during the war and, for a while, was connected with a French diplomatic mission in a satellite country. The description could only fit a limited number of persons, and de Lannurien felt he was under suspicion. While in SDECE he had been Mercier's immediate superior, advocating the creation of a French network in the United States to steal American defense secrets, and American security knew about it.

To justify himself, Georges de Lannurien, bypassing his superior, General Jacquier, had gone to see Prime Minister Georges Pompidou. Of the meeting I only know what de Lannurien told friends and some American journalists. The Prime Minister had rejected his request to set up a commission of inquiry, denying him the chance to clear himself. "Pompidou is trying to cover up for someone," said de Lannurien, "and he does not want the real Soviet agents to be uncovered." I have no particular reason to like Georges Pompidou, but to hint that he was covering for Soviet agents is absurd.

A few days after this meeting, Colonel Georges de Lannurien and Colonel Leonard Houneau resigned from SDECE and from the Army.

Were the two colonels innocent victims of Martel's disclosures, and were they used as scapegoats in the French government's desire to sweep the whole affair under the rug? Or was there really foul play? I cannot say, but on August 31, 1969, when the Czech people were lamenting their lost freedom, and when French journalist Georges Penchenier was kept incommunicado in a Czech jail for having performed his duty, retired Colonel Georges de Lannurien was honored in Prague by President Svoboda and Prime Minister Černík and all the Communist dignitaries. He was awarded the medal of the White Lion order.

One thing is sure, de Lannurien is most welcome in a Communist country, and I would not be. . . .

The departure of SDECE's number two and number three men, who had been so anxious to ruin my accomplishments, was to be followed a year later by the ousting of their boss, General Jacquier, for gross incompetency and grave mistake in the fulfillment of his duties. Because of it, several men died and the Ben Barka affair rocked the French government.

It all happened at the beginning of November 1965.

The king of Morocco had decided to ask Mehdi Ben Barka, an exiled opposition leader, to join his government. The Minister of Interior, General Oufkir, knowing that the return of Ben Barka to favor would mean his own dismissal, was determined to get rid of his opponent before he set foot on Moroccan soil.

Prior to the independence of Morocco, General Oufkir was an officer in the French Army, in which he had many friends. Now responsible for Moroccan police and security, he kept in close touch with SDECE and had helped the French Special Services in more than one way. With his support, they had been able to set up in Morocco a large installation to monitor all the communications of the American bases there. He had also accepted as suicide the assassination of Yves Allain, a former SDECE agent found in the desert with a bullet in his head. Allain had been working behind the Iron Curtain for French intelligence who accused him later of being an American agent.

Oufkir's representative in Paris, Chtouki, was in close contact with Colonel Mercier, alias Mareuil, the SDECE liaison with all foreign special services. Their relationship was excellent, and every New Year, Chtouki loaded Colonel Marcel Mercier with presents to thank him for his help. When Ben Barka became a problem, the Moroccan special services representative had a long talk with Colonel Marcel Mercier, an old hand in this kind of operation. The Moroccans asked that "Action" provide the hoodlums needed for Ben Barka's kidnapping in Paris. These thugs, previously used in Morocco, were well known to one of General Oufkir's friends, a certain Lopez. Lopez's involvement proved to be a mistake. He was Air France station chief at Orly airport, and he had been working simultaneously for the Moroccans; for the "Barbouzes" — the reprobates associated with the service "Action"; and for the special division of SDECE intelligence. Lopez was, in fact, a triple agent covering every bet with another. When working for the Moroccans or for the "Barbouzes" he would cover himself by reporting conscientiously to the chief of the special division, Leroy-Finville.

After the successful kidnapping of the Moroccan leader, Lopez reported the disappearance of Ben Barka to Leroy-Finville without mentioning his participation in the plot. When Lopez fell under police suspicion, he tried to clear himself, arguing that he had kept Leroy-Finville informed.

This is how SDECE's involvement in the plot became known. Immediately, pressure was applied to the police and to the witnesses. One witness was murdered, his death faked to look like a suicide. No inquiry was made of Mercier-Mareuil, who disappeared and became unavailable.

A scapegoat had to be found, and Leroy-Finville, the last civilian to hold a position of responsibility in SDECE, was picked. Although he had provided the government with all information on the plot, Leroy-Finville was accused of having done it too late. He was arrested, spent almost one year in jail, and endured a sensational trial before the case against him was dismissed. As to Ben Barka, no one ever knew what had become of him. His body was never found.

The Ben Barka affair and the mock trial which followed threw light on the outrages perpetrated by SDECE. De Gaulle, embarrassed over the crime committed in his name, after firing SDECE Director General Jacquier, withdrew French intelligence from the control of the Prime Minister and placed it under the Minister of Defense. He appointed General Guibaud as new director. This officer had been in charge of intelligence during the battle of Dien Bien Phu and had been notoriously incompetent, but he was known to be unconditionally obedient.

General Guibaud started his new functions with a ridiculous review of all the SDECE members, having them stand at attention in the courtyard of the SDECE headquarters, Boulevard Mortier in Paris. Then he set to work on more serious matters, such as how to get back at de Vosjoli for his letter of resignation and how to silence his comments on SDECE scandals.

During my stay in Mexico, his predecessor, General Jacquier, had sent a goon squad after me, under a Major Fontes, but friends warned me and I tried to be careful. Nevertheless, my apartment was broken into twice. Nothing was found, since there was nothing to find. Without abating, Major Fontes went to the West Coast and set up a network of informers to identify me when I, as he said, "would be going to Tahiti to spy for the United States on the French hydrogen test in the Pacific." SDECE agents there were under cover of UAT, the French airline with direct flights from Los Angeles to Tahiti, and of Air France.

At the same time SDECE received a report from one of their agents in Washington commenting on my activities in Santo Domingo as head of an American intelligence organization in the Caribbean. More men were dispatched there.

I was then quietly writing a novel in Colorado, and all this commotion seemed to be a waste of time and money. If these people were so anxious to see me, why did they not simply let me know? It would have been easy — they knew my office address.

But General Guibaud decided otherwise. A French colonel was sent to the United States to find a way to get hold of me in the

326

Ben Barka manner. This officer was surprised to discover that American enforcement agencies were aware of his plans, and to proceed with them would have meant serious consequences.

For five years I had lived in the hope that someone with enough influence in the government would expell from SDECE and the French administration all the Soviet-infiltrated agents. This would have been quite simple: all of Martel's statements as well as the statements made by French counterespionage officers had been recorded on tape and taken back to France in heavy suitcases by the Sûreté inspectors who interrogated Martel. I myself had left all my records in my office upon leaving Washington. An honest investigation should have been undertaken by a commission made up of Frenchmen of prestige who were not involved in partisan politics. Acting as a grand jury, they should have decided the persons to prosecute and the ones to clear. This would have been reasonable and just.

But nothing happened, so great was the de Gaulle government's fear of the scandals such an inquiry would reveal. I decided then to make public the facts I knew, and in April 1969 I wrote an article which was reproduced in newspapers and magazines all over the world, with the exception of France, where the government was able to bring enough pressure so that no newspaper dared to print it integrally, and the ones who commented on it objectively went through many difficulties. Still, the French people have a right to know.

Freedom of the press is one of the trademarks of a democracy. Another is the rigorous control the nation must exert on its police and on its special services. An intelligence service is necessary to protect a country against unwarranted attacks from its enemies, but intelligence is only the research of information. Killing and other subversive activities on French soil and against friendly countries have nothing to do with intelligence. An intelligence officer works with his brain and not with guns, knives, or other instruments of death. There is no need to resort to violence to uncover what other nations are trying to hide. The guardian of a secret must be smarter than the agents hunting it — otherwise, the secret is lost.

To keep law enforcement agencies and intelligence services

within their proper framework, and to see that some unscrupulous individuals do not use the tremendous power entrusted to them for their personal advantage, rigid controls must be devised. Intelligence services are tools for the defense of democracy, not weapons to kill it.

The day such controls are established, and when individuals will really be protected against police abuses, the French people will once more know the full meaning of liberty.

INDEX

A2, 308

ABWER, 257

Accra, 265

"Action," SDECE special operations group, 136, 162-163, 252, 253, 320; and political assassination, 259-262, 263; recruitment for, 260, 262; loosening of ties with SDECE, 261-262; and de Gaulle's supporters, 262-263, 266-267; and Moumie's assassination, 264-265; and terrorist activities in Algeria, 266-271; and Mattei, 274-277; and Ben Barka affair, 325

Action Committee in France. *See* Committee for Action in France

Africa, 47; nationalism in, 254-263; independence, 273. *See also* North Africa

Agayants, Ivan, 208

AGIP (Italian Petroleum Agency), 272, 273

Ahcene, Ait, 255-257

Algeria, 45, 298, 313; de Gaulle's arrival in, 45, 69, 71; Gaullist resistance movement (Combat), 53, 68, 69; independence movement in, 228, 246, 249-250; revolutionaries of, 255-256; nationalists in Switzerland, 258; special force to eliminate nationalists, 258-259, 261; Gaullist terrorist groups in, 266-271; independence,

270, 273; oil interests, 273-274; rebels, and Castro, 284-285

Algerian National Liberation Front, 273-274

Algiers, 30, 47, 51, 53, 69, 92, 106; BCRA in, 45, 48-49, 51, 52, 76; de Gaulle headquarters in, 48, 66; and Operation Torch, 65; and French intelligence services, 71; and intelligence networks in foreign countries, 77, 92; author returns to Paris from, 112-113; and Dewavrin's secret war treasury, 145; general's revolt, 150

Allain, Yves, 324-325

Allied intelligence, 120-124, 186, 237-238; and French intelligence, 209-210, 216, 243-244, 246-253; and Colonel Houneau, 322

Allied military mission, China, 86, 88

Allies, 19, 21, 40, 76; forces in England, 27; and Free French in London, 41, 57; in North Africa, 44, 64-68; crush Rommel's forces, 45; and de Gaulle's concept of resistance, 60; and liberation of Indochina, 93, 99; Normandy landings, 101; in France after liberation, 116; French collaboration with in military matters (1944), 120; and the generals' scandal, 186, 194

Alphand, Hervé, 246, 315

329

332

Dubois, Mrs., 258
Duclos (alias Saint-Jacques), 58, 59
Dulles, Allen, 214, 248, 249, 250, 251; and Cuba, 289, 294
Dumesnil de Grammont, Michel, 204, 206-207
Dunderdale, Commander, 71
Dungler, Mr. (alias Schneider), 73-74
Duperier, Colonel, 262

Eckberg, Mary, 178-181
École Polytechnique, L', 17, 58, 67
Eden, Anthony, 59-63
Egypt, 228, 246, 258
18th Airborne Corps, U.S., 121
Eisenhower, Dwight D., 65, 79, 120, 195, 214, 217; and U-2 affair, 177; and Suez crisis, 247, 248; and de Gaulle, 250
Elizabeth, Princess, 222
Emblanc, Colonel, 88, 91, 104
England, 10, 13, 41, 57, 121-124; and Allied and Free French intelligence, 19; Allied forces in, 27; SDECE section covering, 136; and Jewish emigrants to Palestine, 137-138
ENI (Ente Nazionale Idrocarburi — Italian National Hydrocarbon Authority), 271-273; French intelligence agents within, 274; and SDECE "Action" group, 274-275
Entreprise des Travaux Ruraux (T.R.), 71, 161
Escarra, Jean, 85-86, 92, 94-98
Espionage, 10, 180. See also Counterespionage
Excelsior, 288
Expeditionary Force in the Far East, 93
Express, L', 270, 298

Far East, 55, 56, 82-111, 216; theater of operations, 96; tracing of war criminals in, 130-133
Far Eastern intelligence section, Free French Special Services, 84-92, 95-111, 116, 125; Avenue Foch offices, 118; dishonesty within, 125-126
Fauguenot, Émile, 262
Fauvert, Louis, 144-145, 151, 160
Federal Bureau of Investigation (FBI),
213; and Soviet subversive activities, 231
FFI. See French Forces of the Interior
Figueres, José, 233, 234, 235
Finland, 107; intelligence, 107
First Regiment of Moroccan Spahis (RMSM), Gaullist regiment, 48, 49
First World War, 12, 49, 50, 94
FLN (Front of National Liberation), Cuba, 285
Foccart, Jacques, 163, 252-253, 273, 299, 322; and Gaullist intelligence network in Africa, 263, 266-268; and Ben Bella's liberation, 270-271; alleged KGB agent, 307-308
Folliquet, Mr., 201
Fontes, Major, 326
For Victory (newspaper), 78
Force de frappe, 310, 311
Foreign Legion, 46, 89
Fourcaud, Colonel Pierre, 142-144, 148-150, 155, 157; and the generals' scandal, 184-185, 197, 202, 203, 211; and whitewash of General Revers, 199-201, 203, 207; called before Sûreté, 202; and Peyre's exile, 208; and the Communists, 208-209
Fourmachat, Major, 87
Foyer, Colonel, 268
France, 65; 1940 capitulation of, 4-5; division of, 5; British intelligence networks in, 60; postarmistice contempt for Army, 70; and AMGOT, 79; and Indochina, 83-111; author's return to, 112-113; postliberation problems, 126; intensification of Communist activities in, 162; and Poland, 168-182; Red Hand activities in, 261-262; repressive police and judicial policies in, 319-320. See also de Gaulle
France Forever (newspaper), 78
France-Soir, 146, 147
Franco, Francisco, 30, 38, 39
Franco-American relations, 70, 90-92, 97, 105, 106-107; and de Gaulle, 66-67, 88, 298-318; and complexity of American politics, 223; and Eisenhower, 250-251; and French nuclear force, 310, 311
Franco-Cuban relations, 280, 284-285

Franco-Soviet mutual defense pact, 127-128
François, BNCI representative, 98
Francs-Tireur et Partisans (FTP), 115, 128
Franklin, 124-125
Fraternization, 9, 16; postliberation punishment for, 115
"Free Algeria" committee, 261
Free French, 19, 27, 41; in Spain, 40; in North Africa, 47, 48; intelligence, 48-54 (see also BCRA); emblem, 62; and the Americans, 65-67; and postarmistice French intelligence services, 70
Free French Army, 50-51; and Operation Torch, 64-66
Free French intelligence service in the Far East, 85, 88, 90-91, 95, 98; placed under DGSS, 97
Free French Navy, 63, 166
Free French Special Services, 72, 77, 101; Technical Division, 74; Far Eastern intelligence section, 84, 85, 97-98, 99, 104, 106, 109, 125-126; members return from Algiers, 113
Free Zone, 5, 8-9, 12; government of, and the Jews, 14; flight of French Masons to, 16; Gestapo agents in, 19; occupied by the Germans, 20, 71
Freemasons, 16, 238; and Martinism, 17; and generals' scandal, 186, 204-207; postwar housecleaning, 205; archives, 205-206; and Peyre's exile, 207-208; and Soviet-sponsored "disinformation" activity, 208
French Air Force, 84
French Army, 4, 12, 47, 94, 184; postarmistice contempt for, 70; after liberation, 126; and generals' scandal, 184-210; and Dien Bien Phu, 236
French Army in Indochina, 84, 85, 107-108, 187, 189
French Committee for the National Liberation, 69, 73, 78
French Communist Party, 128, 143; Central Committee, 16; opposition to Germans, 19; support for de Gaulle, 61; and de Gaulle's govern-

ment, 127-129, 141; and French scientific community, 129; and L'Humanité, 186; and Freemasons, 205-206; and Latin Communist Parties, 231-232; and Soviet subversive activities, 243. See also Communists
French Community, 263-264
French Embassy, Madrid, 44
French Embassy, Washington, 213; security leaks, 240-243; and Couve de Murville, 245
French Forces of the Interior (FFI), 114-115
French High Command, 49, 50, 70, 186
French-Indochinese war, 50
French Institute, Warsaw, 163, 167, 169
French Military Missions, 77, 92; in U.S., 79; in China, 85-89, 91, 92, 101; in Far East, 104
French Navy, 48, 57
French police, 21-25, 74-75; and punishment of collaborators, 115; de Gaulle's policy, 320; "general intelligence," 320
French secret services, 18, 70-72, 98; security problems, 240-243; networks behind Iron Curtain, 243
French Union Assembly, 186
French-USSR agreement, concerning repatriation of Soviet citizens, 153
Frey, Roger, 266-268, 269
Friedli, Liliane, 264-265
Frischimger, Fritz, 123

G2, 70, 105, 308; Cuba, 292-293
Gallagher, General, 110
Galy, Maurice, 262
Gano, Colonel, 168
Gardes Républicains, 251
Gardier, Robert du, 285, 289, 293
Gatward, Flight Lieutenant, 63-64
Gaulier, Bernard, 6, 7
Gaullists, 78, 146, 147; Swiss bank accounts and corporations of, 150-151, 321; and generals' scandal, 208-209; fanatic, 262-263; and terrorist groups in Algeria, 266-271; and Mattei, 271-277; in Canada, 319; subversive activities, 321

Informers, 16, 157-158
Institut des Hautes Études de la Défense Nationale (War College), 190, 192, 193, 195
Intelligence, 13-14; author's vision of, 55; basic rules of, 81-82; delivery and distribution methods, 158; as commodity, 228-229. *See also* specific intelligence services
Interarmco, 273
International Red Cross, 294
Iron Curtain, 167, 177, 303, 305; SDECE networks behind, 243
Israel, 92, 247
Italy, 4, 45, 48, 271-277; and AMGOT, 79; Communist Party, 129; Christian Democratic Party, 271-272

Jacquier, General Paul, 299, 302, 309-315, 321-322; and author's resignation, 316-317; ousting of, 324, 326
Japan, 83, 84, 85, 93; invasion of China, 86; and Pearl Harbor, 87; at war with U.S., 96; occupation of Indochina, 99, 104-106; and Finnish intelligence, 107; acquires U.S. code, 107; and slaughter of French troops in Indochina, 107-108; surrender of, and future of Indochina, 109; diplomats of, 118-119
Japanese intelligence services, 107, 119
Japanese Navy, 87
Japanese secret services (Kempeitai), 109, 185
Jarrel, Commander, 105
Jewish Agency for Palestine, 137
Jews, 3, 132, 294; and escape into Free Zone, 6-9; persecution of, 14-15; and responsibility for the disaster, 16; in Spanish jails, 40; and Palestine, 137-138
Joliot-Curie, Frédéric, 129
Jour de France, 214
Jovenes Rebeldes, Cuba, 291
Joxe, Louis, 308
Jubelin, Lieutenant Commander, 63
Jungvolk, 131
Justice. *See* Department of Justice

Kennedy, John F., 223, 224-225, 301-304, 310, 311; assassination of, 317

Kennedy, Joseph P., 223, 224
Kennedy, Joseph P., Jr., 223-224
Kerillis, Henry de, 78
KGB, 116, 179, 206, 208; and Polish security services, 170; penetration of French secret services, 302-318 *passim*, 323; and Colonel Penkovsky, 314
Khokhlov, Nicholas, 238-240
Khrushchev, Nikita S., 295
Kolissev, Theodore (Lapchinsky), 152-153
Kominform, 231
Kommandantur, 5, 6, 16
Korean War, 216, 237
Krassine, Ambassador, 152
Kriegel-Valrimont, 202-203
Kriegsmarine, 29, 116
Kunming, 102, 103, 105, 107

Laffont, Colonel (alias Vernueil), chief of counterespionage, 71, 161-162, 170, 176, 232, 257; and Robineau trial, 175; and generals' scandal, 188, 198-201, 205; and the Soviets, 209; and Lannurien, 323
Laguerre, Andre, 196
Lallier (alias Bienvenue), 58, 68; agent in U.S., 77-78
Lamartre, Captain, 54
Landrieu, Captain, 149
Langlois, Captain, 33-39, 41
Lannurien, Colonel Georges de, 312-313, 322-323; attempts to clear allegations against, 323-324; resigns from SDECE, 324; honored in Prague, 324
Lannurien, General de, 322
Laperche, Georges, 261
Latin America, 231-236
Laurent, Colonel, 267-269
Laurent, saboteur, 275-276
Lautissier, Jean, 186-188, 199
League of Arab States, 228
Lebanon, 137, 232-233
Leclerc, Jean, 47, 48
Legion of Honor, significance of, 223-224
Le Grève, M., 261
Lemarchand, Pierre, 267-270
Lemarchand, Mme., 267, 269-270

Organization of American States, 226, 235
Orléans, 4, 112, 113
Orly Airport, 239, 248, 321
Orlynski, Major, 171
Orves, d'Estienne d', 10, 20
OSS. See Office of Strategic Service
Oufkir, General, 324-325

Pacot, 61-62
Paillole, Captain, 70-72, 74, 161
Palestine, 137-138. See also Israel
Palewski, de Gaulle's director of cabinet, 102
Pamplona, 38, 39, 42; Carcel Modela, 39-41
Paques, Georges, 244-245; arrest of, 315-317
Paringaux, Yves, 19
Paris, 11; liberation of, 106, 112, 141; Japanese Embassy, 118; Police Headquarters, 141; Soviet Embassy, 152-153, 238-240; American Embassy, 247
Paris, Comte de, French pretender, 65, 92
Passardière, Guy de la, 282, 283
Passy. See Dewavrin, Captain André
Patti, Major, 109-110
Paul, Marcel, 128, 168
Paul, Mr. See Peyre, Roger
Pelabon, Commander, 67-69, 76-77, 96-98
Penchenier, Georges, 324
Penkovsky, Colonel, 314, 317
Pentagon, 216-218, 245; and Vietnam, 237
Perón, Juan, 81
Perrier, Monsieur. See Paillole, Captain
Pétain, Marshal Henri, 4, 5, 14, 16, 19, 30, 40, 44, 57, 74, 78, 245, 322; and the Synarchy, 17-18, 205; and Giraud, 30; and French forces in North Africa, 47-48, 67; and occupied France, 66; and postarmistice secret services, 70; and postarmistice counterintelligence, 71; and French refugees in U.S., 78
Petchkoff, Alexis. See Gorki, Maxim
Petchkoff, General, 88-89, 91, 105
Petite Gironde, La, 28
Peyre, Roger (alias Paul), 190-194,

197, 202-203; and SDECE, 198-199, 201; and Girardot, 199-200; and Revers testimony, 203; and Freemasons, 206-207; in exile, 207-208; and confidence in French government, 208-209
Philby, Harold, 210, 212, 214-216, 240, 243, 245
Philippe, André, 60, 61, 144
Pietri, 44
Pignon, 186
Pinay, Antoine, 300
Pineau, Christian, 246
Pinson, Mimi, 119
Planchais, Jean, 140
Playa Girón, Cuban jail, 291
Pleven, René, 92, 98
Poland, 115, 164-182; Nazi occupation of, 167; citizens of, in France, 168; jails of, 171; trials of French consulate employees, 171-172; trade relations with France, 172, 175; and Robineau trial propaganda, 173; loss of French intelligence network in, 174; agents in France, 175-176
Police intelligence services, 175, 179
Polish Foreign Office, 166
Polish Ministry of Foreign Affairs, 166, 168
Pompidou, Georges, 251, 252, 323-324
Pontchardier, Dominique, 267-268, 270
Pontchardier, Mrs. (alias Mrs. Rollin), 267
Potsdam meeting, 109, 110
Powers, Francis Gary, 177
PPF, wartime fascist organization, 191
Prisoners of war, 121-124
Puchert, Georg, 257, 260
Pucheu, Pierre, 19, 74-75
Pyrenees, 27-30

Quai d'Orsay, Paris, 166, 170, 172, 315; and Cuban revolution, 280, 284
Quebec Conference, 102, 106
Quok, Nguyen Ai. See Ho Chi Minh

Radio transmitters, 14; for Indochinese resistance operations, 103-105
Ramadier, Paul, 154-155; and generals' scandal, 194-195
Raux, 102

134-138; geographic devision (intelligence), 133-136, 157; section for studies, 133, 136, 157; counterintelligence, 133-135; career officers in, 134; duplication in, 135-136; "Action," 136, 162-163, 252, 253, 259-271, 320, 325; Honorable Correspondents (H.C.'s), 139-140; and Dewavrin's resignation, 140-141, 143-144; and Ribière, 142; and Fourcaud, 142-144, 148-150, 155, 157; and Dewavrin's arrest, 143-150; and generals' revolt in Algeria, 151; and Communists in the government, 154; Communist infiltration in, 155; and Ribière-Fourcaud feud, 155-156; reorganization of, 157-161, 304-305; and Ministry of Foreign Affairs, 158; security problems, 160-161, 170; civilian employees, 160-161; and intensification of Communist activities (late 1940s), 162; discrediting scandals, 163; and the Robineau case, 164-171, 174, 182, 197; and the generals' scandal, 184, 186-188, 196-210; and counterespionage in foreign countries, 187; and commission of inquiry, 204; and French Freemasons, 206; and Fourcaud's firing, 208-209; liaison in Washington, 210, 212, 213, 240; and Dien Bien Phu, 236; and Khokhlov, 238-240; and networks behind Iron Curtain, 243; de Gaulle's reorganization of, 253; and political assassinations, 254-271; and ENI, 274; penetrated by Soviet agents, 300-318, 327; author's resignation from, 316-317; and de Gaulle regime, 321; and de Lannurien, 322-324; and Ben Barka affair, 324-326
Second World War, 12, 70
Secret Committee for Revolutionary Action (CSAR). See Cagoule
Section de Liaison Française en Extrème Orient (SLFEO), 100
Seignon, Henri, 41
Servan Schreiber, Jean-Jacques, 298-299
Service de Documentation Extérieure et de Contre-Espionage. See SDECE
Service for Civic Action (SAC), 263

Service of Compulsory Labor, 20
Sinai peninsula, 247
Sinclair, Sir Archibald, 63-64
Sino-American Cooperation Organization (SACO), 88, 90, 92, 108; and General Chennault, 105
SIS, British secret service, 211-212
Skorzeny, Colonel Otto, 120
Smith, General Walter Bedell, 214, 217, 219-223; and the Kennedys, 223-224; head of CIA, 248
Smuggling, 124, 125, 158
Smuts, Jan Christian, 89
Socialist Party, 141, 143, 144, 190; and newspapers, 147
Soustelle, Jacques, 72, 76, 96, 250, 300
South Vietnamese Army, 221; American training of, 237
Southeast Asia, 217. See also Indochina
Soviet Embassy, Paris, 152-153, 238-240
Soviet intelligence services, 78, 153; alleged operations in France, 302-318. See also KGB; MVD
Soviet Union, 107, 162; and supersonic jet, 127; penetration of French government, 128-129; prestige of (1945), 145; and Poland, 165, 167-169; and NATO, 167-168, 172, 208; French Masonic archives, 205-206; and SDECE, 208; subversive activities, 230-232, 238; and French security problems, 242-245; and Algerian nationalists, 261; and Cuba, 285-286, 295-297, 311, 313; penetration of French intelligence services, 300-318
Spain, 27-30, 32, 35; Free French in, 40; Government cooperation, 44; OSS's Donovan in, 97
Special services. See Free French Special Services
Spring Hill, British prison camp, 123
Stalin, Joseph, 128, 129, 152, 155, 206; and NATO treaty, 167-168
Stalin, Svetlana, 152
Stalin School, Moscow, 208
State, U.S. Department of, 107, 180, 217; and visiting dignitaries, 244; and Couve de Murville, 245
Stillwell, General Joseph, 105